MW01504270

GOD WANTS US

TO FLY

NOTES FROM
THE LECTURES OF LIFE
VOLUME 2

W. T. SVEDIN

Forward

God Wants Us to Fly, Volume II is primarily a compilation of talks and essays prepared and given over a period of many years. With the exception of quotations, the thoughts and opinions expressed are personal and not meant to be authoritative. There are thoughts and stories that are repeated in the talks to illustrate different topics. No attempt has been made to eliminate the duplications.

The things that are written in this book were intended to teach, but in addition to teaching, and more importantly, they were written in an effort to learn and understand. I feel most inspired when I begin to write and articulate the things that I have read and received while pondering those things. More than anything else, my hope is that what I have written might be the catalyst for someone else's inspiration.

Adversity

I remember a conversation I once had with a friend who was very pleased to inform me that his son had just received a perfect score on the A.C.T. test. I thought how remarkable that was and it made me think back a few years to that Saturday when I drove to Olympus High School and took that test myself. We won't be talking about the score I received. I found many of the questions to be difficult to say the least. I am positive I could have done much better on the test had I been allowed to simply skip over the hard ones and be scored only on the easy ones. But, once the test began all I could do was take each question as it came and do my best.

This test and the memory of it is likely something that most of us here can relate to. In a hall filled with others taking the same test, I remember feeling very much alone, particularly when it was difficult. Fully wrapped in the test there was little consolation in the fact that I had chosen to take it, and dwelling on the difficulty of the test only made the time pass more slowly and served no purpose. In the common test setting of life each one of us is engaged in a test uniquely suited to us. Neal A. Maxwell taught, "If God chooses to teach us the things we most need to learn because he loves us, and if he seeks to tame our souls and gentle us in the way we most need to be tamed and most need to be gentled, it follows that he will customize the challenges he gives us and individualize them so that we will be prepared for life in a better world....In the eternal ecology of things we must pray therefore, not that things be taken from us, but that God's will be accomplished through us." (Neal A. Maxwell, BYU September 1,1974)

Elder Maxwell continues, "...We so blithely say in the Church that life is a school, a testing ground. It is true, even though it is trite. What we don't accept are the implications of that true teaching— at least as fully as we should. One of the implications is that the tests that we face are real. They are not going to be things

5

we can do with one hand tied behind our backs, they are real enough that if we meet them we shall know that we have felt them, because we will feel them deeply and keenly and pervasively." (Neal A. Maxwell, BYU September 1, 1974)   When the questions of our test become seemingly too difficult and we wish, *can't I just skip this one,* we do well to remember that the remedial questions we would substitute can never produce the same result. The Lord intends to refine our character, not merely define it. C. S. Lewis borrowed a parable from George MacDonald when he said, "Imagine yourself as a living house. God comes in to rebuild that house. At first, perhaps, you can understand what he is doing. He is getting the drains right and stopping the leaks in the roof and so on: you knew that those jobs needed doing and so you are not surprised. But presently he starts knocking the house about in a way that hurts abominably and does not seem to make sense. What on earth is he up to? The explanation is that he is building quite a different house from the one you thought of—throwing out a new wing here putting on an extra floor there, running up towers, making courtyards. You thought you were going to be made into a decent little cottage: but he is building a palace. He intends to come and live in it himself." Mere Christianity p.176

When considering the tests we have or will experience it is essential that we strive to understand and remember the nature of the atonement. The atonement, accomplished by the Savior is personal; not a one size fits all, but done in such a way that it is customized to the specifics of every individual who makes application for it. Without a personal understanding and witness of the atonement we may find ourselves superficially rejoicing in the grandness of it while feeling personally abandoned by it. We may think ourselves unworthy if we consider ourselves as merely a bit and piece of some unimaginable whole. I testify that the atonement was accomplished for me, for Tom and Susan and for every individual that made the choice to participate in this test. It is the sum of these individuals for whom and with whom our Savior suffered that makes the atonement infinite. Its individual nature necessitates an individual application for its cleansing and healing power. I am inspired by the lessons we are taught in a brief exchange between the Savior and one who felt alone and who made that personal application. In the 5th chapter of Mark we read of a "...woman, which had an issue of blood [hemorrhage] twelve years, And had suffered many things of many physicians, and had spent all that she had, and was nothing bettered, but rather grew worse. When she heard of Jesus, came in the press behind, and touched his garment. For she said, If I may touch but his clothes, I shall be whole. And straightway the fountain of her blood was dried up; and she felt in her body that she was healed of that plague. And Jesus, immediately knowing in himself that [power] had gone out of him, turned him about in the press, and said, Who touched my clothes? And his disciples said unto him, Thou seest the multitude thronging thee, and sayest thou, Who touched me? And he looked round about to see her that had done this thing. But the woman, fearing and trembling, knowing what was done in her, came and fell down before him, and told him all the truth. And he said unto her, Daughter, thy faith hath made thee whole; go in peace, and be whole of thy plague." (Mark 5:25-34) The Lord has promised that if we will draw near to him, he will draw near to us. The nearness he is speaking of is not physical proximity, but of a heart and will coming ever nearer to that of his. Regardless of the loneliness we may feel within the commotion and anonymity of life, we too can reach out in faith. It was not merely the touch that blessed and healed this woman, but the faith demonstrated by her reaching.

Many, if not most of the trials or tests that we face are the result of choices we make individually. Trials of our own making, while not easy to bear, are somewhat easier to understand, because after all, we deserve it. However, when the choices and actions of others entangle us and through no fault of our own we are made to suffer, in humility or desperation, or even defiance, we may wonder why. Time spent in search of the proper place to focus blame is time ill spent. Grudges foster no consolation, no matter how well founded we think they are. When the conditions of our test are simply unfair we do well to remind ourselves that we are the beneficiaries of the suffering of Gethsemane where there was no equity, only mercy. Jesus had no sins of his own, and yet, with no other cause but his love for us, he chose to suffer supremely that the sinner might be forgiven absolutely and the broken hearted healed completely.

Trials incident to life provide for us experience and lessons invaluable in our eternal progression. It is a misconception that all trials are sin related and that personal righteousness will give us immunity. Under such misconception, when we find ourselves being tested, even in spite of our efforts, we might begin to question our own worthiness. As we do, the suffering becomes more intense, as this self-interrogation is based on a false premise. Satan is quick to take advantage of such moments and will promote our suffering purely for the sake of suffering. Among other things, he might tell us that whatever we do, it is not enough and therefore our suffering is an indication of our failings. (In this assumed unworthiness we cannot see ourselves or the Lord in the light of truth.) This kind of suffering can be intense and debilitating. Often there is little comfort in the well-meaning advice of friends and family who are trying to understand and cope as well. Listen to the love in their hearts and know that there is one who does understand. Jesus is forever our advocate and is indeed pleading our cause. Certainly none of us is perfect, but think of the implications of the words we repeat so often, "I am a child of God, and He has sent me here." Hymn 301, LDS Hymn Book In this personalized test, certainly the sincere efforts of God's children are viewed in the perfection of His love, and the offering of our faith and devotion is acceptable and pleasing to Him. May I share a page from a chapter in my journal entitled, "Asparagus?" "The lunches my mother prepared were carefully placed into a brown paper sack. I always folded the empty sack and put it in my back pocket to be used again the next day. The sack would be used and reused until the repeated folding made holes in it. In late spring the sack was put to use as I walked home from school. I kept my eye on the asparagus growing along the ditch bank. When the spears were just right I broke them off and placed them in my lunch sack and proudly carried them home. This was purely for my mother and father. I had no intention of eating any of it. What self-respecting 10 year old boy would? But, how could this repay all the days I came home to the aroma of fresh baked cinnamon rolls or cookies. A few small spears of asparagus could hardly compensate for the endless devotion of my parents. I don't suppose I was really trying to repay them. How could a small boy even know how to do that? I was simply anxious for their response as I presented to them something that appeared to please them. Looking back I am sure that my cuttings were roughly on the same par with a bouquet of dandelions, but my parents always looked passed the gift and saw my heart. It was not until I was a little older and a little wiser that I began to realize that it was me they loved and not the asparagus." However perfect or imperfect our offering might be, as long as we are striving to keep our covenants, it is enough. Certainly God sees our hearts. He loves us, and whatever our trial may be, this truth must never come into question.

Some of the trials we experience come as we witness the suffering of those we love. Our love for them makes their burden our own. In these tests we are able to examine and demonstrate a new dimension and depth of our faith. In the 9th chapter of Mark we read of a man who approached the Savior on behalf of his son, but not just his son. We hear in his plea a cry for help that his faith would be sufficient to heal his son and at the same time, sustain him: "...if thou canst do anything, have compassion on *us*, and help *us*. Jesus said unto him, If thou canst believe, all things are possible to him that believeth. And straightway the father of the child cried out, and said with tears, Lord, I believe; help thou mine unbelief." Mark 9:14-24 This has always been a curious statement to me and one I have pondered often. Over the past year and half I have thought of it in a very personal way. In April of '07 we learned that our second daughter was expecting a baby. Since the birth of her son 7 years earlier she had not been able to successfully carry another baby. We prayed that she would be able to have more children and so we were grateful for this miracle. From the time her son was old enough his prayers and the pictures he drew of the family always included a little sister. Now she was expecting again and our prayers changed to include our gratitude and the plea that she would not lose this baby as she had others. The baby was due in December, but by August she was experiencing those premature symptoms again. We continued to pray with faith, but inwardly I thought *is it enough, help thou my unbelief.* On August 22, four months too early, the very thing we prayed would not happen became a reality. Life is fragile, but never as obviously fragile as in a 1 pound, 2 ounce little girl. What about our faith, were we lacking? My wife and I talked about it often and continued to pray that our faith would be sufficient, and like the woman on the streets of Capernaum, inwardly we felt that we had been healed. A calm and sweet assurance filled our hearts and remained with us and sustained us as we faced each of the challenges that are normal for one so premature. Our little girl met those challenges and overcame them all without any lasting complications. I have paused and pondered a great deal in the last 12 months, and have learned some things. I have learned that we may expect too much of faith when we don't understand it. Faith is not a principle that allows us to simply expect our desires to be granted. In examining my faith I have seen that there is a vast difference between wanting something intensely and having faith. The Spirit is the driving force of all faith. When our desires are one with the will of the Lord we are entitled to and receive a witness by the gift and power of the Spirit. With that witness comes assurance and confidence which validates our desire and it becomes faith. Truly, the desire of our hearts was granted, even when it appeared our prayers were not. In this experience we saw the hand of the Lord multiple times and felt the sweet whisper of peace. We saw the skill and goodness of many who fell in love with our little girl right along with us. How great is our joy now as little Elliana lights the room with her smile. Elliana in Hebrew means "My God has answered."

I am grateful that God has sent me here; that he has sent us here. In our life test, mixed with joy and sorrow, the process of enduring reveals to us how very much God loves us, and what may be more important, how much we love Him.

Atonement, our Foundation

ELDER BRUCE R. MCCONKIE of the Quorum of the Twelve said that "the atonement of Christ is the most basic and fundamental doctrine of the gospel." He said it "is the most transcendent event that ever has or ever will occur from Creation's dawn through all the ages of a never-ending eternity. It is the supreme act of goodness and grace that only a god could perform. Through it, all of the terms and conditions of the Father's eternal plan of salvation became operative." He continues, "It is the least understood of all our revealed truths. Many of us have a superficial knowledge and rely upon the lord and his goodness to see us through the trials and perils of life.... May I invite you to join with me in gaining a sound and sure knowledge of the Atonement." The Purifying Power of Gethsemane, Ensign (CR), May 1985, p.9

I have made this a topic of study and prayer for a very long time, but especially over the past four or five weeks. As we study the doctrines of the atonement we marvel that the Lord has paid the price for the sins of all mankind and we may, if not careful, become lost in the universal scope and grandness of it. Without a conscious desire to know and understand, it is easier to superficially float the tide of a universal atonement than it is to wade upstream against life's perils to make a personal application for its blessings at the source. We are promised and we know that if we will ask in the sincerity of our hearts we may know the truth of all things by the gift and power of the Holy Ghost. Indeed, the Lord has told us that "By my Spirit will I enlighten them, and by my power will I make known unto them the secrets of my will—yea, even those things which eye has not seen, nor ear heard, nor yet entered into the heart of man." D&C 76:10 The Lord wants us to not only know of the atonement, but to have an intimate understanding of it.

Some years ago I took my children on a hike to Lake Blanche in Big Cottonwood Canyon. Half way up I wondered why. Some of you may be familiar with that trail and know that it is steep and often difficult, especially for children. We stopped frequently to rest along the way and in those moments we saw glimpses of the beauty that surrounded us. But, not until we reached the top and stepped out into an unobstructed view did we have any real concept of the scope and grandeur of which we had been a part. From a new point of view it was obvious that a casual walk, or even a labored one, in the woods does not reveal the forest. So it is with the atonement. While immersed in it we are blessed by moments of beauty and peace amid our struggles, but we cannot fully appreciate it until wet come to a point where, "By the power of the Spirit our eyes [are] opened and our understandings... enlightened, so as to see and understand the things of God." D&C 76:12 Then we see that the atonement truly is infinite and eternal. Infinite because there is not one place, creature, or element in all creation that is not blessed by and subject to its principles. These principles are eternal and are truths to which we were introduced in our pre-mortal celestial home. We were taught there of the Savior's sacrifice. The scriptures refer to Him as the "Lamb slain from the foundations of the world," Rev. 13:8 and there in a preparatory spirit estate we received the principles of the gospel and of our salvation by covenant. Spencer W. Kimball taught that, "We made vows, solemn vows, in the heavens before we came to this mortal life." (Spencer W. Kimball, devotional address given at the Institute of Religion, University of Utah, Jan. 10, 1975.) Our ability to understand the atonement and our obligation to it is enhanced as we remember that we accepted its terms and conditions then and there and made ourselves subject to Christ as our Savior and Redeemer.

Each of us have, or will, or may even now carry burdens that seem to validate discouragement and would rob us of hope. The atonement of the Savior and his loving invitation reaches out to embrace all of his children. He said, "Come unto me all ye that labor and are heavy laden, and I will give you rest." Mat. 11:29 "...Be faithful and diligent in keeping the commandments of God and I will encircle thee in the arms of my love." D&C 6:20 Alma taught us that the Savior suffered "...pains and afflictions and temptations of every kind;...and he will take upon him their infirmities, that his bowels may be filled with mercy...that he may know ...how to succor his people according to their infirmities." Alma 7:11-12 The atonement touches every heart and answers every condition. Beyond Gethsemane and Golgotha we find great comfort in the admonition and promises of our Savior recorded in the Doctrine and Covenants: "Listen to him who is the advocate with the Father, who is pleading [not did or will, but is pleading] your cause before him—Saying: Father, behold the sufferings and death of him who did no sin, in whom thou wast well pleased; behold the blood of thy Son which was shed, the blood of him whom thou gavest that thyself might be glorified; wherefore, Father, spare these my brethren that believe on my name, that they may come unto me and have everlasting life." D&C 45:3-5

Along our mortal path we often pause in gratitude for the knowledge that because of the sacrifice of the Savior our sins may be forgiven. Nearly without exception this is what comes to mind when we consider the atonement. Indeed, we are grateful that we need not suffer the pains of sin in order to gain forgiveness. Again, how grateful we are for revelation and the gifts of the spirit that allows us to see beyond the narrow path and teaches us that the promises of the atonement are far more reaching than mere forgiveness. As a youth I spent many hours and days in the tomato fields, hay fields and sugar beets. In my journal one of those days has since been labeled "Sugar Beets and Eternity." Among the many lessons I learned that day was that to be forgiven is not enough when we really want more. I was as anxious as any other kid to make a dollar and when my neighbor offered me an entire field of sugar beets to thin I had visions of dollars that went well beyond my imagination. I knew it would be a lot of work, but I was excited that he would give me the chance and the promise of all that money made it all worth it and doable. I gave him my commitment and he gave me his promise. So Saturday morning with a hoe on my shoulder and visions in my head I walked the half mile to the waiting beets. When I got there the field seemed bigger than I had remembered, but I was undeterred. For those of you who may not know about sugar beets, they had to be thinned, which meant manually cutting out all but one beet every 6 to 8 inches in the row. The rows were about the length of a football field and there were hundreds of them. Alone in the field I started up the first row with precision strokes of life and death and was feeling quite good about myself. Soon it was time to lean on my hoe, catch my breath and see how far I had gone. I looked down the row to where I had started and for a moment I still felt good about myself. I made the mistake, however, of looking the other direction where I could see more work than dollars. The vision that was my initial motivation suddenly was not the same, but I went back to work. I worked what I thought was long and hard and again I stopped to straighten my back and lean on my hoe. I looked down the row and then up again and realized I had come face to face with eternity. There was not enough vision left in my head to sustain more than a token effort the rest of the day. I had made a commitment and so I knew I could not simply quit, I had to stick it out. The task soon became impossible and almost more than I could bear. I thought of all the meaningful things I could be doing; such as fishing, hunting, or even watching TV. I even began to blame my neighbor for what he had done to me. I realized I could never finish the job and spent the rest of day proving it. However, what seemed to be eternal torment, eventually gave way to a new problem. I had done very little of what I agreed to do and was now running out of time to do it. Now I had a new motivation. It wasn't money anymore; it was my day of reckoning. I didn't have time to reverse what I had done, or rather not done all day and so I began to think of what I would tell my neighbor to redeem myself. I don't remember exactly what I came up with and it really doesn't matter, but I remember that it seemed quite clever and again I felt good about myself. I later learned that this is called rationalization. Well, the day of reckoning came and I found myself in front of my neighbor. With some degree of confidence I began to recite the words that I had rehearsed. Not many of them escaped before I began to sense disappointment from him and a kind of consuming embarrassment. That wasn't supposed to happen! As soon as the words hit the air I realized that they were more feeble than clever. I learned then and have observed since that rationalization has no power to alter the truth and in the end the truth will hold us accountable. My neighbor was a good man and he had compassion on young boy. He forgave, but his compassion toward me was limited by my performance and he could only give me a small portion of what he had promised. I was forgiven, but the thought of the promise, now beyond my reach, became a part of the price I personally paid to be forgiven.

How grateful we are for the redeeming power of the atonement that offers more than forgiveness. Those who choose to suffer and pay for their own sins eventually become heirs of salvation. They are forgiven of their sins but are limited by their performance and cannot come where God is. The Lord's atonement offers us a remission of our sins in addition to forgiveness and by its cleansing power enables us to come into the presence of God. Alma taught that "...no man can be saved except his garments are washed white; yea, his garments must be purified until they are cleansed from all stain, through the blood of [Christ]..." Alma 5:21 The Savior counsels us, "...prepare yourselves, and sanctify yourselves; yea, pruify your hearts, and cleanse your hands and your feet before me, that I may make you clean; That I may testify unto your Father, and your God, and my Gjod, that you are clean..." D&C 88:74-75 Only those who are made clean by the atoning blood of Christ may enter into His presence. Knowing this the people of Mosiah "...cried aloud with one voice, saying: O have mercy, and apply the atoning blood of Christ that we may receive forgiveness of our sins, **AND our hearts may be purified**...And it came to pass that after they had spoken these words the Spirit of the Lord came upon them, and they were filled with joy, having received a remission of their sins, and having peace of conscience..." Mosiah 4:2-3   In the atoning embrace of God's love we are filled with hope and I add my witness to that of Alma when he said, "...there can be nothing so exquisite and sweet as was my joy." Alma 36:21

I once observed a young girl with her mother as they walked up and down the aisles of a discount store. The toys and things caught the eye of the little girl and prompted repeated requests. Finally, after the girl had asked for half the items in the store, the mother turned to her and said, "if you had done your chores you could have had a treat." In tears the little girl protested, "but I didn't know we were coming here." The atonement of Jesus Christ will bring us face to face with Him, as the scriptures state, with "...a bright recollection..." Alma 11:43 We will remember all the former commitments and promises and have the privilege of presenting our lives as testimony of our commitment. As we honor the vows we made and are diligent in keeping the commandments the doctrines of the atonement will distill upon us, fill our hearts and sustain us. Not only will we know where we are going, we will long to be there.

****

Become As Children

We were asked to read the four gospels in preparation for conference. I love to read these accounts and picture myself there. Can we imagine the power of the spirit that must have been in the temple when Simeon held the infant Savior and testified, along with Anna, of his divinity? Those present and others who heard their testimonies must have looked forward to Joseph's and Mary's annual visit to Jerusalem. Is it any wonder that the teachers in the temple were audience to a boy who, just 12 years earlier within those very walls, had been proclaimed the Messiah?

The bible dictionary explains that, "The four Gospels are not so much biographies as they are testimonies. They do not reveal a day-by-day story of the life of Jesus; rather, they tell who Jesus was, what he said, what he did, and why it was important." Bible Dictionary p. 683 As we study and ponder the life of Jesus, and walk where He walked, the spirit makes His ministry a reality in our lives and our faith becomes a sustaining power as we choose to follow Him. The eyes of our understanding are opened and we find ourselves eyewitness to His power and divine Sonship. The things He did and said are directed at us individually. The questions He asked, we are compelled to ponder and answer.

The eternal truths of the gospel that Jesus gave us remain true and binding, regardless of their reception. By those truths all of mankind will be blessed or condemned. A casual perusal of His Life will merit little more than an interest in the tears He shed over those who could not see beyond the carpenter of Nazareth. We must accept His invitation to come unto Him and to learn of Him.

The testimonies of the gospel writers invariably leave us to ponder the deeper meanings. We have been blessed with highlights, and as we continue to study, the spirit teaches us and clarifies what we read when we ask questions such as: What does this mean, or is there more?

Toward the end of the Saviors earthly ministry, the disciples approached him with a question, *"Who is the greatest in the kingdom of heaven?"* (Mat. 18:1) John is the only one of the four writers that did not record this exchange. The records of Mark and Luke are very similar, and we find the greatest detail offered by Matthew, in the 18th chapter. In response to their question, the Lord called for a little child. *"...and set him in the midst of them, and said, verily I say unto you, Except ye...become as little children, ye shall not enter into the kingdom of heaven."* (Mat. 18:2-3) For all who hope to enter the kingdom, this is a very important declaration. It leaves us with the question, "what does it mean to become as a child?"

Immediately our thoughts take us to Mosiah 3:19 and in our minds we hear King Benjamin's words, *"...submissive, meek, humble, patient, full of love, willing to submit to all things which the Lord seeth fit to inflict upon him, even as a child doth submit to his father."* I would have loved to have met those children. I was a child once, and as adorable as I was, I don't believe I was thought of in quite those terms, at least not for very long periods of time.

Robert L. Millet poses the question, *"Are little children innocent?"* He continues, *"The answer is a resounding yes. But that question is not really a debated issue. We all know that little children are innocent. The more difficult point is: Why are little children innocent?... there are those who believe little children are innocent because they are that way by nature. They are pure and holy and decent and good and unselfish and solicitous and benevolent and submissive, just by virtue of the fact that they are little children. I don't know about you, but I have not reared any of those types!..."* Robert L. Millet, Selected Writings of Robert L. Millet: Gospel Scholars Series , p.175

President Eyring said, *"I want with all my heart not to shrink, but rather to look up at [God] and see Him smile and say, 'Well done, thou good and faithful servant. Enter in.' King Benjamin makes it clear how we can earn the hope to hear those words if we find the way in this life to have our natures changed through the Atonement of Jesus Christ. That is the only way we can build on the sure foundation and so stand firm in righteousness during the storms of temptation. King Benjamin describes that change with a beautiful comparison, used by prophets for millennia and by the Lord Himself. It is this: that we can, and we must, become as a child-a little child."* Please note Elder Eyring's emphasis on "**little** child." As a Child, Ensign May 2006

While the attributes listed by King Benjamin might easily apply to little children, I think most of us would agree that they quickly outgrow them, even while still in their childhood. I don't want anyone to think that I would presume to disagree with King Benjamin, or with any of those who quote him. However, this is a good place to ask, *is there more*? May I suggest that he was not describing children, per se, as much as he was those who *have become as a child.*

We often refer to children as being sinless, and with good reason too. Mormon said that "...little children are not capable of committing sin..." (Moroni 8:8) and the Lord declared that "...they cannot sin..." (D&C 29:47) If, indeed they are sinless, and that is what it means to become as a child, how do we, at this point of our lives, become sinless. Again, having once been a child myself, I have a hard time with this idea. In addition, my observations of children make it difficult to use that word in its strictest meaning to describe them. I admit that children have their moments, but they can also be cruel, calculating, and selfish. I realize that I am not talking about your children; I'm talking about those other kids. Nevertheless, the Lord declared that, *they cannot sin.* That may have us scratching our heads a little, particularly when we read King Benjamin's affirmation that, "the blood of Christ atoneth for *their sins.*" (Mosiah 3:16) So, do children sin or don't they? .

A few years ago I watched my grandson playing basketball. His father, along with the father of one of the other boys, was coaching and officiating. I was grateful for what I learned and I wrote it my journal. It was humorous to watch ten small boys trying to play the game as well as their understanding and coordination would permit. For the most part, what they were doing was mimicking what they had seen their fathers, and others, do while playing the game called basketball. These small boys played at varying levels and limits of understanding and ability. Most of them merely wanted the ball, but few of them knew what to do with it when they had it. Some listened dutifully to the coaches and obediently held their arms high, not really knowing why. The boy with the ball was the most entertaining. His first instinct was to run and protect his prize. After six to twelve steps, and shouts from on looking parents, and coaches, he remembers something about dribbling. He stops. The other nine players hesitate for a moment in anticipation of what he might do next. He bounces the ball a couple times, which is the signal for five boys on the opposing team to rush him. He panics, hugs the ball and runs again. While he is doing this the other four members of his team are aimlessly running about, waving their arms above their heads and shouting, "I'm open." The defense remembers something about, "stick to your man," and tenaciously chase after the boys whose arms are in the air. But, even completely surrounded, the roaming four offensive players continue to proclaim how open they are, not really knowing what that means; they're really saying, "Throw it to me; it's my turn." A teammate runs up to the boy with the ball and with arms still flailing, and his face within inches of the other, he shouts again, "I'm open." There is a handoff, and another boy takes his turn. He hugs the ball with both arms and runs straight for the basket. The defense backs away, knowing that a shot at the basket will put the ball up for grabs. With a clear shot available he must choose; do I bounce the ball, pass off, or shoot? In a split second he decides to bounce the ball a couple times which signals the defense again, and immediately they swarm him. The boy with the ball becomes frantic; he needs to get rid of it. He runs side to the side, bocks at the basket a couple times and then lets it fly. Both the defense and offense were waiting for this moment. As soon as the ball is airborne it is fair game; there is a free-for-all as nine boys scramble for the coveted sphere. A boy on the other team immerges from the chaos with the ball. He runs out of bounds and then back in again, and the drama repeats itself in the direction of the basket at the other end of the floor.

It is not hard to imagine what would have happened if these small boys had been made to play by the rules. The ball would have changed possession more than it would have been in play and most of the boys would have fouled out within minutes. They would have learned almost nothing and had little fun in the process. But, in spite of the violations the game went on. Why; because it had been determined in advance that the small boys would not be subject to the rules and regulations of the game. In a sense they could not violate them, in spite of the fact that they obviously did. For them, there was no accountability; the coaches had relieved them of that in advance. Likewise, by virtue of the atonement little children are blameless, in spite of themselves. As Mormon said, they are *"…alive in Christ, even from the foundation of the world…"* (Moro 8:12) This is one of the great mercies of the plan of salvation; a period of time granted when Satan cannot influence us, when we can learn the rules of the game and set our course. And all this "that great things might be required at the hand of their fathers." We are commanded to teach our children, to bring them up in light and truth.

King Benjamin taught that children are blameless and through repentance, we too may become as a child; blameless. This is the underlying message of his sermon. I believe that he teaches us that, in addition to becoming submissive, meek, humble, etc. we must strive to become as a child in order to become the saint who has 'put off the natural man.' Chapters three through five in Mosiah speak of becoming blameless and retaining a remission of sins which is what it means to become as a child.

In the process of becoming blameless as a child, the repentant acquires other attributes, such as:
- Peace of Conscience—We would all love to be able to sleep like a child

- Ability to believe: Believing is the natural response of the child; his intellect has not yet trumped his faith. Our intellect serves us well when used in harmony with the spirit to discern what is true. However, the intellect of the natural man becomes a detriment when it assumes an arrogance that demands he argue with, rather than listen to the promptings of the spirit. Do we believe in God; that He is our father and creator? Is he all powerful and does he know all things? Of course He does; he is God. ------------Last Sunday my daughter in Ogden pushed a few buttons and instantly I was talking to her. She couldn't find a letter I had written about 10 months ago. I pushed a few buttons in my office; she pushed a few more, and printed the letter in her home. I can't explain this. I know there are radio waves, or some other kind of waves, bouncing off of towers and satellites, but this is what's happening and I have no idea how it is possible. But, I don't need to know and I don't demand to know; I simply accept the miracle. Unfortunately it is not always the same for the miracles we read in the scriptures. A great flood, parting of the sea, water changed to wine, etc.; are these really any less believable than instantaneous conversations and transmission of documents over many miles. As King Benjamin said, we need to believe in God; that he is all powerful; that He knows all things and we do not.
- A child is at home in the embrace of parents:The little child longs for the comfort of loving arms. In them he finds peace and security in loves affirmation. Becoming as a child is longing for home and those loving arms; to hear the words as mentioned by elder Eyring. I have seen what it means to be as a child in the life of my father. I love his story of the lost sheep: *Forgetting to stake the sheep, or thinking a rope was sufficient he left the sheep unattended. It had been used to roaming the mountains and took off. Knowing how much the*

sheep and its lambs would mean to the family, he set out to bring it back. He must have walked 3 miles or more and was gone long enough for his parents to become very concerned. Along the trail he discovered an old crippled ewe that barely had the strength to stand and thought it would be a good substitute for the sheep he had lost. He forced the poor creature to its feet and prodded it along. At the top of the hill he saw his father and mother coming. They had been searching for their boy, who had been gone far too long. Thinking his father would be as pleased as he was that he had found a stray sheep, he shouted, "Look, dad, I have a sheep." His father showed little concern for the sheep, but there was a profound relief and love in his voice when he said, "Let's go home."

One who has become as a child is filled with peace and assurance that comes from a quiet longing to go home.

****

Charity, Christ Centered Life

When I sit on the stand in a chapel filled with faithful mothers and fathers, I see a much larger congregation, one of children and grandchildren receiving the powerful sermon of example. Speaking of children the Lord said, *For it is given unto them even as I will, according to mine own pleasure, that great things may be required at the hand of their fathers."* (D&C 29:48) What greater thing can we do for them than keep the commandments and honor our covenants? This is how we show our children the depth of our love. And we do love our children. It is sometimes a challenge, nevertheless, the responsibility of children, young and old, to be loveable! We are all children and we never outgrow the commandment to honor our parents. Our lives should be indicative of our love and honor for them, whether they are living or no longer with us.

The Lord is My Light, then why should I fear…The Lord is my strength. I know in his might I'll conquer at length…."LDS Hymn 89 The words of this hymn are powerful; a source of comfort to those whose faith is weak as well as those who have a firm conviction of them. The Lord said, "Let not your heart be troubled: ye believe in God, believe also in me." (John 14:1) Even in the midst of the uncertainties of life, a conviction of God and Christ will speak peace and calm.

I have a personal witness of God and Jesus Christ and of their love for each of us. My heart goes out to those who have not felt or experienced that love for themselves. We are uniquely blessed as a Church because the restoration of the gospel includes the revelation of the nature of God and His plan for us. Indeed He is a God of love. Our son recently shared with us parts of a conversation he had with a man of another faith who believes that a person qualifies himself for heaven by confessing Christ and that must be done in this life. And, since there is only heaven and hell all others are damned.

But, what about the infant who dies at birth? The answer was cold and decisive, Hell. What about the men and women in remote parts of the world who have never heard of Christ or Christianity? Again the answer, Hell. It seems strange to me that such religious creeds are referred to as a faith.

How grateful we are to know that our Father's plan for our happiness is eternal and universal in its scope. Regardless of individual circumstances, God's love embraces all His children. In the perfection of His love there is no such thing as preferential entitlement. The scriptures also teach us that redemption in the Kingdom of God is a matter of individual choice. The Lord said, "I am the good shepherd, and know my [sheep]…" John 10:14 "…and they are numbered." Ne 18:31 "… and they follow me" John 10:27 Speaking to his son, Corianton, Alma said, "Therefore, O my son, whosoever will come may come and partake of the waters of life freely; and whosoever will not come the same is not compelled to come…" (Alma 42:27)   The blessings and privileges of our heavenly home did not exclude one soul and yet even in His presence some excluded themselves because they would not follow God's plan. (see Alma 13:4-5) Speaking of those who choose to pursue their own path of happiness, the Lord said, "Behold, there are many called, but few are chosen. And why are they not chosen? Because their hearts are set so much upon the things of this world…" (D&C 121:34-35) Our circumstances are different from what they were in the spirit world, but our options are the same as they were there. Many exclude themselves in favor of things the world has to offer. God's plan does not require the forfeiture of life's comforts. It will redeem us from the world and qualify us for salvation in His Kingdom if, in spite of the world, that is our desire. However, for those whose hearts are set on the world the redemption he offers is not seen as such and He will not force it upon a single soul. They are left to follow the path of happiness they have chosen. Alma taught, "And he shall come into the world to redeem *his people*; and he shall take upon him the transgressions of *those who believe on his name… * and *salvation cometh to none else.*" (Alma 11:40)

On my desk at work I have a holder for my business cards. I made it from a piece of decaying wood from my back yard and it now serves as a constant reminder to me. This piece of wood is all that remains of what was once a large and vibrant tree. I planted it as a seedling and it grew rapidly. Our young children enjoyed climbing and swinging from its branches. But then, after years of healthy growth, the leaves began to yellow and with each succeeding spring more and more branches appeared lifeless. Finally I had no choice but to take it down. For a long time the stump remained anchored solidly in the ground. However, the sustaining flow of life was gone. Instead of drawing nourishment from the earth it began to be consumed by it. In time everything that once defined it as a beautiful tree was lost in its assimilation. Instead of sustaining the tree the earth simply claimed it. Jesus said that He is the light and the life of the world. Without that light and life in us, the world that would otherwise nourish us will claim us.

The Lord pleads with us to come out of the world and live our lives centered in Him. Through the prophet Alma he said, "…come ye out from the wicked, and be ye separate, and touch not their unclean things…" (Alma 5:57) To the Romans the Apostle Paul wrote: "I beseech you therefore, brethren, by the mercies of God, that ye present your bodies a living sacrifice, holy, acceptable unto God…And be not conformed to this world: but be ye transformed by the renewing of your mind, that ye may prove [try or experience] what is that good, and acceptable, and perfect, will of God." (Romans 12:1-2) The Savior invites us, "…come unto me…and I will give you rest…learn of me and ye shall find rest unto your souls." (Mat. 11:28-29)

How do we live a life centered in Christ? Early in His ministry the Savior taught us; "Blessed [are] the poor in spirit, Blessed [are] they that mourn: Blessed [are] the meek: Blessed [are] they which do hunger and thirst after righteousness: Blessed

27

[are] the merciful: Blessed [are] the pure in heart: Blessed [are] the peacemakers:" Mat. 5:3-9

These Beatitudes are reiterated by Moroni in his description of the attributes of charity: "Charity suffereth long, and is kind, and envieth not, and is not puffed up, seeketh not her own, is not easily provoked, thinketh no evil, and rejoiceth not in iniquity but rejoiceth in the truth, beareth all things, believeth all things, hopeth all things, endureth all things." (Moroni 7:45)

Paul teaches us that charity is the more excellent way. Charity is the Christ centered life and is well defined for us. In fact, so well defined, we might, in our imperfection be prone to ask; how can I do and be all that? If our focus is on the attributes, charity it is indeed daunting. Our focus should be on charity itself. With the bestowal of charity comes the bestowal of its attributes. As we are reminded, "perfect love casteth out fear." 1 John 4:18 That perfect love is charity as defined by Moroni, *everlasting love* and *the pure love of Christ.* This pure love is the transforming power that Alma experienced and described as *exquisite joy.* By this pure love we come to know that while God cannot look upon our sin with the least degree of allowance, in the perfection of His Love He looks upon our repentance with the maximum degree of mercy.

As we accept the Savior's invitation, and truly come unto him, we begin to experience His pure love. His suffering in the Garden of Gethsemane and death on the Cross are central to His atoning sacrifice. But, in a very real way the atonement is something He is doing as opposed to something He did. He is our advocate and continues to plead our cause D&C45:3 and when that pure atoning love penetrates our hearts it comes with enabling power and the bestowal of charity. When we know His love, we are able to see ourselves and others the way He sees and love the way He loves. The pure love of Christ adds graciousness and long-suffering to our nature. Neal A. Maxwell said: "…ponder how the absence of graciousness in human relationships automatically exalts rudeness, bringing so much brittleness in human interactions and communications." The

Promise of Discipleship p. 51 He also taught, "Vengeance is directly opposite to long-suffering. 'Getting even' does not really balance the scales at all; it only distorts them even further—whether practiced between nations, tribes, or spouses!" The Promise of Discipleship p. 51

There is no saving grace in vengeance and no heavenly sanction; whether it is in the retaliatory 'eye for an eye' or the demeaning subtlety of sarcasm or the cold daggers of silent grudges. Vengeance in any of its forms is nothing more than the self-righteous desire to dominate rather than elevate. It is always self serving, requiring of others the sacrifice and long suffering it is not willing to give.

Joseph Smith said, "The nearer we get to our Heavenly Father, the more we are disposed to look with compassion on perishing souls; we feel that we want to take them upon our shoulders, and cast their sins behind our backs..." Documentary History of the Church, Vol. 5, p. 24 We become more than just lovers of peace; we become peacemakers avoiding confrontation by considering the tender feelings of others above our own.

As I ponder what it means to live a Christ centered life my thoughts are of the many individuals in my life who have been and are examples of the pure love of Christ. I am grateful for my wife and her unyielding devotion to the Lord. Many have been able to feel the depth of her testimony and have been fed spiritually by her gift of expression through music. I am blessed constantly by her personification of the admonition of King Benjamin; "...and now, if you believe all these things see that ye do them." (Mosiah 4:10) And of Mary's instructions to the servants at the wedding in Cana; "...whatsoever he saith unto you, do it." (John 2:5)

With love and respect and even reverence I think of my parents who taught me what it means to live a life centered in the love and teachings of the Savior. I don't remember any specific lessons or lectures, but in my father and mother I observed lives centered in Christ. And that was fortunate for me since I was one who was prone to test the limits of their patience. I never did test them intentionally, although they may have thought so. My journal is a personal treasure trove of stories and the lessons I learned by observation. I include one of my entries:

As a boy I spent countless hours at the river and the several ponds that were nearby. One of these ponds was fed by springs and then emptied into the river through a twelve inch pipe under a dirt access road. One day I was struck with a brilliant idea as boys often are. I thought if I put something in front of the culvert to dam the water the pond would become huge. The idea and the possibilities were so exciting there wasn't time to consider consequences. I found the perfect piece of scrap lumber and positioned my makeshift dam. In a short time I could see that it was working nicely and I was quite pleased with my engineering skills. However, watching water rise really isn't all that entertaining and soon a myriad of other things took me away from the pond. I didn't give it another thought all the rest of the day, until late that night after I had gone to bed. A sudden recollection of my brilliant idea made my eyes open wide. I had forgotten all about the dam. Because of my experience with irrigation I knew about the destructive power of water. I wanted to think the dam had broken and that everything was fine, but I had engineered the thing to last. I had visions of water spilling over the dirt road and washing it out entirely. I knew I had to do something. My brilliant plan had suddenly become just another stupid idea. There was no way I could explain a nighttime trek to the pond without full disclosure and confession. Reluctantly I stood at the side of my father's bed and explained the whole thing. Without a word we dressed and then he drove me to a spot just a short walk from the pond. By the time we got there the water was within inches of going over the road. I held a light while my dad used a rake to fish out the dam. The sound of the water gushing into the river was a relief and we went home and back to bed.

What I had done was incredibly dumb and irresponsible. My father could have pointed that out to me and pounded it home belaboring what might have happened. Instead he let me ponder those things on my own and silently taught me a far greater lesson that has stayed with me all my life; the power of love, patience and the unspoken word. I had done a rather boyish thing, but my parents never did subscribe to the idea that boys will be boys. I had proved many times that I was a boy but they had a vision of me that was much more. They never preached it or harped on it, but by the way they treated me and lived their lives, I knew. Had my father delivered the wrath and anger that might have been a more natural response, I might have felt relieved of obligations to that higher level of trust and expectation. As it was my desire to honor and please my parents became a stronger motivation than the enticements of sin and mischief. My father taught me that patient and loving disappointment is much more powerful than even the most controlled anger. I think of my father's wordless sermon and feel the same love and compassion I feel in the Savior's nearly wordless discourse that concluded with *"neither do I condemn thee."*

I testify with Paul and Moroni, *Charity never faileth.* In spite of the weakness of our imperfections the pure love of Christ enables us to see ourselves as He sees us and makes us instruments of His love in the lives of others.

****

CHRISTMAS

As I read of our Savior's birth and ponder the events surrounding it I am impressed by the very personal considerations given amid an event of such universal importance. Five years prior to the birth of the Savior, Samuel, the Lamanite, prophesied of heavenly events *...insomuch that in the night before he cometh there shall be no darkness...Therefore, there shall be one day and a night and a day, as if it were one day and there were no night;* Hel. 14:3-4 As that time drew near *...there was a day set apart by the unbelievers, that all those who believed in those traditions should be put to death except the sign should come to pass...And it came to pass that [Nephi] cried mightily unto the Lord all that day; and behold, the voice of the Lord came unto him, saying: Lift up your head and be of good cheer; for behold, the time is at hand, and on this night shall the sign be given, and on the morrow come I into the world...* 3 Ne. 1:9, 12-13

This amazing event preceding the birth of Jesus appears to have been a phenomenon of the Western Hemisphere. Roughly 15 hours later a new star appeared in the night sky over the Eastern Hemisphere proclaiming the Holy Birth in Bethlehem. And, approximately nine hours later, that star became visible in the Promised Land; a witness to them that the Savior had come.

I love to read of Gabriel's visit to Mary and I can feel the tenderness. I'm not sure that we can even imagine the depth of emotion that must have come over Mary when she was told that she was to be the mother of the promised Messiah. Her humble question was *...how shall this be...* and in the same humility replied, *be it unto me according to thy word.* What else but tender mercy was the angel's announcement that *...thy cousin Elisabeth, she hath also conceived a son in her old age...for with God nothing shall be* *impossible.* Luke 1:34-39 Understandably, Mary went with haste to be with Elisabeth and spent the next three months with her. Their relationship which was already close must have developed into a bond that only they could fully appreciate. They rejoiced together in their miracles and must have pondered deeply the sacred trust and privilege that was theirs. Elisabeth had most likely consigned herself to the apparent reality that she would never have children and now, not only would she have a son, but he would be the one, long prophesied, to be the predecessor to the Savior of the world. That must have been a weight of responsibility that only the Holy Spirit could help her bear. And Mary, to be the mother of the Son of God, the long awaited Messiah, other than Elisabeth, was there another mother anywhere that could help her know how to nurture her son? Indeed, as Luke tells us, Mary had much to ponder in her heart.

We are told of others who, in addition to the universal proclamation of the star, were given a personal witness. An angel appeared to shepherds and said, ...***unto you*** *is born this day in the city of David a Savior, which is Christ the Lord.* Luke 2:11 The Holy Ghost revealed to Simeon ... *that he should not see death, before he had seen the Lord's Christ.* Luke 2:26 Approximately a month following the birth of the Savior, the spirit prompted Simeon to go to the temple where he was able to see and hold the Son of God. Anna was there and bore her witness ...*to all them that looked for redemption in Jerusalem.* Luke 2:38

Prior to that first Christmas, disciples of Christ looked forward to the signs of His coming. Thirty years following His birth, on the eve of his ministry, according to Luke, the people were in expectation. They sought the Messiah as we do. How grateful we are for the signs and witnesses of His coming.

I bear my personal witness that Christ was born in Bethlehem. I pray that we will all look to the signs and witnesses and follow the example of the shepherds who went with haste to find the babe in the manger. As we do, the joy of our salvation will fill

our hearts as we with Andrew and Phillip attest, *We have found Him.*
John 1:45

****

Criticism

WHY AM I so quick to criticize? It doesn't make me feel better about myself and it doesn't help me to know the other person.. it is easy to find fault, but I have found there is little value in it. I've also observed that if virtues are not obvious, it is often because they are buried unto my own criticism. Take the time to see the good; it is a happier place.

Dew Drop

IN THE COOL OF MORNING, moisture laden air saturates everything it touches. Dew drops form on grass and leaves and sparkle in the sunlight like precious gems. At first the tiny drops simply look at the sun and sparkle, but as they swell they begin to creep toward the edge of their perch. I watched closely as some quickly sped away, pausing only briefly on the lip of the leaf before plunging to the ground. Smaller droplets moved more timidly to the right and left, as if looking for direction and the strength to keep moving. They found their strength in the moistened path left by drops that had preceded them and moved with increasing confidence. Some of the smaller drops began to merge and their contribution to each other gave them power and momentum to race away. They too clung to the edge of the leaf as long as they could, briefly suspended in the sunlight before splashing and nourishing the soil far below the leaf. But, I saw that some of the droplets didn't move. Stubbornly they stuck to their spot on the leaf, and in isolation would not give nor receive the assistance that would make them free. Their own fulfillment evaporated with them in the heat of the sun.

True and lasting happiness is achieved when we discover that it is found in the happiness of those around us. Our happiness is limitless when our objective is the happiness of others. In the grasp of hands and the embrace of hearts we give and we find the assurances of experience, the enabling power of compassion and the inspiration of hope. But, all of that is out of reach to the one who confines himself to the tiny world of self.

****

Doctrine of Christ

I felt impressed that I should write a letter to a friend, a good man who has not yet seen the necessity of baptism in the Church of Jesus Christ. It is my hope that the spirit will impress upon everyone the importance of this topic. I begin by quoting the prophet Nephi. Near the conclusion of his ministry he said, "…the things which I have written sufficeth me, save it be a few words which I must speak concerning the **doctrine of Christ**; wherefore, I shall speak unto you plainly…if the Lamb of God, he being holy, should have need to be baptized by water, to fulfill all righteousness, O then, how much more need have we, being unholy, to be baptized, yea, even by water!...Know ye not that he was holy? But notwithstanding he being holy, *he showeth unto the children of men that, according to the flesh he humbleth himself before the Father, and witnesseth unto the father that he would be obedient unto him in keeping his commandments.*...I know by this that unless a man shall endure to the end, in following the example of the Son of the living God, he cannot be saved. Wherefore, do the things which I have told you I have seen that your Lord and your Redeemer should do; for, for this cause have they been shown unto me, that ye might know the gate by which ye should enter. For the gate by which ye should enter is repentance and baptism by water; and then cometh a remission of your sins…And then are ye in this strait and narrow path which leads to eternal life;…And now, behold my beloved brethren, *this the way; and there is none other way* nor name given under heaven whereby man can be saved in the kingdom of God. And now, behold, *this is the doctrine of Christ, and the only and true doctrine of the Father, and of the Son, and of the Holy Ghost…"* 2 Ne 31

Following his resurrection, Christ appeared to the inhabitants of the American continent. Those privileged to be there on that sacred occasion were allowed to "...see with their eyes and did feel with hands, and did know of a surety and did bear record, that it was he..." 3 Ne 11:15 The first thing Jesus did was to establish the authority and proper order of the ordinance of baptism. He said, "And this is my doctrine, and it is the doctrine which the Father hath given unto me;...and I bear record that the Father commandeth all men, everywhere, to repent and believe in me. And whoso believeth in me, and is baptized, the same shall be saved; and they are they who shall inherit the kingdom of God....And again I say unto you, ye must repent, and be baptized in my name, and become as a little child [which means a saved condition within the enabling power of the atonement], or ye can in nowise inherit the kingdom of God. Verily, verily, I say unto you, that *this is my doctrine, and whoso buildeth upon this buildeth upon my rock,* and the gates of hell shall not prevail against them. And *whoso shall declare more or less than this, and establish it for my doctrine, the same cometh of evil...*" 3 Ne 11"32-40

The doctrines of Christ are clearly taught and defined in the scripture. However, today, as in every age since the gospel was given to Adam and Eve, they are being undermined by the philosophical and misguided doctrines of men. An angel of the Lord taught Adam and Eve, *"...thou shalt do all that thou doest in the name of the Son, and thou shalt repent and call upon God in the name of the Son forevermore. And in that day the Holy Ghost fell upon Adam..."* Adam and Eve rejoiced together in the Doctrines of Christ and *"...they blessed the name of God, and they made all things known unto their sons and their daughters. And Satan came among them, saying: I am also a son of God; and he commanded them, saying: Believe it not; and they believed it not, and they loved Satan more than God..."* Moses 5:8-13

Ever since that time, Satan has devoted himself to deceptions, both subtle and blatant, designed to discredit the Doctrine of Christ. Even when Christ himself was on the earth, Satan was active in his opposition. While there were many who recognized that Christ

38

taught with authority, there were many who found his doctrine to be more than they could bear (see John 6:60-71). But, Jesus made no apologies. He said, *"…My doctrine is not mine, but his that sent me. If any man will do his will, he shall know of the doctrine, whether it be of God, or whether I speak of myself."* John 7:16-17 *"…no man can come unto me, except he doeth the will of my Father."* JST John 6:65

There are people all around us who are genuinely good and yet they do not embrace the gospel of Jesus Christ. This has always been the case and the Doctrine of Christ teaches us how we should respond to them. Speaking to Jesus, John said, *"…we saw one casting out devils in thy name, and he followeth not us: and we forbad him…but Jesus said, Forbid him not…for he that is not against us is on our part…he shall not lose his reward."* Mark 9:38-41 Jesus recognized and gave sanction to the good this individual was doing, for which he would not lose [his] reward, but Jesus came short of saying that his goodness would qualify him for the blessings promised in His doctrines. To those who want to believe that they are entitled to a place in God's kingdom on the basis of goodness outside of the doctrines of Christ, he said, *"Not everyone that sayeth unto me, Lord, Lord, shall enter into the kingdom of heaven; but he that doeth the will of my Father which is in heaven. Many will say to me in that day, Lord, Lord, have we not prophesied in thy name?… and in thy name done many wonderful works? And then will I profess unto them, I never knew you: depart from me…"* Mat 7:21-23

Keeping the doctrine pure has always been a struggle. Jesus himself noted, *"This people draweth nigh unto me with their mouth, and honoreth me with their lips; but their heart is far from me…in vain they do worship me, teaching for doctrines the commandments of men."* Mat 15:8-9 Following the death of Jesus and the martyrdom of many of the apostles, there was a complete falling away, resulting in ages of darkness. Centuries later, the rise of Christianity sparked, in some cases, misguided and even evil interpretations of the Doctrine of Christ. The influence of the spirit guided others to look for the pure doctrine, giving rise to a reformation and setting the stage for a restoration. Joseph Smith described it as, *"an unusual excitement on the subject of religion…which created no small stir amongst the people…"* JS-H 1:5 Guided by the spirit and his desire to know the truth, young Joseph Smith concluded that the only way to discover the truth was a direct appeal to God. I am grateful that I am able to testify, for I know it is true, that the Father and the Son appeared to Joseph Smith. In that revelation began the restoration of the Doctrine of Christ.

Young Joseph's question was simple and unassuming; which of all the churches was true. In response to his question, Jesus told him that they were all wrong, *"…that all their creeds were an abomination in his sight; that those professors were all corrupt; that: 'they draw near to me with their lips, but their hearts are far from me, they teach for doctrines the commandments of men, having a form of godliness, but **they deny the power thereof**.'"* JSH 1:18-19

The answer Joseph Smith received was a defining declaration to all of us and speaks of all philosophies or doctrines that do not fully embrace the doctrine of Christ. Those who espouse such doctrines may well be sincere and so there is a form of godliness. However, it is only the doctrine of Christ that has the power to sanctify us and promote the ideals and behaviors that will grant God access and ability to exalt us. The doctrines of men are content to merely justify chosen philosophies and behaviors and effectively deny God any real power in the lives of those who promote them.

I have come to realize that my reading of the Lord's response to Joseph Smith has been rather superficial. Until now I have thought that when the Lord spoke of professors of abominable creeds, he was speaking about the leaders and preachers of the various religions. I now realize that they were just a small representation of those the Lord spoke of. Anyone who has an idea or philosophy and promotes it by word or conduct is a professor of that philosophy. With this understanding came the realization that, if I am not careful, I could be one of those professors the Lord spoke of.

We have a natural tendency or inclination to develop personal philosophies of life, primarily to make us feel good about ourselves and to cope with a world out of harmony. Most of the time these are good and even healthy, but we must be careful that these ideas do not contradict or prevent us from embracing the doctrines of Christ. Too often these personal doctrines allow those who profess them to feel comfortable in places and things where black and white choices are made gray by their indulging them, where rationalization justifies their contention that they are still entitled to the promises within the doctrine of Christ. I learned something about this a long time ago—*I was as anxious to make a dollar as any other kid my age, and at thirteen the opportunities were limited. When my neighbor offered to let me thin his beets and have first go at the entire field, dreams were inspired by visions of cold hard cash.*

I gave my neighbor my commitment and he gave me his promise. So, on a Saturday morning, with a hoe on my shoulder, I walked the short half-mile to the waiting field of crowded beets. When I got there the field seemed larger than I had remembered, but I was undeterred while dollars still danced in my head. I stepped up to the first row and with great precision the life and death strokes of my hoe began.

After a few minutes I stopped to lean on my hoe and check my progress. I wanted to have some idea of how long I would be there and how fast the money was adding up. I was sure I had already done a lot. I looked back at where I had begun and I was quite pleased with myself. I should have been satisfied with that, but I made the mistake of looking up the row at what remained. Looking in that direction my progress was all but undetectable. Unconsciously I told myself that I had to work harder and faster. This second energy burst lasted a good while and another evaluation was in order. This is when the concept of eternity first entered my head. I had already gone forever up the row of endless beets and looking up I saw another forever ahead of me. There I was, standing in the middle of forever, forgetting what landed me there. Suddenly

41

the visions in my head were not the same. The dollars stopped dancing. They were so remote now they weren't doing anything. How could they?

I had told my neighbor that I would thin his beets. ...I was stuck; trapped by my own promise and surrounded by what had become objects of misery. It no longer seemed worth it. I knew I had to stick it out long enough so I could at least say (even if it wasn't true) that I had tried.

As the job became more impossible I moved more slowly. The opportunity to make a little money was not even a thought anymore and the job had become a great imposition. How could he (my neighbor) expect one person to do so much! I became angry for what he had done to me. I didn't care about the money. ....no effort would ever achieve it. I silently went about validating my own predictions. Less than half-heartedly I made token strokes with my hoe. By midday there were few beets in the field that were in any danger.

I didn't think the day would ever end, but after what seemed to be eternal torment there came a point when I actually knew it would. Then I was faced with a new problem. I had done very little of what I had committed to do and was running out of time to do it. I would have to face my neighbor; he would want an explanation. Time began to go by more quickly as I contemplated my day of reckoning. I had wasted the day, but how could I say that to him? He would be disappointed, not to mention the embarrassment for me. So, I worked a little longer with a new kind of motivation and as I did I thought about what I would say to redeem myself. By the time I finished that last row I had come up with some reasoning that I thought was quite cleaver. As I walked back home I polished my speech and was feeling more than vindicated. I told myself that I had endured an acceptable portion of the day and had accomplished quite a lot compared to the actual time and energy I devoted to it.

Reckoning time came and with a degree of confidence I began to recite the words I had rehearsed. Not many escaped before

I could sense his disappointment and a profound embarrassment. That wasn't supposed to happen! However, when my words hit the air, it was obvious that they were more feeble than cleaver. I learned very quickly that it didn't matter what I said. Words were powerless to change the reality of what I had done, or should I say, not done. Rationalization is always self-serving and its persuasive power is limited to those it serves. My excuses were easily dashed by the truth. I had wasted the day. I had not done what I said I would. Words designed to establish nobility based on a fabricated truth fell with a thud. At this point words were as worthless as was the performance that necessitated them and they held no power to justify anything more than a meager wage for a meager effort. I learned that even the cleverest rationalization is powerless to alter the truth and the truth will always hold us accountable.

My neighbor was a good man and forgiving, but his compassion was limited by my performance. For my meager effort I received but a small portion of what had been promised. I also learned that to be forgiven is not enough when it leaves us short of the promise. The thought of those promises, no longer available to me, became a part of the price I paid to be forgiven.

Where the doctrine of Christ is concerned, if we find ourselves rationalizing our behavior, we can be sure that we are doing it on Satan's side of the line and, for all our talking; we are powerless to reposition ourselves. No amount of arguing, regardless of its eloquence, will ever make the doctrine of men equal to the Lord's. Rationalization is always self-serving, but we do well to remember that it can only serve within the limitations of the one who argues in his own behalf.

In a day and time when society attempts to normalize and idealize perversions of God's laws, it is important that we understand that his doctrine is non-negotiable. He said, *"all who will have a blessing at my hands shall abide the law which was appointed for that blessing, and the conditions thereof, as were instituted form before the foundation of the world."* D&C 132:5

Fathers

The scriptures tell us that following the expulsion of Adam and Eve from the Garden of Eden they *"...called upon the name of the Lord...And he gave unto them commandments, that they should worship the Lord their God, and should offer the firstlings of their flocks, for an offering unto the Lord. And Adam was obedient unto the commandments of the Lord. And after many days and angel of the Lord appeared unto Adam, saying; Why dost thou offer sacrifices unto the Lord? And Adam said, I know not, save the Lord commanded me. And then the angel spake saying; This is a similitude of the sacrifice of the Only Begotten of the father, which is full of grace and truth. Wherefore thou shalt do all that doest in the name of the Son and thou shalt call upon God in the name of Son for evermore. And in that day the Holy Ghost fell upon Adam, which beareth record of the Father and the Son, saying...as thou hast fallen thou mayest be redeemed, and all mankind, even as many as will..."* Adam and Eve blessed God because their eyes had been opened and they knew that in life they would have joy in their posterity and in the knowledge of their redemption and *...the eternal life which God giveth unto all the obedient. And Adam and Eve blessed the name of God, and they made all things known unto their sons and their daughters. And Satan came among them, saying: I am also a son of God; and he commanded them, saying: believe it not; and they believed it not, and they loved Satan more than God. And men began from that time forth to be carnal, sensual and devilish. "* Moses 5:5-15

Ever since the time of Adam, men and women have been choosing sides; aligning themselves with those things that they deem most important and rewarding. We see the great wisdom in God's plan acting out in the lives of his children. Many of the choices and pleasures men love were actually a part of the spirit condition, but

44

mortality and the physical element gave them new expression. Enhanced by the physical those enticements have a strong appeal for many. There are those who are spiritually indifferent while others actually become offended by the idea that the gift of life comes with accountability. In this world there are those who have literally chosen to love Satan more than God. All of us have and will continue to make choices which find expression in the conduct of our lives. Consciously or unconsciously we identify ourselves. Everything we do and say, particularly when we think no one is watching, is an expression of our inner most desire and commitment.

In a conference address, President Packer reminded us of the fascinating story of Gideon. In the book of Judges we read, *"...the Midianites came up, and the Amalekites, and the children of the east, even they came up against them...and destroyed the increase of the earth...and left no sustenance for Israel...they came as grasshoppers for multitude...without number; and they entered into the land to destroy it...And the angel of the Lord appeared unto [Gideon] and said unto him, The Lord is with thee, thou mighty man of valour....And he said unto him, Oh my Lord, wherewith shall I save Israel? ...And the Lord said unto him, Surely I will be with thee, and thou shalt smite the Midianites...* Judges 6:1-16

When Gideon had assembled his army *"...the Lord said unto Gideon, The people that are with thee are too many for me to give the Midianites into their hands..."* Judges 7:2 A process of elimination or identification was begun. Quoting Elder Packer, "Gideon had an interesting way of selecting his recruits. When the men drank water at a stream, most 'bowed down...to drink.' Those he passed over. A few scooped up water in their hands and drank, remaining completely alert. They were the ones chosen....Gideon's small force succeeded because, as the record states, 'they stood every man in his place.'" President Packer continues, "While the priesthood is presently all over the world, we call on every elder and high priest, every holder of the priesthood to stand, like Gideon's small but powerful force of 300, *in his own place.* We now must awaken in every elder and high priest, in every quorum and group, and in the father of every home the power of the priesthood of the Almighty....We need everyone. The tired or worn out or lazy and even those who are bound down with guilt must be restored through repentance and forgiveness. Too many of our priesthood brethren are living below their privileges and the Lord's expectations....The authority of the priesthood is with us...it is now our responsibility to activate the power of the priesthood in the Church. Authority in the priesthood comes by way of ordination; power in the priesthood comes through faithful and obedient living in honoring covenants...Now, fathers, I would remind you of the sacred nature of your calling. You have the power of the priesthood directly from the Lord to protect your home. There will be times when all that stands as a shield between your family and the adversary's mischief will be that power. You will receive direction from the lord by way of the gift of the Holy Ghost." Power of the Priesthood, Ensign May 2010

The challenges we face as fathers and priesthood holders were anticipated by our Father in Heaven. Elder Richard G. Scott said, "He included a provision for you to receive help with such challenges...That assistance will come to you through the Holy Ghost as spiritual guidance. It is a power, beyond your own capability, that a loving Heavenly Father wants you to use consistently for your peace and happiness...What may appear initially to be a daunting task will be much easier to manage over time as you consistently strive to recognize and follow feelings prompted by the Spirit. Your confidence in the direction you receive from the Holy Ghost will also become stronger...as you gain experience and success in being guided by the Spirit, your confidence in the impressions you feel can become more certain than your dependence on what you see and hear." To Acquire Spiritual Guidance, Richard G. Scott, Ensign November 2009

In the Kingdom(s) of God there is no higher honor or authority than that of father. This is a principle that possibly is not understood to the extent that it should be. Joseph F. Smith taught,

"In the home the presiding authority is always vested in the father, and in all home affairs and family matters there is no other authority paramount. To illustrate this principle, a single incident will perhaps suffice. It sometimes happens that the elders are called in to administer to the members of a family. Among these elders there may be presidents of stakes, apostles, or even members of the first presidency of the Church. It is not proper under these circumstances for the father to stand back and expect the elders to direct the administration of this important ordinance. The father is there. It is his right and it is his duty to preside…" (The Juvenile Instructor, March 1902, p. 146.)

Elder Packer quoted this statement in his talk and as I read it again I believe I began to understand more fully what we are being taught. I felt the Spirit guiding me to the 88th section of the Doctrine and Covenants. I love the scriptures and find that even when they seem to deal directly with one subject the Spirit is able to enlighten us beyond the obvious. Section 88; "All kingdoms have a law given; And there are many kingdoms; for there is no space in the which there is no kingdom; and there is no kingdom in which there is no space, ether a greater or a lesser kingdom." (36-38)

One of the great blessings and fundamental purposes of this earth experience is in our individual opportunity to establish the foundations of our own kingdom; to become as God is and eventually receive all that He has. Within these kingdoms there is no higher authority than the office of father. The responsibility and challenges are great but come with promises and power in our priesthood. *"For whoso is faithful…magnifying their calling, are sanctified by the spirit…"* D&C 84:33

Safeguard and honor your priesthood. Fathers, protect your home and family. I find it interesting and sobering that the reason sited by the Lord that children are protected from the direct influence of Satan is *"…that great things may be required at the hand of their fathers."* D&C 29:48

I pray that we will make the establishment of our home a conscious and deliberate effort. That effort begins long before marriage and is the duty of every priesthood holder. Elder Nelson, of the Quorum of the Twelve has said, "To bear the priesthood means you have a personal responsibility to magnify your calling. Let each opportunity to serve help to develop your power in the priesthood. In your personal grooming, follow the example of the living prophets. Doing so gives silent expression that you truly comprehend the importance of 'the Holy Priesthood, after the Order of the Son of God.'" Elder Russell M. Nelson, Personal Priesthood Responsibility, Ensign (CR), November 2003, p.44

It is the seemingly small things that often speak the volumes of our lives. Never let the inner commitments of your heart become obscured by conflicting outward expressions. It is our outward expressions that nurture those commitments and the power in the priesthood that will bless your family now and in eternity. The scooping of water and drinking from a ready hand may have seemed a strange selection process, but it identified those the Lord would empower to save Israel. We too must identify ourselves and as we do we will be filled with the enabling power to save our kingdom and as many as will.

****

Forgive

Lorenzo Snow said, "I believe that when you and I were in yonder life we made certain covenants with those that had the control that in this life, when we should be permitted to enter it, we would do what we had done in that life— find out the will of God and conform to it." Lorenzo Snow, The Teachings of Lorenzo Snow, edited by Clyde J. Williams, p.91 The idea that covenants were requisite to earth life and made by us in the pre-mortal part of our lives is an important consideration. It indicates that the purpose of mortality was taught and understood. The accepting and making of those covenants to a great extent constituted the keeping of our first estate. Having made those covenants and having accepted the conditions of mortality we have indeed come here with something to prove. It is often said that we are here to be tested. While this is true it does not express our purpose in its entirety. Life is a test but, the test is not our purpose. What we prove or demonstrate by means of the test is. We knew that life would be difficult and that our mortal condition would be fraught with trials that would test our resolve and our commitment to the principles of eternal life. We also knew that this was the whole purpose, that we would be tested in order to prove ourselves. As difficult as it seems at times, in all actuality we should be grateful for those trials, for without them we prove nothing. However, there are many who see them as evidence of abandonment and justification for doubt and complaint. How unproductive and ironic. Would anyone ever think, after voluntarily registering for a required examination, that they could or should complain about the questions being asked?

The trials we experience as a natural part of living create a bond of charity among family and friends and if we permit, they bring us closer to the Lord. They make us aware of our dependence upon Him and make the atonement a daily reality in our lives. These trials are the bitter that enable us to recognize and appreciate the sweetness of life. A member of the Martin handcart company said of his ordeal, "Was I sorry that I chose to come by handcart? No; Neither then, nor any minute of my life since. The price we paid to become acquainted with God was a privilege to pay, and I am thankful that I was privileged to come in the Martin Handcart Company." (Relief Society Magazine, Jan. 1948, p. 8.)

These trials of life that just happen are unavoidable and intended for our experience. (See 1 Peter 4:12) They are random and always within our ability to cope because in them we are entitled to divine intervention. There are other trials however, that are avoidable. They are the ones we bring upon ourselves and inflict upon others. They are the ones we experience when we step off the path of the Lord's plan of happiness. They are worse than unproductive, and very often are the result of a need to make or prove a point that is pointless, never to prove a Christ-like nature. When we add these trials to our test we can expect heartache because they promote spiritual solitude and cause the innocent to suffer.

These trials that ensnare the innocent and compromise our faith are meant to be avoided and indeed they will be when our faith is anchored firmly in the principles of the gospel. If we allow ourselves to be offended and abandon those principles we turn our backs on the recipe for coping. To be easily offended is not Christ-like and does not give us special license. We remain accountable to the principles of truth no matter how far we distance ourselves.

In His Sermon on the Mount the Savior taught us that human relations should be more than human. He taught us that we can and should be our own master; that in the face of offense our response should be one of kindness and patience, tolerance and forgiving. What a wonderful world this would be if everyone operated under the assumption that men are basically good. Unfortunately many are quick to jump to a conclusion based on doubt and suspicion. Jumping to conclusions is easy. The trick and difficult thing is to land on the right one. We serve and are served better by being forgiving. One who is forgiving is less likely to be offended. Most often those who have offended us would be as shocked by our perceptions as we are by their actions. When we ask ourselves, 'how could he do such a thing,' more often than not he didn't. Usually the bits and pieces by which we judge are so incomplete that the truth is entirely misrepresented. On those occasions when our perception is not tainted and the offense was real and deliberate we do ourselves no service in being unforgiving and equally offensive.

In a conference address, President Hinckley spoke of forgiveness. He said, "I think it may be the greatest virtue on earth, and certainly the most needed. There is so much of meanness and abuse, of intolerance and hatred. There is so great a need for repentance and forgiveness. It is the great principle emphasized in all of scripture, both ancient and modern. In all of our sacred scripture, there is no more beautiful story of forgiveness than that of the prodigal son found in the 15th chapter of Luke. Everyone should read and ponder it occasionally." Forgiveness, Gordon B. Hinckley, Ensign November 2005 In the depths of his despair and remorse, the prodigal acknowledged his unworthiness. "And the son said unto him, Father, I have sinned against heaven, and in thy sight, and am no more worthy to be called thy son." Of the many responses this father could have given, we are taught and inspired by how he chose to receive his son. "...his father saw him, and had compassion, and ran, and fell on his neck, and kissed him." (Luke 15:14-21)

The prophet Nephi gives us another wonderful example. After repeated criticism, ridicule and abuse by his brothers he refused to surrender to natural instincts. In a rare moment of humility Laman and Lemuel "...were sorrowful, because of their wickedness, insomuch that they did bow down before me, and did plead with me that I would forgive them of the thing that they had done against me. And it came to pass that *I did frankly forgive them* all that they had done, and I did exhort them that they would pray unto the Lord their God for forgiveness..." (1 Ne. 7:20-21) What would have happened if Nephi had allowed his brother's behavior to determine his; if he had chosen to set aside the principles of the gospel to satisfy a more natural desire to get even? One thing is certain, Laman and Lemuel would have been denied those few and far between moments when they actually felt a spiritual influence in their lives. How unremarkable Nephi would have been, had he chosen to be like his brothers. Had he done so it is not likely that we would be reading about him today in any other way than we do of Laman and Lemuel. With his life now lived and recorded it is easy for us to see what he would have forfeited. All of us should consider what we stand to lose when we are unforgiving. It is so much more than just our composure.

In the Book of Mormon we have an example of another great man by the name of Pahoran. Moroni had plead with Pahoran as chief governor to send support to defeat the Lamanites. When Moroni received no response he sent another scathing letter. "Do ye suppose that the Lord will still deliver us, while we sit upon our thrones and do not make use of the means which the Lord has provided for us? Yea, will ye sit in idleness while ye are surrounded with thousands of those, yea and tens of thousands, who do also sit in idleness, while there are thousands round about in the borders of the land who are falling by the sword, yea, wounded and bleeding. Do ye suppose that God will look upon you as guiltless while ye sit still and behold these things?..." Moroni was not aware of the civil rebellion in Zarahemla threatening the inner fabric of the government and preventing Pahoran from sending aid. This is a good story made great by Pahoran's response. Moroni had threatened to come against him saying, "I do not fear your power nor your authority..." Pahoran responded simply and humbly, "...you have censured me, but it mattereth not; I am not angry, but do rejoice in the greatness of your heart..." (see Alma 60 and 61)

Pahoran's forgiving response exemplifies the Savior's teachings in the Sermon on the Mount recorded in the 5th chapter of Matthew. The Savior said, "...resist not evil: but whosoever shall smite thee on the right cheek, turn to him the other also. And if a man will sue thee at the law, and take away thy coat, let him have thy cloke also....Love your enemies, bless them that curse you, do good to them that hate you, and pray for them which despitefully use you, and persecute you." (Mat. 5:38-44) While these are principles designed to bless and save the world, as we live them they save us individually in spite of the world. The apostle Paul instructed us: "...be no more children, tossed to and fro, and carried about with every wind of doctrine, by the sleight of men, and cunning craftiness, whereby they lie in wait to deceive;...This I say therefore, and testify in the Lord, that ye henceforth walk not as other Gentiles walk, in the vanity of their mind...Let all bitterness, and wrath, and anger, and clamour, and evil speaking, be put away from you...And be ye kind one to another, tenderhearted, forgiving one another, even as God for Christ's sake hath forgiven you." (Eph. 4:14-17, 31-32)

Developing the ability to unreservedly forgive will introduce and maintain peace in our hearts and is required of us. The Lord said, "Wherefore, I say unto you, that ye ought to forgive one another; for he that forgiveth not his brother his trespasses standeth condemned before the Lord; for there remaineth in him the greater sin. I, the Lord, will forgive whom I will forgive, but of you it is required to forgive all men." (D&C 64:9-10) President Spencer W. Kimball warned us, "A common error is the idea that the offender must apologize and humble himself to the dust before forgiveness is required. Certainly, the one who does the injury should totally make his adjustment, but as for the offended one, he must forgive the offender regardless of the attitude of the other. Sometimes men get satisfactions from seeing the other party on his knees and groveling in the dust, but that is not the gospel way." (Miracle of Forgiveness p. 282) I wonder who is blessed most by the principle of forgiveness. Certainly the one forgiven has reason to rejoice in an outpouring of love, but he who is able to forgive is made free to rejoice. To condemn requires pride and pride demands our constant devotion. This pride convinces the unforgiving that the Savior's Sermon on the

Mount does not apply in all situations, that there are circumstances when judgment and justice is our prerogative and obligation. The one who freely forgives is not so preoccupied. Those who have learned to forgive quickly are unencumbered and free to be happy regardless of influences to the contrary.

There is no happiness in condemnation, only heartache. If a person is worthy of condemnation, he will not need our help to achieve it. In the 8th chapter of John we read an account of one who was caught in sin and brought before the Savior. From this brief exchange we are given five words that speak volumes of hope and consolation to all of us, "Neither do I condemn thee." John 8:11

"And the scribes and Pharisees brought unto him a woman taken in adultery; and when they had set her in the midst, they said unto him, Master, this woman was taken in adultery, in the very act. Now Moses in the law commanded us, that such should be stoned: but what sayest thou? This they said, tempting him, that they might have to accuse him. But Jesus stooped down, and with his finger wrote on the ground, as though he heard them not. So when they continued asking him, he lifted up himself, and said unto them, He that is without sin among you, let him first cast a stone at her. And again he stooped down, and wrote on the ground. And they which heard it, being convicted by their own conscience, went out one by one, beginning at the eldest, even unto the last: and Jesus was left alone, and the woman standing in the midst. When Jesus had lifted up himself, and saw none but the woman, he said unto her, Woman, where are those thine accusers? Hath no man condemned thee? She said, No man, Lord. And Jesus said unto her, Neither do I condemn thee: go, and sin no more." (John 8:3-11)

There was no question of guilt and no plea of false accusation by the woman, and yet, the Lord spoke no condemnation. He sent her away to complete the repentance already begun in her heart. The shame she must have felt in the presence of the Lord surely gave way to joy in the hope of the Savior's compassionate response. We too, caught in sin, are assured that the Lord will not condemn us but longs to forgive us. The woman was sent away with the charge to sin no more. Her forgiveness or condemnation was placed into her hands and rightly removed from those who sought to use her in their evil design.

There are obvious lessons in these nine verses and more to be gleaned as we ponder and liken them to ourselves. Where was her husband? Was he a victim in this affair? Was he among the accusers, or was he nearby pleading and praying for them both? What kind of man was he? What kind of people are we? How do we respond when we find ourselves victimized by another? Do we insist that he suffer at least as much as we have, or does compassion and charity prompt us to say in our heart, *neither do I condemn thee*?

What about the accusers? Having walked away, condemned in their own hearts, did they simply let it go? It is interesting to note that the practice of stoning, on grounds of adultery, had been abandoned long before the time of Christ. The Scribes and Pharisees sought only to use the woman and the situation to entrap the Savior. Their wicked design ignored both the woman and the law. The Savior's wisdom did not allow them to use either for their self-righteous cause. How did they react in the solitude of conscience? How do we react? Do we harbor ill will and adopt a cause of justice even when the author of justice and mercy has proclaimed to all of us, *neither do I condemn thee*?

Having been caught in the act we may wonder if the woman was repentant. James E. Talmage says that she was. "...She remained, humbly awaiting the Master's decision, even after her accusers had gone. Jesus did not expressly condone; He declined to condemn; but He sent the sinner away with a solemn adjuration to a better life." (Jesus the Christ p.406) Exposed and yet repentant, what effect did this have on her relationship with friends and neighbors? Did they abandon her? Did she abandon them? We don't know if she had the humble courage to allow her friends the opportunity to prove their love and loyalty. Avoiding them to conceal her shame would have added tragedy to her embarrassment. How do we respond when our failings are exposed? Are we humble enough to seek and receive the love of true friendship? Human weakness does not compromise love and friendship, but defines and reveals it.

The Lord told us that, "...he who has repented of his sins, the same is forgiven, and I, the Lord, remember them no more." D&C 58:42 And in the words of Paul; "Be ye kind one to another, tenderhearted, forgiving one another, even as God for Christ's sake hath forgiven you." Eph. 4:32 I testify that the Lord lives. It was He who descended below all things and took upon Himself our weakness and imperfections. We, the beneficiaries of His Benevolence, have reason more than He to say, *neither do I condemn thee*. As we do this our hearts will be open to receive the peace and consolation of the gospel of Jesus Christ.

****

Funeral Service-Allen Stocking
August 6, 2010

The prophet Joseph Smith said, *"All men know that they must die. And it is important that we should understand the reasons and causes of our exposure to the vicissitudes of life and of death, and the designs and purposes of God in our coming into the world, our sufferings here, and our departure hence. What is the object of our coming into existence, then dying and falling away, to be here no more? It is but reasonable to suppose that God would reveal something in reference to the matter, and it is a subject we ought to study more than any other. We ought to study it day and night, for the world is ignorant in reference to their true condition and relation. If we have any claim on our Heavenly Father for anything, it is for knowledge on this important subject.....*" Teachings of Joseph Smith

REVEALED TRUTH and our hearts tell us that we are eternal beings and that we came from the place where God dwells. In our hearts we also know that each of us will again take our place in the realms of eternity. For some the thought of heaven is sweet anticipation while for others it is a matter of grave concern. In the middle of a very brief moment in eternity our vision is limited by the horizons of time. If we were permitted just a glimpse in either direction, I'm sure our perspective of life and death would change dramatically and that is precisely the reason for our limitations.

As children in our mortal experience we respond to parents and others in compliance or defiance. In their presence neither of these accurately reveals our character. It is when we are alone that we begin to know who we are. In our earthly isolation outside the immediate presence and influence of God we are free to discover and reveal our individual nature and identity. Our potential is infinite. If there are limitations they are those we impose upon ourselves.

In our heavenly home our Father taught his children the principles of life and happiness within His Kingdom. When we open our hearts and seek to know those principles here, they instill within us a peace we do not fully comprehend and yet it is somehow familiar; calling up distant memories now obscured by life and time. These principles enlighten our minds. They give us glimpses of something better. Then, when God calls us home and we look back we will see the great wisdom of his plan. There, in his presence, immersed again in the principles of his home we will understand that in the eternal scheme of things we simply needed a few moments alone to know for ourselves if the principles of his home would constitute our eternal happiness.

Lorenzo Snow taught, "*I often ask myself, what am I in the world for? Where did I come from, and where am I going? Well, we have learned something in regard to this. We have learned that we existed with God in eternity before we came into this life, and that we [were true to him]. Had we not [been true] and observed the laws that governed there, you and I would not be here today. We are here because we are worthy to be here, and that arises, to a great extent at least, from the fact that we [were true to God in heaven]. I believe that when you and I were in yonder life we made certain covenants with those that had the control that in this life, when we should be permitted to enter it, we would do what we had done in that life-find out the will of God and conform to it.*" Teachings of Lorenzo Snow p.91

The Book of Mormon prophet Amulek taught us that "…this life is the time for men to prepare to meet God…" (Alma 34:32) It is here in this life that we make the defining choices that will prepare us for the kind of life we will live in eternity. Each day is an entry in the book of our lives and carries with it eternal consequences. When our book is complete we will present it to the Lord as evidence of the station we have chosen for ourselves.

Few of us will have as many entries in our books as Grandpa Stocking. He had 36,337 (if my calculations are correct). I'm sure that along the way he has done some editing and I for one am grateful that the atonement of Christ affords us that ability. Grandpa showed us all the art of living. He loved life all the time. If the sun was shining he was happy for a beautiful day. If there were clouds he was happy for the cool breezes. Rain and snow was a delight because it meant a good start for the winter wheat on the dry farms and tall grass for the sheep and cattle on the range. He showed us what it means to work and serve others. This building [1800 W. 13400 S.] stands as a monument to his example; there is hardly an inch of it that has not come under his loving touch either in its construction or its maintenance. Many of us have been the recipients of tomatoes, melons and flowers that he grew solely for the purpose of sharing.

Over the past several months I've been looking back on my life a little more thoughtfully. I begin to see how important it is that we have a grasp of the obvious; that the only living we can do is today. We can look ahead to tomorrow, but if we are to have any influence there it will be in the living we do today. Once today is done and deposited with our yesterdays we cannot change it, but each of them will profoundly influence today. Grandpa showed us how to live one day at a time. Even when he became too weak to care for himself he showed us how to be humble and gracious.

This life is not easy and I don't believe it was ever meant to be. It was meant to refine us and define us and whether we know it or not it is always doing that. Many years ago I had an experience that in retrospect has taught me a great lesson. I took four of our five children on a day hike to Lake Blanche in Big Cottonwood Canyon. Some of you might be familiar with the trail. It is 3.3 miles and climbs in elevation 2600 feet. The kids were fresh and energetically skipped along and at times looked back impatiently at their much slower father. The trail was well marked, but steep. The first mile was good; a peaceful hike. While the children entertained themselves along the trail I was able to stop briefly here and there to take in the beauty that had swallowed us. The muffled thunder of a rushing stream combined with the rustle of leaves as trees dipped and swayed to catch the wind. Tiny birds, some blue and some yellow, piped and sang while squirrels chattered nervously. Somewhere near the end of the second mile things began to change. If the birds were still singing I was not aware of it. Why did I even try this? What had seemed an easy thing, was now far more difficult than I had anticipated. If it had not been for the children, quitting might have been a preferred option, but we pressed on.

Standing on the edge of a huge granite boulder I looked back at where we had walked. The struggles and hardship of the trail were entirely lost in the grandeur. The view commanded our silent awe and prompted feeble attempts to express our emotion.

As we go through life we encounter hardship, heartache, disappointment that we did not anticipate. In the middle of things unexpected we are faced with a choice; the choice to quit and be defined or push on and be refined. The difficulties of life will forever shackle us if we stop to entertain them. However, they will be lost entirely when we move on to places where the view is unobstructed. Grandpa showed us how to keep moving.

He has stepped out of this life into another and has left us asking again, where is he? What is it like there?

The prophet Alma taught us that as soon as men die, whether good or evil, they return to that God who gave them life. According to the prophet Brigham Young the world of spirits is right here. Modern revelation tells us that the same sociality that exists here is there too and that the work of the Lord goes on there as it does here. Jedadiah M. Grant was privileged to see into the spirit world. *"He also spoke of the buildings he saw there, remarking that the Lord gave Solomon wisdom and poured gold and silver into his hands that he might display his skill and ability, and said that the temple erected by Solomon was much inferior to the most ordinary buildings he saw in the spirit world. ...In regard to gardens, says brother Grant, "I have seen good gardens on this earth, but I never saw any to compare with those that were there. I saw flowers of numerous kinds, and some with from fifty to a hundred different colored flowers growing upon one stalk."* Journal of Discourses, 26 vols., 4:, p.136

Neil A. Maxwell has taught us that the spirit world is an extension of our testing. He said, *"The veil of forgetfulness of the first estate apparently will not be suddenly, automatically, and totally removed at the time of our temporal death. This veil, a condition of our entire second estate, is associated with and is part of our time of mortal trial, testing, proving and overcoming by faith—and thus will continue in some key respects into the spirit world."* Promise of Discipleship, p. 111

We wish so often that we could see them, and we wonder; can they see us?

A couple weeks ago I was blessed to witness an inspiring moment. I watched the children of Allan Stocking surround him as he lay in his bed in his living room. I thought of those that had gathered around him in another place 99 ½ years ago and of those gathering to receive him now. He was too weak to speak but I felt and clearly understood the love and tenderness in his final testimony and prayer.

The last words spoken to him in this life are those I like to think were the first he heard in the next.

Ninety nine years, five months and twenty days ago (at the time of this writing) angels gathered to offer their best wishes to one of their own. Was there any degree of sadness in that intimate gathering when they sent him away? These were just a few of my thoughts as I watched five angels gather around the bed of their dying father to wish him well once again. Too weak to even speak aloud he offered a prayer of love and gratitude. I could not hear the words but I felt them clearly. I thought of over 36,000 yesterdays that brought him to the door about to open from the other side, where there is gathered and gathering another group as intimate and loving as the one surrounding his bed. What words could possible express the gratitude for those days that reveal themselves now in tenderness and almost heart rending compassion? Nowhere is there a greater testament to the profound importance of the todays we live and deposit in the repository of yesterday.

****

Funeral Service, Anona Leishman
November 29, 2008

It is an honor to be asked to speak at this important and sacred meeting. However, the real honor and blessing has been and is in knowing Anona and the Leishman family. It was roughly 35 years ago when Jan and I first became acquainted with the Leishman's. Over those years we have been able to laugh and play and serve together. Each time Anona called me friend I knew I had achieved one of life's choicest blessings. She taught us how to play chicken foot and in general the joy of a smile. She taught us how to have fun with life and if we didn't learn it, it was our fault. I can't help but think of her now when I read again Elder Wirthlin's counsel in our last general conference. He said, "Over the years I have learned a few things that have helped me through times of testing and trial…The first thing we can do is learn to laugh." Ensign, November 2008 The prophet Lehi taught us that "men are that they might have joy." 2 Ne. 2:25 I'm sure he was referring in large part to an eternal reward, but Anona showed us that we don't have to wait. Our son enjoyed calling on the office where Anona worked. He said it is hard to think that she won't be there. He loved, as he put it, her sassy sense of humor. He was right; very little ever escaped her. If anyone needed a humility check she knew how to put a person in his place and leave him wanting to come back for more. I am sure that her counsel to us here today would be to live life, love it, and laugh.

In moments of grief incident to the passing of those we love, questions arise. In our search for answers even the love of God may briefly come into doubt, but in reality it is His influence that sustains us. My father told me of his first real experience with the passing of one close to him. When he was 17 his grandmother passed away. Most 17 year olds have a lot of questions and he was no exception.

He remembers the emptiness that filled him with the fear that he would never see her again. However, in the moment of that fear he heard a voice of reassuring peace; a voice and message to each of us, "you will see her again."

In the middle of the very brief now of eternity our vision is limited by the horizons of time. If we were permitted just a glimpse in either direction I'm sure our perspective on life and death would change dramatically and that is precisely the reason for our limitations. In our earthly isolation, influenced by only those things we choose, we are able to find out who we really are. Many or most of our limitations are self imposed. We can breach them if and when that becomes our true desire.

In our heavenly home our Father taught his children the principles of life and happiness within His Kingdom. When we open our hearts and seek to know those principles here they instill within us a peace we do not fully comprehend and yet it is somehow familiar; calling up distant memories now obscured by life and time. These principles enlighten our minds. They give us glimpses of something better. Then, when God calls us home and we look back we will see the great wisdom of his plan. There, in his presence, immersed again in the principles of his home we will understand that in the eternal scheme of things we simply needed a few moments alone to know for ourselves if the principles of his home would constitute our eternal happiness.

Over the past couple days I have considered the similar process of sending and receiving that takes place at both ends of this life experience. For all of the joy with which we receive our little ones there are those in another place who experience a separation. Granted their view is loftier and more enlightened which likely voids any pain or sorrow. Even within our limitations that kind of view is available to us and to the extent we achieve it our pain and sorrow gives way to peace. But, even within our assurances we find consolation in the tears of joy and of grief. As we mourn we find ourselves in company with our Savior who, in spite of his view, wept with Mary and Martha at the death of their brother and his friend Lazarus, and as the Jews observed of Jesus we repeat, "Behold, how we love Anona."

When our Father in Heaven sent us away to enter and experience mortality he blessed each one of us with the means of our escape. None of us knows the timing or the means of our departure from this life and the manner of our passing is not important. Neal A. Maxwell said, "Surely none of us will rush eagerly forward to tell Jesus how we died." (Ensign, November 1983, p. 66.) What will be important however is how we've lived! Our Father wants us to do more than merely experience mortality and escape it; he wants us to come home again. We have no recollection of our spirit past and none of us is able, of our own accord to find our way. Thomas asked the Savior, "How can we know the way?" To which the Savior responded, "I am the way; the truth and the life." John 14:5-6 Since God does want us to return he has made it possible. Alma taught, "After God had appointed that these things should come unto man, behold, then he saw that it was expedient that man should know concerning the things whereof he had appointed unto them; therefore he sent angels to converse with them, who caused men to behold of his glory…Wherefore, he gave commandments unto men,…placing [them] in a state to act, or being placed in a state to act according to their wills…" Alma 12:28-31 Our faith and hope and the manner of our living is validated by the assurance that God has provided for our return and he will receive us. As explained by the prophet Abinidi, God himself had broken the bands of death, and "…having gained the victory over death; giving the Son power to make intercession for the children of men… being filled with compassion towards the children of men; standing betwixt them and justice…having redeemed them, and satisfied the demands of justice." Mosiah 15:8-9 Nephi explained that Christ, "…hath power given unto him from the Father to redeem [us] from [our] sins because of repentance;…" Hel. 5:11 Christ himself assures us, "…if ye will come unto me ye shall have eternal life. Behold, mine arm of mercy is extended towards you, and whosoever will come, him will I receive; and blessed are those who come unto me." 3 Ne 9:14 God will receive us individually and we will have the privilege of expressing our love and gratitude for all he has done for us.

Prior to coming here our lives and the way we lived them prepared us in large measure for our mortal experience just as we are now in preparation for the kind and quality of life we will enjoy in eternity. We know by revelation that we, as spirit children, had the ability and the power to influence and bless our brothers and sisters. That ability came with us into mortality to the extent we developed it there and acknowledge it here. Those of us who have been privileged to know Anona as wife, mother, visiting teacher, chauffeur, confidant and friend have been influenced by an unconditional love that is surely a heavenly treasure and gift she brought with her to be a blessing to us. We have been taught by Anona and others that when our treasures on earth compliment those of heaven and are centered in things we can take with us we approach the inevitable with more longing than sorrow. As has been stated so many times before; this is not the end, but is more like another beginning. Neal A. Maxwell taught, "We tend to overlook the reality that the spirit world and paradise are part, really, of the second estate." The Promise of Discipleship p. 111 He continues, "The veil of forgetfulness of the first estate apparently will not be suddenly, automatically, and totally removed at the time of our temporal death. This veil, a condition of our entire second estate, is associated with and is part of our time of mortal trial, testing, proving, and overcoming by faith—and thus will continue in some key respects into the spirit world." The Promise of Discipleship p. 111 Anona's gifts and wonderful influence continue with even greater potential. Quoting Elder Maxwell again, "On the other side of the veil, there are perhaps seventy billion people. They need the same gospel, and releases occur here to aid the Lord's work there. Each release of a righteous individual from this life is also a call to new labors. Those who have true hope understand this. Therefore, though we miss the departed righteous so much here, hundreds feel their touch there. One day, those hundreds will thank the bereaved for gracefully forgoing the extended association with choice individuals here, in order that they could help hundreds there. In God's ecology, talent and love are never wasted." The Promise of Discipleship p. 105 I am confident that Anona is happy and very busy.

Much of the goodness we know in our lives has come as a direct result of the influence Anona Leishman has had on us. Likewise, the degree of goodness others will experience is dependent upon each of us. Second only to the securing of our own salvation is our responsibility and joy in the salvation of our family and friends. Jesus said of himself, "I am come that **they** might have life, and that they might have it more abundantly." John 10:10 We rejoice today in an abundance that is ours because of one elect lady.

Bob, I love you and your family. I know that you have experienced the sweetness that rightfully comes to those left behind when one is received into the presence and love of God. I leave my witness and testimony that Jesus is the Christ. He is the Savior of all mankind and he lives. His declaration to his good friend Martha is an invitation and promise to each of us; "I am the resurrection, and the life: he that believeth in me, though he were dead, yet shall he live: And whosoever liveth and believeth in me shall never die." John 11:25

****

GOSPEL OF CHRIST
EXPERIENCE AND PHILOSOPHY

PERHAPS THE GREATEST teacher that we will know is Experience. However, this master teacher is seldom recognized for what it presently is and is appreciated most with the passage of time. Experience offers everyone a potential treasure trove of wisdom, deposited in personal life accounts. The sooner we begin to recognize and reinvest the growth, the greater the treasure will be when our port folio reaches maturity.

Experience makes philosophers of all its students. Some proudly promote their philosophies while others quietly cope within the shelter theirs has created. What makes one philosophy better than another is a matter of how near to the truth it comes and that, for most people, is also a matter of philosophy. The philosophies that immerge from the experiences of those around us can be influential in the development of our own, as they help us process similar experiences. Eventually, every student develops his or her own philosophy by which the lectures of experience are received. For this reason we see individuals spiral down to the depths of despair while similar experience is a crescendo of joy for others.

Ideals praising and promoting personal indulgence are incapable of transcending this world and often amount to nothing more than rationalization. The Gospel of Jesus Christ is the Grand Philosophy of life and eternity; it is His philosophy. Our mortal presence is evidence that we entered into a covenant that we would make his philosophies our own. There are two questions we should ask of ourselves: first, is my personal philosophy in compliance with the Gospel of Jesus Christ? Second, am I prepared and anxious to sit down, face to face, with Christ to compare and discuss the merits of my philosophy? The day will come when we will have that opportunity and unlike today, we will not be able to dismiss Him or deny the covenant we once made regarding His Gospel. Does this thought spark the anticipation of joy or something else?

****

Hand of the Lord

When I was very young I remember thinking and wondering, as I listened to conference, how anyone was able to stand and speak for so long. I was always encouraged when the speakers name would appear at the bottom of the screen, because that generally meant that his talk was nearly over. Now I marvel that so much is said in such a short period of time.

President Uchtdorf spoke of the vastness of space and God's creation, a subject of fascination to me. (Ensign, November 2014) Andromeda galaxy is two million light years away (a light year is 5.8 trillion miles). The closest star to us within our own galaxy is Proxima Centari, 4.2 light years. Traveling to Proxima Centari by the fastest known means of travel would take 81,000 years. It is estimated that ten million stars make up the center of our galaxy; all within one light year of each other. *"What is man that thou art mindful of him?"* (Heb. 2:6)

It is humbling to address a congregation who expect to be taught and enlightened. I feel a burden of responsibility. As I consider who might receive my words, feel safe in placing a portion of that burden upon them. I will make some remarks, but I ask each of you to listen to what the spirit is saying to you personally.

I have had the blessing of visiting with most of you, individually, in temple recommend interviews. In each of these interviews I have felt the confirming witness of the Holy Ghost and on many occasions I have seen testimony sparkle in moistened eyes.

The questions we review in the temple recommend interview have been carefully and prayerfully prepared by prophets. These questions help us to know and understand a minimal level of worthiness. They are not intended to be a means of determining the level of perfection we have achieved, but rather, our state of preparedness and worthiness to enter the Lord's house to participate in the advanced studies leading to perfection.

Having the privilege of being a part of these interviews multiple times each week gives me the opportunity to ponder the questions in depth. Many times I have asked myself, "What do I mean when I say I have faith in God, that I have a testimony of the atonement and of the restoration of the gospel?" It is not my intention to answer these questions for you, because I'm not sure that I can. Certainly I could offer some insights, but regardless of how enlightened they may be, they remain, after all, insights. The real answers come very personally as a result of introspection and soliciting the influence and enlightenment of the Holy Spirit. So, instead of answers, I pose the questions personally: what do you mean when you say you have faith in and a testimony of God the eternal Father, his Son, Jesus Christ and the Holy Ghost? What do you mean when you say you have a testimony of the Atonement of Christ, and of His role as our Savior and Redeemer? What do you mean when you say you have a testimony of the restoration of the Gospel in these, the latter days?

President Eyring has encouraged us to take note and make a record of the times we have recognized the hand of the Lord in our lives. (O Remember, Remember; Ensign November 2007) The story of Peter Mourik certainly illustrates just how involved the Lord is willing to be. In the Sunday morning session of conference, President Monson related this story associated with the dedication of the Frankfurt Temple. Having been informed that Peter Mourik was not in attendance, President Monson was still impressed to announce him as the first speaker. Knowing what he had done, President Monson said he was not worried. Ten minutes away, in another place and a different meeting, Peter Mourik felt impressed that he needed to leave immediately for the Temple. He arrived just in time to hear his name announced as a speaker in that session of the dedication. (Stand in Holy Places, Ensign, November 2011)

71

I'm not so sure we always recognize the Lord's hand at the time. Hopefully we do when we have time to consider the things that happened as opposed to what might have happened.   1968 was a pivotal year in my life. At the height of the Vietnam conflict, boys graduating from high school were subject to the draft by lottery. Young men who served as missionaries were deferred for the duration of their mission, however wards were allowed only two per year. My parents were determined that I would have the opportunity to go on a mission, even though our ward had already met its allotment. We moved from our home in Crescent (now South Jordan) to Millcreek; the Millcreek 1st ward. There I received a call to serve in Sweden, where my mother and father had served. I wanted to go to Sweden, but didn't think it possible, since my sister was already serving there. My first assignment was in the same city my father had served. At the conclusion of my mission I had 5 days to report to the draft board. To that point in my life had never been grateful for flat feet, but because of them, I was not required to go to war. I didn't think about it at the time, but now I see the hand of the Lord.

That same year, 1968, I attended a region youth conference at BYU. While there I met the most beautiful girl I had ever seen. From the moment I saw her, my life was not same and I knew it never would be. Three years later we were married. We recently celebrated our 40th wedding anniversary. Together we have seen the hand of the Lord preserving and guiding us. Over those years I have observed that those who most readily recognize the hand of the Lord in their lives are those who make themselves instruments in it.

I have seen that people discover pretty much what they are looking for in life. Recently Jan and I went out to dinner. There were a lot of people there and the receptionist said it would be about a 25 minute wait. We took a number and sat on a bench outside the entrance. It was beautiful and pleasant evening, but then three ladies sat on a bench behind us, close enough that we had no choice but to listen to their conversation. During the course of their conversation there was not one positive comment or observation. I thought how different their world was from mine and Jan and I were both grateful when their number was called.

Recently I've read again the opening chapters of the Book of Mormon. I love to read about Lehi's dream and of Nephi's vision of the things his father had seen. In addition to wonderful truths revealed by these revelations we are taught by the contrasting examples of Nephi and Laman and Lemuel. In these examples, good and bad, we learn how we can recognize the hand of the Lord. We read the response of Nephi and can imagine the intensity with which he listened to his father. *"And it came to pass after I, Nephi, having heard all the words of my father, concerning the things which he saw in a vision, and also the things which he spake by the power of the Holy Ghost, which power he received by faith on the Son of God-- and the Son of God was the Messiah who should come--I, Nephi, was desirous also that I might see, and hear, and know of these things, by the power of the Holy Ghost, which is the gift of God unto all those who diligently seek him…after I had desired to know the things that my father had seen, and believing that the Lord was able to make them known unto me, as I sat pondering in mine heart I was caught away in the Spirit of the Lord…"* (1 Ne. 10:17, 11:1)

Laman and Lemuel, on the other hand argued among themselves regarding the meaning of what their father had told them. They admitted to Nephi that, *"…we cannot understand the words which our father hath spoken…"* (1 Ne. 15:7) Nephi's response, simple and profound, speaks to each of us today. *"Have ye inquired of the Lord?"* (1 Ne. 15:8)

I find it both interesting and sad what Laman and Lemuel had heard. Instead of being filled with peace and love, they stuck with fear and were concerned about the torment of judgment. How much better it would have been if they had been able to hear the message and could envision the Tree of Life. It would have been so much better for them and everyone else if they had recognized the Lord and sought him out as did Nephi.

Because Nephi went to the Lord with his questions and desires, he was shown, not only what his father had seen, but much more. Among other things, he saw us. His description of today's world wide church is a source of strength, testimony and courage to us in the face of pointing fingers from a spacious and outspoken world.

Nephi's ability to recognize the hand of the Lord sustained him and prepared him to not only see the Lord's hand, but to be a real part of it.

****

Home Teaching

There is a wonderful association in our great priesthood brotherhood. Elder Bednar has said, "Brethren, we as priesthood leaders should improve our personal purity and our preparation and our performance. In the latter-day war against wickedness in which we are engaged, we fight against the forces of evil and the seduction of sin. As the Adversary increases the intensity and the sophistication of his attacks, we must increase in spiritual strength and power. What has been effective for us in the past will not be effective in the future. Thus, if you and I simply stay the same spiritually, we are destined to fail....My objective for us would not be that we leave...with a list of supposed answers, with a notepad filled with lists of things we are supposed to go and do. Rather, my desire is that we...would seek to identify the inspired questions upon which we should focus and ponder and about which we should pray in the coming months. What must I do in my ministry? How must I change? What must we do in our ministries to help invite the blessing and gift of hope in a world that grows increasingly dark?"

David A. Bednar, Address to General Authorities and Area Seventies, March 31, 2005

If I do my job here today and you do yours, each of us will be instructed and edified. I would hope that if you keep any notes it will be of those things you hear that are not spoken. These quiet whisperings will be your personalized inspiration pertaining to your ministry.

I have been asked to talk about increasing the effectiveness of home teaching. This is a topic by which most of us have at one time or another been frustrated, or distressed, or possibly downright discouraged. For years, as priesthood leaders we have struggled with the question of how to get our home teachers to do their home teaching. These struggles have resulted in ideas and approaches that have come as a result of both inspiration and desperation. Some of these have been creative and all have been intended to remind and motivate. Unfortunately many of these ideas are short lived and have little lasting influence. By their nature they must be resurrected periodically and do little except to add to the initial distress and frustration.

Several months ago we asked the quorum and group leaders of each ward to place an emphasis and focus on an attitude of 100% home teaching. We have not yet achieved it, but I am pleased to report that we are seeing improvement in our statistics. This is a place to start.

For years we have *talked* about the importance of *doing* our home teaching. Brethren, this is where we need to begin making corrections if we expect to see any lasting improvement in our home teaching. Neal A. Maxwell said, "I worry sometimes that we get so busy discussing the doctrines...that talking about them almost becomes a substitute for applying them." Neal A. Maxwell, "Becoming a Disciple," Ensign, June 1996 Elder Bednar has counseled us, "In our customary Church vocabulary, we often speak of going to church, going to the temple and going on a mission. Let me be so bold as to suggest that our rather routine emphasis on going misses the mark....The issue is not going to church; rather, the issue is worshiping and renewing covenants as we attend church. The issue is not going to or through the temple; rather, the issue is having in our hearts the spirit, the covenants, and the ordinances of the Lord's house. The issue is not going on a mission; rather, the issue is becoming a missionary and serving throughout our entire life with all of our heart, might, mind, and strength. It is possible for a young man to go on a mission and not become a missionary, and this is not what the Lord requires or what the Church needs." David A. Bednar, "Becoming a Missionary," Ensign, November 2005

In the spirit of Elder Bednar's instruction, the issue is not doing our home teaching; rather, the issue is serving magnifying our priesthood and becoming a home teacher. If we continue to ask the brethren, or even strongly urge them, to do their home teaching we miss the mark, and in spite of our good intentions a sacred calling is reduced to a task among many others that we must do. The implication is that at some point we might consider it done. Elder James A. Cullimore said, "Priesthood home teaching is not just another program of the Church, something to get done so you can send the report in. It is a principle of action, the vehicle by which all of the programs of the Church are taken to the family and the individual, and, in addition, it has the power to bless and guide and strengthen souls." (Regional Representatives Seminar, December 12, 1970.) Can we ever really consider home teaching done?

I'd like to tell you about a home teacher in our stake. Ten days into the month of August he has visited one of his families 4 or 5 times, he wasn't sure. In those visits two priesthood blessings have been given. A message and testimony of the atonement was delivered. Witness was born of the Lord's love and personal awareness of the adult children. In the absence of the father the lawn was mowed. A visit was made to the hospital to check on the very ill mother. Many phone calls have been placed to a father and husband who is many miles away and very concerned. Home teaching is never done. When I asked if he had given the "First Presidency Message," he answered as if he had neglected something and that another appointment would be made to do that. This good brother has been so busy being a home teacher that I doubt he has given a second thought to doing his home teaching. Each of us who have or who are now serving in an elders quorum presidency or high priest group leadership know what I am talking about when I say that we are grateful for those individuals who know what it is to be a home teacher and, on the other hand, we continue to agonize over those who struggle with the difficulty of finding the time to do their home teaching

Home teaching was introduced to the Church in 1963. Prior to that we had *ward teaching*. Not to over-simplify it, but some of you will remember as I do that ward teaching consisted primarily in the delivery of a uniform message intended for every family. In 1973 Elder James A. Cullimore, speaking of home teaching said, "This differs from ward teaching in that greater emphasis is placed on watching over the family, rather than just making a monthly visit. Instructions have been given that the duty of the home teacher is to keep in touch with the families, to watch over them, to contact them in whatever manner necessary, in order to watch over them....We are to have concern for these families every day as long as they are assigned to us." Elder James A. Cullimore, Home Teachers—Watchmen over the Church, Ensign (CR), January 1973, p.124

The First Presidency message in the Ensign is a wonderful resource. However, it was never intended to be the impetus behind our home teaching, nor the basis of, as Elder Marion G. Romney put it, "a perfunctory visit once a month." Elder Marion G. Romney, Conference Report, October 1962, General Priesthood Meeting, p.77; Elder James A. Cullimore, Home Teachers—Watchmen over the Church, Ensign (CR), January 1973, p.124 When I asked that good home teacher about the message, I did so primarily to get his reaction. Home teaching does not require that we deliver the Ensign message or any other pre-printed message. The message may not be what the family needs and is not required to satisfy the statistical check mark in the home teaching column.

President Harold B. Lee said, "Maybe the home teacher should be charged more clearly to describe his mission to watch over and to strengthen, to see that members do their duty....Maybe we ought to be calling them home guardians or sentinels...We must do something to change the emphasis from teaching to guardians, 'watching over the church kind of concept.' Until we get that into our minds, we are not going to do the kind of home teaching that is going to get results." Harold B. Lee, The Teachings of Harold B. Lee, edited by Clyde J. Williams, p.498

Harold B. Lee instructed, "Three things should be kept in mind in thorough preparation for home teaching. *First, a knowledge of those whom you are to teach*. ...Each pair of home teachers should become intimately acquainted with every child, youth, and adult in the family to whom they are assigned, and have in them the same personal interest they have in members of their own families....we should be continually aware of the attitudes, the activities and interests, the problems, the employment, the health, the happiness, the plans and purposes, the physical, temporal, and spiritual needs and circumstances of everyone...in the homes and families who have been placed in our trust... *Second, a knowledge of what they are to teach.* Home teachers should have a feeling of urgency about the importance of knowing and living the gospel. Our lives are fleeting, and we must live the gospel while we are here. There is no other way to check the downward trend of society. Even though there may not be enough people who accept and comply with the principles of the gospel to save the nations, still thousands and millions of individuals will be saved, if they live the gospel. Hence, the urgency. This we must get over to the people. It isn't enough to merely engage in some activities in the Church. We must have a knowledge of the gospel and dedicate our lives to living it. This we must teach. It is therefore the home teacher's duty to teach that Jesus Christ is the Redeemer of the world....and that Joseph Smith and his successors are Prophets of God, and that the gospel has been restored, and to prepare our Father in heaven's children to receive the sacred ordinances of the gospel....*Third, a knowledge of how we're going to teach*. This brings us to a consideration of the method by which we can get the saints to accept and profit by what the Church offers for their benefit by way of knowledge and training in the gospel. If we may take some language from the Doctrine and Covenants and apply it to this purpose, the home teachers should 'visit the house of each member' and 'teach, expound,' and exhort each to pray vocally and in secret; to attend to all family duties and 'watch over the Church always, and be with and strengthen them'— and this means always— however, and whenever, and with whatever may be necessary. ...It is our duty as home teachers to carry the divine spirit into every home and heart. To love the work and do our best will bring unbounded peace, joy, and satisfaction to a noble,

79

dedicated teacher of God's children." Harold B. Lee, Priesthood Session, April 6, 1963

I hope we will never fall into the trap of excuses; particularly the excuse of time. Time can be an elusive thing, so hard to find when it is needed, and yet so very abundant when it is needed for things we prefer. Those who cannot find time are like a man, chest deep in water, wishing he could go for a swim. Our time naturally and automatically gravitates to and absorbs the things and/or people we love.

Home teaching is inherently a part of our priesthood covenant. As with all principles of the gospel by which we are bound, we determine the extent to which we keep and honor it, but we cannot dismiss it. Increasing the effectiveness of our home teaching requires more vision and purpose than we typically see. Vision and personal conversion will take our sense of duty to a level of love and charity that will make of a home teacher a true shepherd. When we are converted we are not only in a position to strengthen our brethren, but we are also empowered by the desire to do so. There is applicable power in the words and experience of Enos: "And my soul hungered; and I kneeled down before my Maker, and I cried unto him in mighty prayer and supplication for mine own soul...And there came a voice unto me, saying: Enos, thy sins are forgiven thee, and thou shalt be blest...And I said: Lord, how is it done? And he said unto me: because of thy faith in Christ... Now, it came to pass that when I had heard these words I began to feel a desire for the welfare of my brethren..." (Enos 1:4-9) Likewise, the son's of Mosiah felt that yearning that took them outside and beyond themselves. When they were converted they "Were desirous that salvation should be declared to every creature, for they could not bear that any human soul should perish." (Mosiah 28:3)

I know in my heart that if we are to improve the effectiveness of our home teaching it will be done more readily and with more lasting effect by helping each home teacher rise to a level of personal conversion by which the pure love of Christ becomes his motivation.

When this happens the statistical visit will take care of itself as individuals and families are nurtured. I testify that home teaching, when viewed and pursued as it was revealed is the means by which we in very large measure fulfill the covenant of the priesthood as we have been charged. It is a means by which we represent the Lord as instruments to bring to pass the eternal life of man.

****

I GIVE MEN WEAKNESS

And if men come unto me I will show unto them their weakness. I give unto men weakness that they may be humble; and my grace is sufficient for all men that humble themselves before me; for if they humble themselves before me, and have faith in me, then will I make weak things become strong unto them. Ether 12:27

MORONI EXPRESSED his concern that his words might not be well received because of his weakness in writing. However, the Lord promised him that the Gentiles, "...shall take no advantage of your weakness." Indeed, the words of the Book of Mormon have become powerful in many lives; the *Lord has made weak things become strong*.

While confirming Moroni's humble assessment of his weakness, the Lord neither confirmed nor denied the weakness itself. Who among us would think to call the words of Moroni weak?

The Lord's promise, to make weak things become strong unto [us], has been of source of strength for me as it has for countless others. However, I have often wondered what the Lord meant when he said; *I give unto men weakness...* Surely the Lord does not make us weak just to turn around and make us strong and yet, at a glance it seems that that is what the scripture is telling us. Logically speaking, if God is actually the source of our weaknesses, he would be assuming a role in opposition to his own plan. If we accept the idea that He is the author of our weakness, we must also acknowledge him as the source of our genius and talent, which is much easier to do, but in doing so we make him a 'respecter of persons.' God is very much involved in our lives, particularly when we ask him to be, however this kind of involvement makes us more experiment than children, with God looking on to see how we will react to conditions for which he is responsible.

While God does give us weakness, I don't believe that He is the actual source. (What I mean by that will hopefully become clear as we proceed.) The same can be said of our strengths and talents. Moroni's message to us is not so much about the source of weaknesses as it is about what God will help us do with them. Making God the source of our weakness, places him in a position of responsibility and accountability in our lives that is not his and would contradict our purpose.

So, if God is not the source of our weaknesses, how does he give them to us? A look at another verse of scripture will be helpful. "The Lord said unto Enoch: Behold these thy brethren; they are the workmanship of mine own hands, and I gave unto them their knowledge, in the day I created them; and in the Garden of Eden, *gave I unto man his agency*;" Moses 7:32 Emphasis added Here the Lord is talking about the eternal principle of agency and yet he said he *gave* it to man in the Garden of Eden. Adam and Eve were mortal beings in the Garden of Eden as a result of their agency, but they were also in a state of innocence. In their innocence, they were neither aware of nor needed their agency. As they increased in knowledge, the choices they faced made them acutely aware and enabled their agency and in this sense, God indeed gave it to them.

This same line of reasoning can be applied to our weaknesses. That part of us where our weakness and strengths reside is the eternal intelligence from which we were created; *[intelligence] is independent in that sphere in which God has placed it, to act for itself...* D&C 93:30 As I read the scriptures, they tell me that God is not able to alter the basic nature of the intelligences, but then why would he want to? The abilities and strengths of the intelligences were plain and known to God and their individualization brought about by the spirit creation, made those attributes apparent to all of us; they made us unique. However, we begin our earth experience without memory of those things, in a state of innocence, dependence and 'weakness.' So, in this sense the Lord did give us weakness, but it is intended to be temporary, while we catch up with ourselves, so to speak.

We should talk a little about what it is that actually constitutes a weakness. I am privileged to know many gifted people. When I compare my strengths to theirs, I honestly wonder a little bit if I actually have any. Is this how we discover our weaknesses? I don't think so and if we try to, we do ourselves a grave injustice. We might view weakness as a virtue, attribute or talent we have not yet attained. We might also think of weaknesses in terms of a vice or character flaw that we are striving to overcome. These would be accurate assessments as long the discovery is not the result of comparison to individuals we have put on a pedestal for the sake of the comparison.

I enjoy gardening and there are some who say I'm good at it; that it is a talent or strength. Does this mean that for my neighbor, who does no gardening at all, it is a weakness? I am not a mathematician, I am not a great musician; are these weaknesses? I admit that they are not strengths, but does that automatically make them the kind of weaknesses we're talking about? If a productive and successful mortal experience required everyone to be proficient in math and music, then yes, they would be weaknesses but, since that is not the case, in and of themselves they are neither strength nor weakness and I don't have to be concerned about that. The strengths we admire in others are not to be seen as indicators of weakness and/or deficiency in us.

Outside of our being born into a state of weakness, how does God give us weakness without actually being the one who makes us weak? He does so by giving us glimpses of our strengths. A glimpse at our potential inspires desire, which in turn reveals a weakness we are able to take to him.

When I was very young I had a fascination and love for flowers. That love grew and developed in the sweat and toil of annual gardens alongside my father. When I reached the point in my life when I became the gardener, my weakness became very apparent to me. I studied and prayed. I experimented and prayed. As I continue this process, my weakness becomes more and more of a strength to me. The Lord gave me a weakness by helping me become aware of a potential strength.

Our weaknesses are the adolescent form of our potential strengths. Weakness is the generic term for individual strengths just getting started. Note that the Lord spoke to Moroni on a very personal level. *"…if men come unto me I will show unto them their weakness…"* He did not say he would reveal just how weak mankind is. The more we seek the Lord and the light that reveals all truth, the more we become aware of ourselves; the spirit begins to catch up. We begin to see where we should excel and when we take that weakness to the Lord, he then is able to make a weak thing strong in us.

****

IMAGINATION

"For me, reason is the natural organ of truth; but imagination is the organ of meaning. Imagination, producing new metaphors or revivifying old, is not the cause of truth, but its condition." C. S. Lewis

I OFTEN WISH I could have had the privilege of meeting C. S. Lewis; to hear him speak, to have an hour one on one. I am inspired by the depth of his insights and his ability to express them. He takes us well beyond the confinement of our circumstances. I marvel at his ability to explore the complexities of subjects such as love and happiness and then take us into the magical world of Narnia. I think he has demonstrated that wisdom and imagination are not distant cousins, many times removed, but are inseparable siblings. Hand in hand they help us discover the meaning in our lives and to manage our discoveries. A closer look reveals that first we imagine and then we live.

"Imagine yourself as a living house. God comes in to rebuild that house. At first, perhaps, you can understand what He is doing. He is getting the drains right and stopping the leaks in the roof and so on; you knew that those jobs needed doing and so you are not surprised. But presently He starts knocking the house about in a way that hurts abominably and does not seem to make any sense. What on earth is He up to? The explanation is that He is building

quite a different house from the one you thought of – throwing out a new wing here, putting on an extra floor there, running up towers, making courtyards. You thought you were being made into a decent little cottage: but He is building a palace. He intends to come and live in it Himself." C. S. Lewis, Mere Christianity p. 176

We first imagine and then we live. This is true no matter the course and direction of our lives, whether spiraling downward or ascending toward lofty pursuits; imagination maintains the course or alters it. We will never achieve more than we are able to imagine. Common sense keeps our imagination in check, but a healthy imagination makes our sense not so common. It enhances our ability to learn and fuels our desire to achieve.

Imaginations are often described as vivid, healthy or possibly void. But, regardless of the condition of our imagination, it is a good indicator of the condition of our lives. For this reason the prophet Alma asked, "…can you imagine to yourselves that ye hear the voice of the Lord, saying unto you, in that day: Come unto me ye blessed, for behold, your works have been the works of righteousness upon the face of the earth? Or do ye imagine to yourselves that ye can lie unto the Lord in that day, and say—Lord our works have been righteous works upon the face of the earth—and that he will save you? Or otherwise, can ye imagine yourselves brought before the tribunal of God with your souls filled with guilt and remorse, having a remembrance of all your wickedness, yea, a remembrance that ye have set at defiance the commandments of God?" Alma 5:16-18

In a world that is turning its back on wisdom and attempting to imagine virtues in the abandonment, we would do well to examine the substance of our imagination. If we can imagine that God wants to make of us a living palace in which he intends to live, it will be because our lives are filled with the materials he prescribes and needs to construct such a place.

****

Journals

Among the first instructions I received as a missionary was the counsel to keep a missionary journal. I was obedient. It required several books, but I wrote in my journal every day. I was somewhat less faithful when I returned home. However, important events such as marriage and children and church callings helped me to keep this principle again.

President Spencer W. Kimball, "We ask you again to do the things that we have suggested…such as keeping up your homes and writing in your journals. Every person should keep a journal and every person can keep a journal. It should be an enlightening one and should bring great blessings and happiness to the families. If there is anyone here who isn't doing so, will you repent today and change—change your life?" President Spencer W. Kimball, Let Us Move Forward and Upward, Ensign (CR), May 1979, p.82

For those of us who have found it difficult to keep our personal record and have procrastinated a little more than we should, please consider this; obviously writing about life events as they occur is the best way to preserve the details of those events. However, the details of living are far less important than the lessons they provide. Those lessons should and will outlive the emotions of the day and are the residue of experience. It is important to write and remember, not so much for the sake of the event, but for what it teaches. I write with an advantage of sorts in that total recall has become lost in a jumble of experiences relieving me of my obligation to those day-to-day details. I am left to recall and to rejoice in the residue of my life experience. From this vantage point I can write that which is most pleasing and of the most worth to me and to others.

I recall an event in my early childhood. The details have been trivialized by time and are all but lost, but the lessons impressed upon me are still very real. The journal entry is called "Only a Toad." I found a tiny toad and subjected the poor creature to the things only a boy would think of. The toad lost its life in the course of my games. I was convinced I was going to hell for killing the toad. I soon found out that I wasn't; at least not right away. Lessons of heaven and hell, God's loving forgiveness and pains of anxiety, came much later and helped me to understand other events in my life. The lessons I learned have indirectly helped members of my family and others because I have recorded them.

The old house next door to where I grew up was home to my curiosity and imagination, but what I've recorded is the great lessons of Charity I learned there.

There are many ways of keeping a journal. Most of the scriptures we read, which are essentially journals and letters, are not daily entries in the lives of the author. For example, most of what we read in the four gospels was written well after the fact and much of what was written was not personally witnessed by the author. So what do we include in our journal? I think we include anything that impresses us and we feel would be a blessing to others as well. Think of the great loss that we would not even know about if Nephi had not included the words and visions and experience of his father.

When my father was a young, only about 13, he was asked by his future aunt, not a member of the Church, to accompany her as she visited her priest. My father was seated by the door while she and the priest visited on the other side of the room. Part way through their conversation the priest turned to my father and asked, "Sonny, when did your church begin?" My father heard a voice; "When father Adam was placed on the earth the gospel was preached to him and that is when our Church began." He repeated the answer he was given and the priest did not ask him any more questions. This experience is part of my journal and my testimony. It has blessed lives now in three generations.

We don't know what will touch and impact the lives of those who will follow us. I have enjoyed reading the journal of my great grandfather, Herman F. F. Thorup. On Sunday, January 22, 1888 he wrote, "A fine day. Attended the meeting at the 14th ward assembly hall with Brother A. Kimball: there were many present of those high in authority, and I must confess that I felt my weakness. But, I prayed to the Almighty for his assistance and he did bless me with his spirit, and with power to perform my duties, and to him I ascribe the honor and the praise. On Wednesday I attended meeting at the Social Hall. President Cannon had returned home from the east where he had seen old David Whitmer who, in Cannon's presence bore his testimony to the divinity of the Book of Mormon, that he saw the angel of God, etc."

When I read this, the spirit bore witness to me again of the truth of the Book of Mormon and the authenticity of the witnesses to it. It was as if I now had a personal link to one of the three witnesses.

We have talked briefly now about two of three reasons to keep a journal. First, we are commanded. Second, our experience is intended to touch and bless others. These are important reasons, but in my mind the third is the most important and compelling. We write for what it does for us. No one will ever be blessed by a journal more than its author. Have you ever thought why it is we don't have a first and second Laman or the words of Lemuel? What we do know of them and the absence of their own words speaks the volumes that are understandably omitted and undoubtedly unwritten. Omni said, "I of myself am a wicked man, and I have not kept the statutes and the commandments of the Lord as I ought to have done." Omni 1:2 The 44 years in which he was charged to keep the small plates are summarized in three verses. The first 239 years of the Book of Mormon are recorded in the books of Nephi, Jacob, Enos and Jarom. The words of Omni, Amaron, Chemish, Abinadom, and Amaleki, cover the next 231 years in 30 verses. I mention this merely because it is interesting. The brevity alone of their accounts does not justify judgment on our part. After all, Mormon was inspired to include them in the Book of Mormon. Nevertheless, we take our example from Nephi. In the first verse of the Book of Mormon he wrote, "…having been highly favored of the Lord in all my days; yea, having had a great knowledge of the goodness and the mysteries of God, *therefore* I make a record of my proceedings in my days." We learn later that Nephi had been commanded to keep a record, but in his opening statement we are given to know that he received the commandment as a natural part of his knowledge of the goodness and mysteries of God. When we, like Nephi, make a record of our knowledge of God's goodness, we are prone to ponder those things as he did. This makes us more than receptive to the things of the spirit. The door of revelation is opened to us. Writing teaches us more effectively than almost anything else we can do. A wise man was once asked about a certain subject. His response was, "I don't know. I haven't written about it yet." I have found this to be true and so my journal includes such things as a synopsis of the four gospels and a commentary on the ministry of the Savior. I have written papers on the doctrine of the atonement, the principles of faith, charity, prayer, and others. None of this has made me an authority, but does make me a qualified witness of the reality and divinity of the Lord. I mention it only to illustrate that a journal is so much more than a daily diary. Truly, the more we write, the more we know.

I think Nephi and other prophets had a lot to say largely because they were looking. Their habit of writing, or keeping the record made them more aware of things worthy of mention. It became a refining influence in their lives. Elder Eyring taught us, "As I kept at it, something began to happen. As I would cast my mind over the day, I would see evidence of what God had done for one of us that I had not recognized in the busy moments of the day. As that happened, and it happened often, I realized that trying to remember had allowed God to show me what He had done. More gratitude began to grow in my heart. Testimony grew. I became ever

more certain that our Heavenly Father hears and answers prayers."
(O Remember, Remember; Ensign November 2007)

All of us have and will have "only a toad" experiences. In them are lessons that will shape and make us. We need to look, see the hand of the Lord in our lives, and write.

****

JUDGE A BOOK BY ITS COVER

"YOU CAN'T JUDGE a book by its cover." This is a very interesting statement because it is both true and false. Most often it means something entirely different than what it says. In 2015-2016 I published my Chronicles of Gigania series. I had a professional artist design the cover of each of the three books. He did an excellent job, but the design work was not a simple process, because the intent was for people to judge the books by their covers. I wanted people to be drawn to the books because of what the covers suggested they would find inside. I think this can be said of all books. There will be something about the cover, at the very least, a title to identify the content.

The statement, "you can't judge a book by its cover," almost never refers to a book. It is a figurative comparison of our lives to a book. The statement acknowledges that our lives are housed within a facade and warns against making assumptions based on the visible part of the book. However, in spite of the seemingly sage advice, we can, we do and in many cases, we must, judge the books around us by the covers we see.

When I published my books, I first submitted the manuscript; the book itself. Once the content was proofed and formatted, it was ready for a cover. The cover art was submitted separately and could have been any design I wanted; essentially the book and the cover were not related in the publishing process. Not so with the cover of our life's book. Our cover and the book are inseparably connected. One cannot be altered without altering the other.

It is difficult, if not impossible, to avoid having a first impression. Very often the benefit of doubt affords us the ability to make adjustments to first impressions, but I don't know of anything that can totally prevent them. The more generic the cover, the more generic and benign will be the initial judgment. But, unlike the cover of a book, we cannot submit a cover independent of the book. We are constantly writing and editing the book of our lives and as a result our cover is developing too; hence, the danger inherent in first impressions. The attempt to create a cover more appealing than the book itself, at best, can yield only temporary results. Such a cover will flap in the wind, exposing the pages inside and eventually fall away entirely.

The cover of our life-book is as complicated, if not more so, than the cover of a book we hope to publish. Our cover is made of clothing and appearance, grooming, words and the tone of those words, facial expression, body language, levels of commitment and preferred associations and the list goes on. The more deliberate these things are, the more spontaneous and accurate are the judgments they promote. When a person defends the cover of his book by saying he should not be judged by it, he is really asking that others overlook the statement the cover is making and believe as he would like to, that it is not reflective of the book. All the while he is fully aware that at least some of the chapters are illustrated by the cover. Some will come to the defense of a family member or friend requesting, sometimes adamantly, that they not be judged by their cover because they see that potentially the person may edit and rewrite chapters in the future. This may be true, and we hope it is. When that happens the cover will undergo its own transformation, but for the present, the cover always reflects what's inside and is subject to judgment.

Right or wrong, we judge and are judged on the basis of our cover. A book filled with wind and thunder might host a cover of sunshine; not so with a stormy life. If our life-book is not what we know it should be, we are kidding ourselves if we think we change things by attempting to dawn a "more suitable" cover. The only way to change the cover by which we are judged is to change the content of our book.

So, in what sense is it true that we cannot judge a book, a life book, by its cover? It is true because we cannot really know the extent of another person's struggles. A person who struggles, and that is all of us, is not necessarily a bad person; very often quite the opposite. His/our cover does not always reflect the struggles because subplots don't necessarily affect or change the story. But even these unsolicited insertion in our life story are at least temporarily noticeable. How often have we said, or heard, "What's wrong," with nothing more than the 'book cover' doing the talking?

The bottom line is that we can judge a book by its cover and if we don't like that idea, the only real recourse we have is to edit our book.

****

Laws of God and Salvation

A conversation with C. S. Lewis, Mere Christianity

C. S. LEWIS said, *"It is not humanity in the abstract that is to be saved, but you— you, the individual."*

God's plan for his children is universal and yet personal. Through the atonement, it affords everyone the option and possibility of salvation, but more specifically, exaltation. Mortality permits full expression of one's own will and the degree of salvation that will suit him best. However, mortality also makes it easier to superficially float the tide of a universal atonement rather than wade upstream against life's perils to make a personal application for its saving grace.

C. S. Lewis, in "Mere Christianity," offers some wonderful insights that help bring to bear the heart and reality of every issue that presents itself in our mortal experience:

"He has room for people with very little sense, but He wants everyone to use what sense they have." p 75

"...If a thing is free to be good it is also free to be bad. And free will is what has made evil possible. Why, then, did God give them free will? Because free will, though it makes evil possible, is also the only thing that makes possible any love or goodness or joy worth having..." p.53

"...Now it is quite true that there will probably be no occasion for just or courageous acts in the next world, (I'm not so sure I agree) *but there will be every occasion for being the sort of people that we can become only as the result of doing such acts here. The point is not that God will refuse you admission to His eternal world if you have not got certain qualities of character; the point is that if people have not got at least the beginnings of those qualities inside them, then no possible external conditions could make a "Heaven" for them..." p. 77-78*

It takes very little living to discover that life is not easy. It has been my observation that, without exception, people develop personal philosophies about themselves and their lives to help them get through it and to feel better about themselves than they otherwise would. These philosophies demonstrate their will, whether they conform to or oppose that of God. Drifting superficially the tides of life tends to validate one's philosophy even when it is in opposition to God's law. They wash over and dilute the laws and ideals that God has set. Debating the merits of the philosophical floods of the world is fruitless. They cannot produce what God decreed and ordained by law.

The atonement is a vicarious, universal ordinance, accomplished by the only person that was (is) worthy and capable to officiate and carry out such an ordinance. Just as with any vicarious work, it is of no effect unless those, for whom the work is done, accept it and embrace its power. All others remain as if there had been no atonement. Self-adapted philosophies, outside the laws that God has set are the demonstration of one's denial, or at least ignorance, of God's law.

In section 88 of the Doctrine and Covenants, the Lord tells us that the earth will be "quickened" and "…crowned with [celestial] glory…" Why? Because it "…abideth the law of a celestial kingdom…" It goes on to say, "That which breaketh a law, and abideth not by law, but seeketh to become a law unto itself…cannot be sanctified by law, neither by mercy…unto every kingdom is given a law; and unto every law there are certain bounds also and conditions. All beings who abide not in those conditions are not justified." (See D&C 88:17-39)

Regardless of the philosophies that present themselves, the question is the same; do they comply with the laws of the kingdom and glory we most want to obtain? Remember, it is our will that is being tested and it is our will that will be rewarded. The terms and conditions were set long ago and remain unaltered by the intellectual benevolence of man.

Learn Wisdom in thy Youth

I remember being young once. I remember that it was not always easy, particularly when there were older people telling all the youth what a chosen generation we were and how much would be expected of us. Sometimes the weight of expectation can be a heavy burden and I have felt the anxiety and confusion that often is the result. In such times I have found relief and consolation in a simple verse of scripture from the Book of Mormon; "And behold, all that he requires of you is to keep his commandments…" Mosiah 2:22 It is true, there is a lot expected, but all that is really required is to keep the commandments, to be good. If we just do our best then the Lord will be able to use us when we're ready and when the time is right. We simply don't need to worry about it. King Benjamin continued, "Believe in God; believe that he is, and that he created all things, both in heaven and in earth; believe that he has all wisdom, and all power…" Mosiah 2:22, 4:9 That's not so difficult; we can believe in God, and when we do, we can begin to believe in ourselves. The Lord said, "Take my yoke upon you…for my burden is light…" When we think of a yoke, we think of the large burdensome block of wood that was once used on oxen, but that's a different kind of yoke. In the time of Christ the Rabi referred to the principles of his doctrine as his yoke and so when Jesus said take my yoke, he was inviting everyone to accept his doctrine; his gospel. He says that his burden is light because when we accept his gospel we are on the path where he is and he will help us. He said he would be on our right hand and our left, that he is our advocate with the Father.

What a wonderful time of life. You can be and become whatever and whoever you want to be and when all is said and done, you will. The key is to decide early because you, like all of us, will gravitate toward those things you desire most. This is why Alma counseled his young son Helaman to *learn wisdom in his youth*, to learn in his youth to keep the commandments.

The prophet Ammoron came to Mormon who was only ten years old and made an observation that is good counsel to all of us. He said that Mormon was **quick to observe**. Ammoron then told Mormon that he should remember the things he observed concerning the people and that he had a mission to perform when he was twenty four. You young people have missions and life ahead of you. You know when that's coming. The rest of us have missions ahead as well and so now is the time for all of us to be quick to observe, to keep the commandments.

As a boy I watched and observed my father. I was sure that my dad could do anything. When I was with him I felt confident and secure. I watched him closely; I wanted to be like him. There were certain jobs that only he did; I had to wait until I was bigger. One of these was milking the cow…. He placed a five gallon bucket under the cow and then with each hand he took hold. With left right left right rhythm, powerful streams of warm milk began to flow. As the bucket filled, the force and consistency of the streams produced a head of foam on the milk. I learned later that this was the sign that one had arrived at milking excellence.

The job required large strong hands. Eventually my little boy hands were up to the challenge. My first attempt was only that. … The pitiful little squirts I produced did not compare to the powerful streams that gushed under my dad's hands. Dripping milk does not produce a head of foam on the bucket. The next day my sore hands were even more so, but I tried again. … In time the rhythm and power came, and a head of foam on the bucket told me I had arrived.

What did I learn? I learned that even though I was inadequate and that my efforts were somewhat pitiful, when I persisted I became strong and capable.

I continued to watch my father. He is gone now, but I still look to his example and realize that in many ways I am still looking for foam on my bucket.

My father served for many years on the high council and so I had the privilege of hearing him speak many times. I loved to listen to him. He spoke with power and conviction and without the aid of notes. Very often, a day or two before his speaking assignment I would find him sitting on the end of his bed, no books, no pen or paper, just thinking; he was preparing his talk. I wanted to be like him. In those days we went to priesthood meeting in the morning, Sunday School in midmorning and Sacrament meeting in the evening. As part of opening exercises for Sunday School there were two and a half minute talks. When I received the assignment for one of these talks I did what I saw my dad do, but when I stood up to speak, my mind was blank. I think I gave the shortest two and half minute in the history of two and a half minute talks. That would be I nice experience to forget, except that it taught me something. I learned that if you want something to come out, you have to put something in first. I also learned that my dad's preparation didn't take place on the end of his bed. It was in the way he lived his life, his regular study of the scriptures and his quiet meditation and prayer. He was always putting something in. I had a lot to do before there would be foam on that bucket.

I think that was about the time when I started to observe people and things around me. I think the Lord was on my side, I think he knew that I needed a little extra help. You young men of the Aaronic Priesthood; I hope you know and appreciate the power and authority that is yours. You have it in you to bless lives, and you do. I remember very clearly one sacrament meeting when I was a teacher, listening to the words of the Sacrament prayer. I felt such a power and witness that I was sure that if I opened my eyes I would see the Savior standing at the table.

You young women please don't underestimate the power of your influence. I remember a young man who had received a call to serve a mission. In the MTC he wanted to come home because he missed his girlfriend. She told him that if he came home she was not his girlfriend. He served a wonderful mission.

Young or old, we're all in this together. We are all children of God and share in the promises and responsibilities. President Hugh B. Brown spoke to the missionaries at the Ricks Language Training Mission while I was there. He said, "Your mission will give to you what it finds in you and develop in you what you want to become."

I would like to share parts of a letter I received from one of our missionaries:

This week, amazing things have happened in the area where I am serving.... There are 168 members in our branch, but if we are lucky we get about 60 to show up on a good day. We are spending most of our time right now trying to re-activate our 100 plus inactives and at the same time, to receive referrals from them, from people we talk to on the street, and from the members. **We needed a lot of help though, and the branch wasn't giving us a lot of support. Finally, on Saturday we met with the Branch President and told him what our vision for the branch was, what we needed from him and from the members. We needed the members to work with us, to be willing to come on visits with us, and go out on the streets with us, to talk to their friends and invite everybody they can to work with the missionaries. We reminded him that we were temporary- missionaries come and go, but these branch members are his and they need to help each other serve. Then, the very next Sunday, there was no Sunday school teacher. The branch President went up to the pulpit and called the members out. "The missionaries need help!" He told them. "They need help. They need it from you. And they need it now, and every single day this week.** *You raise your hand and say you sustain the prophet? Well, sustaining him is more than that- it means that you do what he asks, and he asks you to work with the missionaries. You say you love the Lord? Then serve Him and help the missionaries to bring our*

101

brothers and sisters back!" He was magnificent! I actually had to have the meeting re-capped for me later, since my Russian is not yet that fantastic, but while I may not have understood the words he actually spoke, **I definitely felt the Spirit and energy in the room. Then, in Relief Society, the Relief Society President went up and said, "You heard! The missionaries need our help. Who can go with them Monday night? Tuesday? Wednesday...?" She found us a member for every day of the week, and when the meeting ended, more members came up asking how and when they could help. Oh, it was so, so good! I know that this is the Lord's work and I am so grateful to have a part in it, to help move it forward.**

Quick to observe, quick to do, this is what we need to learn, no matter what stage of our lives we are in. "…Behold, I say unto you that it is my will that you should go fourth and not tarry…lifting up your voices as with the sound of a trump, proclaiming the truth according to the revelations and commandments which I have given you. And thus, if ye are faithful ye shall be laden with many sheaves, and crowned with honor, and glory, and immortality, and eternal life." D&C 75:1-5

****

LET US RECEIVE HIM

AS I HAVE STUDIED the life and mission of our Savior, I have come to know Him well enough to love Him. In my study I have found it both interesting and curious the varied reactions and reception He received as His ministry took Him into Judea, Galilee, Samaria and surrounding regions. There were those who were indifferent and even antagonistic toward Him, but there were many who more or less received Him. Most of the people of Israel at the time of the Savior's earthly ministry had no issue with, and even rejoiced, in the idea of a promised Messiah. However, the idea of a living Christ proved to be more than some were able to comprehend. Disciples of Christ identified and distinguished themselves by their ability to recognize and acknowledge Him. While there may have been a general knowledge, at least among the house of Israel, of the promises and prophesies regarding the Savior's birth, there were relatively few who were actually looking for him. The star, visible to the entire world, captured the imagination of scholars in the east and brought them to Bethlehem, but went undetected in Jerusalem by many of the very ones who should have been among the first to rejoice. On another continent the sign of the Holy Birth spared the lives of believers and changed the hearts of thousands who had been hardened by unbelief, while in Bethlehem, in virtual anonymity the Savior of the world was born. Appropriately we sing, "How silently, how silently the wondrous gift is given."

I contrast the silence on earth with the great anticipation and jubilation that must have filled the eternities on that first Christmas.

Unrestricted by mortality the host of heaven witnessed, with eyes fully open and hearts filled with the love of God, that humble and holy birth. Fully endowed by the love of God and the knowledge of His wondrous gift, voices of praise and glory to the new born king could not be restrained. Humble shepherds became the small, but favored audience, as a choir, described as a multitude of the heavenly host, praised the God of Heaven and earth. All eternity came to bear on that pivotal point in time and on the humble birth of the King of Kings. And as we ponder in song, "Were you there, were you there, that Christmas night," in our hearts we answer in quiet reverence, yes. Now with mortal voice again we sing, "Joy to the world, the Lord is come," and our hearts have prepared Him room. As in days of old our discipleship is defined by how we receive our King.

****

NEPHI AND LABAN

Why did Nephi have to kill Laban?

THE OPENING CHAPTERS OF THE BOOK OF MORMON have left many with the question, *why did Nephi have to kill Laban?* I recently read an article addressing this question which discusses it allegorically and admits that the question itself remains unanswered. We can, and its alright to read the scriptures allegorically or literally, or even both. However, we should search the scriptures to find all the meaning, and while it is nice to be able to find some hidden meaning, I'm not so sure that the Lord would tell Nephi to kill a man for the sake of an allegory.

The very short answer to the question is that the Lord commanded him. Nephi was there. The Lord had delivered Laban into his hands; he was the only one that had the means and opportunity to kill Laban. (1 Ne. 4:12) I think we all understand that, so when we wonder why Nephi had to kill Laban, we are really asking, *why did Laban have to die?*

The article I read suggests that, "perhaps Nephi included this event in such detail to answer even more important questions, eternal questions…" Perhaps, but Nephi actually told us why he included this event or should I say saga. He said, "…But behold, I, Nephi, will show unto you that the tender mercies of the Lord are over all those whom he hath chosen, because of their faith, to make them mighty even unto the power of deliverance." (1 Ne. 1:20)

Nephi told us that we should liken the scriptures unto ourselves. In doing that we find metaphors and allegories that are invaluable to spiritual enlightenment, but in many cases, such as this one, we put ourselves in a better position to learn if we liken

105

ourselves to the scriptures. By stepping into his shoes and walking where he walked we are in a better position to understand why Nephi really had to do what he did.

1 NEPHI, CHAPTERS 1-4: Lehi is warned in a dream of the impending destruction of Jerusalem and obediently does his best to warn the people. Not only do the people mock him, but they seek to kill him as they had other prophets before him. The Lord commanded Lehi to escape with his family into the wilderness which he does, leaving house, land, gold, silver and precious things that would have only been unnecessary burdens. His survival and that of his family was all that was important. Laman and Lemuel complained, but Nephi sought and received spiritual confirmation that his father was inspired and was doing the right thing.

Three days into their journey Lehi is told to send his sons back to Jerusalem; back to the hostile environment they had just escaped. They needed to procure the Brass Plates containing the scriptures and genealogy of Lehi's family and take them with them to the land of promise. Laman and Lemuel go reluctantly while Nephi and Sam go obediently.

The lot falls to Laman to go and ask Laban to surrender the plates. He is accused of attempted robbery and Laban tells him, "I will slay thee."

A second attempt to secure the plates is made by essentially offering to buy them for the price of all the gold, silver and property Lehi had abandoned. Laban refuses to let the plates go, seizes their property and sends his servants to murder Lehi's sons.

The third attempt is by Nephi, alone. Laman and Lemuel had given up and essentially taken the side of the Jews, attacking Nephi and Sam. An angel intervenes, but Laman and Lemuel remain unsupportive. Under the cloak of darkness, Nephi returns to the city where at any moment he could be discovered and killed. He finds Laban lying in the street, intoxicated and unconscious. The Lord tells Nephi to kill him.

What has happened? As a result of their efforts to acquire the Brass Plates, Laban has, in effect, declared war against Lehi and his family. He falsely accused them of attempting to steal the plates for which he threatened to kill Laman. He illegally seized Lehi's property and attempted to murder his sons in order to retain the Plates and the property. Laban became a casualty in his own war. This may demonstrate that Laban's death was justified, but the question remains; why was his death necessary? Nephi answers this question too.

Laban's death was necessary—key verses:
1 Ne. 2:1, ...*behold they seek to take away thy life.* The Jews wanted to kill Lehi and then Laban added the family to the death list.
1 Ne. 4:12-13, ...*slay him, for the Lord hath delivered him into thy hands...the Lord slayeth the wicked to bring forth his righteous purpose. It is better that one man should perish than that a nation should dwindle and perish in unbelief.* The Lord took the responsibility for the death of Laban. The fate of a *nation* hung in the balance; Laban's death was essential. (more on this to follow)
1 Ne. 4:24-25, ...*I spake unto him [Zoram] that I should carry the engravings...to my elder brethren...And I also bade him that he should follow me.* Why would Nephi, after he had secured the plates, invite Zoram to follow? Why not just leave Zoram, and Laban's body and just high tail it back to the wilderness?
1 Ne. 4:31-32, ...*I did seize upon [Zoram] and held him, that he should not flee....I spake with him, that if he would hearken unto my words...we would spare his life.* Making Zoram an accomplice may have resulted in a magnanimous gesture on the part of Nephi, but it was not motivated as such. Nephi was fully prepared to kill Zoram just as he had Laban. Why?—
1 Ne. 4:36, *Now we were desirous that he should tarry with us for this cause, that the Jews might not know concerning our flight into the wilderness, lest they should pursue us and destroy us.* Zoram posed a threat and needed to be neutralized. He opted for life and

liberty among the Nephites. If he hadn't, he would have been the second casualty in Laban's war.

Now, back to the dark streets of Jerusalem; Nephi discovers the unconscious body of Laban. Conceivably he could have simply removed Labans robes, taken his sword and gone about his impersonation without killing him. However, the Lord said it was better that Laban die than a nation dwindle in unbelief. Nephi recounted Laban's offenses and reasoned that his people would need the law in order to keep it and so he was obedient; he took Laban's life. But, suppose Nephi had let Laban live and merely took his robes and sword, tricked Zoram and took off into the wilderness with the plates. Eventually Laban would have regained consciousness. He would have realized that he had been robbed. He would have gone on to find Zoram and the Plates missing. Given the very recent attempts by the sons of Lehi to obtain the Plates, he would have been convinced that they had taken them. Laban had already shown what he was capable of doing in order to retain the plates; he would have sent as many servants and armed men as he could to pursue and destroy Lehi and his family. For their survival it was essential that Laban die for the same reason Nephi was prepared to kill Zoram.

What did the Lord mean when he said a *nation should dwindle and perish in unbelief?* Nephi saw the importance of the plates to his people [nation] but the Lord has an eternal perspective. If Laban had not been killed, it is likely that Lehi and his family would not have survived his retrieval of the plates. Lehi's family and subsequent nation would have perished before they started. The nation [generation] the Lord referred to was not Lehi's, but ours. Laban had to die to insure the survival of Lehi's family and the resulting Book of Mormon that we cherish. Without the Book of Mormon our nation, this generation, would dwindle and perish in unbelief just as countless others who have sought for truth not knowing where to find it. One man, Laban, had to die; Nephi had to kill him for the sake of the Book of Mormon of our generation.

Ordinances

Two weeks ago I had the opportunity of driving to St. George with my son. As is frequently the case when we are together, our conversation turned to the gospel. My son has a wonderful testimony and a strong desire to know the Savior. He asked me an interesting question; "Why do we have ordinances?" I gave him an answer and we talked about it at some length. His question stuck in my mind and I have been pondering and studying to know more. President Jaussi has asked me to discuss this today.

When Adam and Eve were driven out of the Garden of Eden they were commanded to offer sacrifices. Moses tells us, "After many days an angel of the Lord appeared unto Adam saying, why dost thou offer sacrifices unto the Lord? Adam said, I know not save the Lord commanded me." Often this is the same explanation and answer we give to gospel questions and it certainly is a good answer. The prophet Joseph Smith was frequently asked, "Can we not be saved without going through with all those ordinances, etc." He responded, "No, not a fullness of salvation. Jesus said, 'there are many mansions in my Father's house, and I will go and prepare a place for you.' *House* here named should have been translated kingdom; and any person who is exalted to the highest mansion has to abide a celestial law and the whole law too." Joseph Smith, Discourses of the Prophet Joseph Smith, compiled by Alma P. Burton, p.146 Speaking of ordinances Elder Boyd K. Packer asked, "Can you be happy, can you be redeemed, can you be exalted without them? Answer: They are more than advisable or desirable, or even than necessary. More even than essential or vital. They are crucial to each of us." Boyd K. Packer, Things of the Soul , p.186

Clearly we understand the importance and crucial nature of our ordinances, but these responses leave us with the same question;

Why ordinances? Sometimes we might wonder if we really can know the answers to our questions in this life; as if answers might infringe on our faith and should be reserved for another place or another life. Certainly faith is much more than commendable, but it is only a beginning. Brigham Young urged us to not "live beneath our privileges." Brigham Young, Discourses of Brigham Young, selected and arranged by John A. Widtsoe, p.32 The Lord said, "...I...am merciful and gracious unto those who fear me, and delight to honor those who serve me in righteousness and in truth unto the end...And to them will I reveal all mysteries, yea, all the hidden mysteries of my kingdom from days of old, and for ages to come, will I make known unto them the good pleasure of my will concerning all things pertaining to my kingdom." (D&C 76:5-7) I would never presume to know all the answers, but I can testify that by the spirit we can "know the truth of all things."

The angel that appeared to Adam came with a question, but more importantly, he came prepared to teach. The angel's appearance and question to Adam is an indication to us that not only can we know the answers to these things, but that the Lord actually wants us to know. The angel explained to Adam that his sacrifices were, "a similitude of the sacrifice of the Only Begotten of the Father." Moses 5:7 The sacrifices of ancient Israel were a constant reminder to them of the Atoning Sacrifice of the Savior. In further explanation the prophet Abinadi said, "...there was a law given them, yea, a law of performances and of *ordinances*, a law which they were to observe strictly from day to day, to keep them in remembrance of God and their duty towards him." (Mosiah 13:30) Our ordinances serve as stabilizing reminders in a world that is worse than complacent and which promotes itself at the expense of things spiritual.

In 1841 the Lord commanded the saints to build a temple in Nauvoo "For I deign to reveal [condescend to give] unto my church things which have been kept hid from before the foundation of the world." (D&C 124:41) In reference to the temple and its ordinances

Brigham Young stated, "Your endowment is, to receive all those ordinances in the house of the Lord, which are necessary for you, after you have departed this life, to enable you to walk back to the presence of the Father, passing the angels who stand as sentinels, being enabled to give them the key word, the signs and the tokens pertaining to the Holy Priesthood, and gain your eternal exaltation…" Brigham Young, Discourses of Brigham Young, selected and arranged by John A. Widtsoe, p.416 The ordinances of the priesthood administer the covenants by which the power of godliness is manifest "And without the ordinances thereof…the power of godliness is not manifest to men in the flesh;" (D&C 84:20-21) When received and honored, these ordinances with their covenants offer the assurance that we may receive all that the Father has.

The ordinances of the priesthood must be performed physically here on earth; essentially because, whether for the living or the dead they must be recorded here. The Lord instructed Joseph Smith, "…whatsoever you bind on earth shall be bound in heaven, and whatsoever you loose on earth shall be loosed in heaven. Or, in other words, taking a different view of the translation, whatsoever you record on earth shall be recorded in heaven, and whatsoever you do not record on earth *shall not be recorded in heaven*; for out of the books shall your dead be judged, according to their own works, whether they themselves have attended to the ordinances in their own *propria persona*, or by the means of their own agents…" (D&C 128:8) If the covenants associated with these ordinances are not received and honored by the individual in this world and likewise those in the next, the ordinance itself becomes merely a physical exercise.

My father has mentioned to me his gratitude for the young boy of eight who was baptized as proxy for the man he became; enabling him to open his heart and receive the covenant as an adult, fully aware of the blessing received those many years earlier. We perform the physical part of priesthood ordinances for those who did not have the privilege in life. They too must receive the covenants.

To my knowledge it has not been revealed to us how these ordinances performed for the dead are actually received by them individually; however, we do know that the priesthood functions as actively and vitally where they reside as it does here.

I recently had the opportunity of speaking with a young man about the blessings of temple marriage. His wife is a member of the Church, but he is not. Because he does not understand the principles of eternal marriage he is somewhat offended by the idea that his civil marriage is not binding in the next life. He reasons that God's love for him would not permit their separation merely on the basis of this technicality. He does not understand that it is God's love that will allow him to affect his own separation on the basis of his own agency.

Some years ago my wife and I became acquainted with two young sisters from Laos. We had the opportunity of witnessing as they, along with others from all around the world, stood before a judge and were sworn in as citizens of the United States. I cannot speak for all of those people, but I know that our two friends studied hard. They learned the process and acquainted themselves with all the requirements and then did all they could do to qualify for official residency in America. It does not take much of an imagination to know what would happen if an individual made application for citizenship based solely on his desire and the good nature of the judge. It is simply understood that admission is limited to those who are willing to comply with the established laws pertaining to citizenship and naturalization. No one would presume to ignore or rewrite these laws and yet there are some who assume the prerogative to do exactly that when it comes to God and entrance into His Kingdom.

If we are to gain entrance into the celestial kingdom and receive an exaltation there it will be by a voluntary effort on our part to discover and comply with the laws and ordinances of the gospel. These laws and ordinances were prescribed and ordained in the spirit world before this world began. (D&C 128:22) The great Atonement was detailed then and there for all of God's children. We know by revelation that 1/3 would have nothing to do with it. Adam and Eve were placed on the earth and the Father's plan was put into motion for the 2/3 that chose to participate in it. Alma explains that "After God had appointed that these things should come unto man, behold, then he saw that it was expedient that man should know concerning the things whereof he had appointed unto them; therefore he sent angels to converse with them, who caused men to behold of his glory." (Alma 12:28-29) The saints in all ages have been commanded to build temples wherein the foreordained ordinances are revealed. In our day the Lord said, "…build a house…that those ordinances might be revealed which had been hid from before the world was." (D&C 124:38) These ordinances are hidden from the world, but available to all who desire citizenship in God's kingdom and are willing to make application. By means of this earth experience we have the privilege of proving ourselves by accepting the ordinances that were ordained for that purpose. For those who will not receive these ordinances this life is little more than a test. The Lord wants so much more for us. He said, "…build a house to my name…that you may prove yourselves unto me that ye are faithful in all things whatsoever I command you, that I may bless you, and crown you with honor, immortality, and eternal life." (D&C 124:55)

The Savior taught us by His example that there are no exceptions; that the laws pertaining to God's kingdom applied to him as much as any other child of God.

I am grateful that God has revealed and restored the ordinances of the priesthood by which we declare an active desire to be one with Him in full fellowship in His kingdom. In the ordinances of the priesthood God's love for us and ours for Him is manifest.

****

Perception vs. Reality

IN A VERY REAL and sometimes unforgiving world, there are few who live their lives in total harmony with it. Everything we do is based on the way we see the realities around us. Hopefully, we navigate life in relative safety behind lenses of perception. But perception is not always reliable; it might not serve us the way we think; it is just as likely to be detrimental as it is advantageous. Generally speaking, we cannot, or possibly do not permit ourselves, to see anything more than what our perception tells us. Ideally, we occasionally dare to look beyond our perceptions to see how they stack up against reality and when we do, sometimes our perception changes. Sometimes our perception lens gets shattered by reality slamming up against it. Then, as reality bears down on us, we have no choice but to accept it as it is, at least for a time. Usually the result is a new perspective, hopefully a better one; a heightened perception with which to navigate. However, sometimes pride stubbornly throws up the same old lens and our perceptions are none the better for it. When that happens, the person behind the lens becomes defensive and protective of his perception and reality becomes an enemy.

The process of shattered lenses and grasping for new ones is a regular occurrence, particularly for children. While it often represents the tragic end of life as the child knows it, these moments, from a more adult perspective can be humorous. Meal time often pits adult perspectives against those of the child; a contest not easily managed by either. On one such occasion, our daughter was compelled to send her six year old daughter into another room for the much dreaded 'time out.' Our granddaughter's lens had shattered. After just a few minutes her sobs went silent. The brief silence was followed by a desperate cry, "I want to live!" In that instant her perception of the world around her had collapsed and in the trauma of the moment, she was not able to see anything else. In a few more minutes she began to realize that her world was still intact and without knowing it her perception of it was changing.

We accept this as a childhood thing; a growing process. What we may not recognize is that we never entirely outgrow it. At best we learn to manage it, but the older we get the more difficult it becomes. The child absolutely hates it when his lenses break or even crack, but for a child, new ones are found easily and he quickly forgets the old ones. Children are good at breaking lenses and they do it mercilessly. Most children learn that rather than enduring broken lenses, it is better to not be too attached to perceptions and be willing to let reality have some say in them; to make adjustments if needed. We all did, or rather, do this. We polish our lenses in an effort to broaden our view. The earlier in life we do this; the easier it is for us to alter our perceptions; to accept and live with reality. The longer we hold onto our perceptions, true or false, right or wrong; the more they become our reality. Trying to put an adult in a proverbial time out has the reverse effect; it limits his view to the one that would land him there.

Most people are content with their perceptions and confident that they have a firm grasp of reality. I say most because there are those who know that their perception is skewed and yet they remain devoted to the reality they have created for themselves.

What is reality? Someone will quote another person and then add, "But in reality he is saying…" Another person shakes his head and says, "That guy needs to get a grip on reality." When we talk about reality, what we really mean is, 'the truth of the matter.' What is interesting and often ironic, is that when a person questions someone else's perception, he is doing so on the basis of his own, which is not always (often isn't) the real 'truth of the matter,' but just another perception.

Some things are very important and fall under the heading of 'the truth of the matter.' However, most of what is considered a part of life and living is not part of a grand reality and quite simply doesn't matter. But, there are some so entrenched in their reality that they are less than patient with others who dare to see things differently.

Some live behind customized lenses they have designed to protect them from the 'real truth of the matter' when reality is too painful. This is generally done when a person bases his perception of reality on someone else's misguided perceptions. Sadly, they become victims of perceptions. They create a place that can be lonely, where they are constantly defending themselves against reality. Sadly, reality becomes a bad thing when the truth of the matter is that reality is their escape from the heartache they have bundled up in their perceptions.

The truth of the matter is that mankind was meant to have joy. Anything that says otherwise should be dismissed as a false perception of reality.

***

Prayer and Personal Revelation

It is estimated that the Milky Way Galaxy, of which our solar system is a part, contains some 400 billion stars. That estimate comes with the caveat that the number might be only half as much but could as easily be double that. Within the Milky Way galaxy there are billions of solar systems and from our position in the universe with today's technology there are over 125 billion observable galaxies. The Lord said, *"...For there are many worlds that have passed away by the word of my power. And there are many that now stand, and innumerable are they unto man; but all things are numbered unto me, for they are mine and I know them."* (Moses 1:35) By revelation the prophet Joseph Smith recorded, *"And this is the gospel, the glad tidings, which the voice of the heavens bore record unto us—That he came into the world, even Jesus, to be crucified for the world, and to bear the sins of the world...that through him **all** might be saved whom the Father had put into his power and made by him;"* (D&C 76:40-42)

The Psalmist said, *"When I consider the heavens, the works of thy fingers, the moon and the stars, which thou hast ordained; what is man, that thou art mindful of him..."* (Psalms 8:3-4) This is a question that I have asked and pondered at some length. The Lord indeed is mindful of us, but that will mean very little to us unless we are mindful of Him. This is illustrated in the circumstances surrounding the birth of the Savior. It is likely that in addition to Zacharias and Elisabeth there were others who were faithful and were privileged to know of Jesus' birth in advance of it, but in spite of that, as far as we know, Joseph and Mary came to Bethlehem unannounced. They were two among many who had come by the same mandate of Rome. They found the city a bustle of people and activity. There was no room to be found and so a stable became the temporary shelter and birth place of the Savior of the world. The quiet and anonymous arrival of Mary and Joseph to Bethlehem is contrasted by a universal proclamation of Jesus' entry into mortality. A sign that only God, His Father, could provide was given as a star in heaven, placed in its appointed course in the eternities to appear at precisely the right moment in time to herald this great event in the eternal lives of all mankind. The star was visible across the world and was seen by those who were mindful and cared to see it. Scholars in countries to the Far East saw it and followed its prophesy to find the Child Savior. An angel accompanied by a heavenly host proclaimed to shepherds the royal birth. The long awaited Messiah had been born in obscurity but certainly not in secret. And yet, less than 10 miles away in Jerusalem Herod and his court were unaware and later *"When Herod the king had heard these things, he was troubled...."* (Mat. 2:3)

In spite of the incomprehensible vastness of God's creations any anonymity on our part is self imposed. Earth and heaven proclaim Him, but only to those who are mindful of Him. The Lord has promised, *"Draw near unto me and I will draw near unto you; seek me diligently and ye shall find me; ask, and ye shall receive; knock, and it shall be opened unto you. Whatsoever ye ask the Father in my name it shall be given unto you, that is expedient for you;"* (D&C 88:63-64)

The phrase "Come unto me" is referenced 64 times in the scriptures. Most of these are direct invitations to us with promises such as: "I will give you rest" "Mine arm of mercy is extended toward you" "Be saved" "I will receive you" "I shall heal them" "Be sanctified by the reception of the Holy Ghost" "Ye may receive a remission of your sins" "show unto them their weakness" "Their souls may live" "Ye shall have eternal life" In the 76th section of the Doctrine and Covenants we read, *"I, the Lord, am merciful and gracious unto those who fear me [are mindful of me], and delight to honor those who serve me in righteousness and in truth unto the end....And to them will I reveal all mysteries, yea, all the hidden mysteries of my kingdom from days of old, and for ages to come, will I make known unto them the good pleasure of my will concerning all things pertaining to my kingdom."* (D&C 76:5,7)

The gift and principle of prayer enables God's children to come unto him. It is simple in its operation, but let's consider its miracle and mighty power. Let's assume for a moment that the celestial world on which God lives is somewhere in our galaxy and we are able to locate it and travel there at the speed of light. Depending on where that is exactly it could take as much as 100,000 years for us to get there, and yet our humble prayer penetrates the vastness of the cosmos and each of us have felt the instantaneous witness of the spirit in response. Obviously the laws of physics as we know them do not apply to prayer and are beyond the understanding of our physical condition. To say that God's Spirit is everywhere and ever present is no less of a miracle. I for one am grateful that I do not have to understand the principle of prayer in order to harness its power and rejoice in its miracle.

Brigham Young said, "There is no doubt, if a person lives according to the revelations given to God's people, he may have the Spirit of the Lord to signify to him His will, and to guide and to direct him in the discharge of his duties, in his temporal as well as his spiritual exercises. I am satisfied, however, that in this respect, we live far beneath our privileges." (Journal of Discourses)

The revelation and blessing of those privileges will come in large measure as a result of personal prayer. The witness and testimony of others casts a dim light upon them but through the prayer of faith they are fully illuminated and become our own.

This great power and privilege of prayer must never be taken lightly or for granted. It is made available to us by the Lord. It is our gift and in no way does it obligate Him to us. The Lord has warned, *"...except this people repent and turn unto the Lord their God...it shall come to pass that when they shall cry unto me I will be slow to hear their cries...and except they repent ...I will not hear their prayers, neither will I deliver them out of their afflictions."*

(Mosiah 11:23-25)   James instructs us that we must *"...ask in faith, nothing wavering. For he that wavereth is like a wave of the sea driven with the wind and tossed. For let not that man think that he shall receive any thing of the Lord."* (James 1:6-7)

Coupled with faith our prayers should and must be offered in the deepest appreciation and reverence. We are addressing our Father, the God of earth and universe. Speaking of the language of prayer Elder Dallin H. Oaks has said, *"...Some languages have intimate pronouns and verbs used only in addressing family and very close friends. Other languages have honorific forms of address that signify great respect, such as words used only when speaking to a king or other person of high rank. Both of these kinds of special words are appropriately used in offering prayers in other languages because they communicate the desired feelings of love, respect, reverence, or closeness. Modern English has no special verbs or pronouns that are intimate, familiar, or honorific. When we address prayers to our Heavenly Father in English, our only available alternatives are the common words of speech like you and your or the dignified but uncommon words like thee, thou, and thy which were used in the King James Version of the Bible almost five hundred years ago. Latter-day Saints, of course, prefer the latter. In our prayers we use language that is dignified and different, even archaic. The men whom we sustain as prophets, seers, and revelators have consistently taught and urged English-speaking members of our Church to phrase their petitions to the Almighty in the special language of prayer. President Spencer W. Kimball said, 'In all our prayers, it is well to use the pronouns thee, thou, thy and thine instead of you, your and yours inasmuch as they have come to indicate respect.'"* Elder Dallin H. Oaks, The Language of Prayer, Ensign (CR), May 1993, p.15

Elder Rulon S. Wells reminded us many years ago that *"The Lord has commanded us to pray without ceasing"* and he went on to explain what that means. *"Prayer is the soul's sincere desire, uttered or unexpressed....The real prayer, the true prayer is a*

condition of the heart. When we bow the knee and offer up our verbal petitions, we are giving expression to prayer and this should be done at frequent intervals, every morning and every night, but the prayer itself is in the heart and must be constant and unceasing."
Elder Rulon S. Wells, Conference Report, October 1930, Afternoon Meeting, p.87

Prayers that are offered habitually may never find a place in the heart and are made rhetorical in substance. These prayers, like all prayers, are received and considered with the same sincerity as that of their offering. If our prayer truly is the soul's sincere desire then thoughtful pondering is the expression and measure of that desire.

Pondering is the nurturing of a prayer that occupies the heart. As we nurture it there, we are not only petitioning, we are also listening. Spiritual conversation is most likely to occur when our prayer for guidance or for understanding or consolation continues and persists in a humble heart. Here our prayers are able to develop and mature. As they do we learn to ask inspired questions and we begin to understand and appreciate the nature of the answers we receive. What do I mean by the nature of the answers? An answer from the Lord will never come as an FYI. God will never reveal anything to us as a matter of information only. The answers to our prayers will always come with inherent obligation and responsibility; if nothing else, the responsibility to believe it and to act upon. Answers may come with the responsibility to share it or bear witness of it. The nature of our response to what we are given will ultimately validate what we receive or do not receive in response to our next petition.

Elder B. H. Roberts said, *"For what is prayer, the only prayer worthwhile, but the Infinite in man struggling outward to find God's Infinite, and stand united with that?...What is prayer, but the very limited righteousness of man seeking the righteousness of God? What is prayer but the little strength in man seeking to supplement that strength-which but reveals man's weakness, -by union with God's strength, that man may be adequate for his duty? Such is prayer. Its effort and its mission is to invoke the felt need and felt presence of the Infinite, leading to realized acceptance with God—*

the crowning glory and the end of worship." The Spirit of Worship By B. II. Roberts of the First Council of Seventy Improvement Era 1914

I testify that these things a true. May we ever be mindful of the Lord, the Great Giver of all that is good and come unto Him in humble and mighty prayer. As we do we will feel His presence and the sweet assurance of His voice.

****

Rising Generation

I will be speaking primarily to the adults; you fathers and leaders, but the young men should pay attention as well, because what is to be said here is vitally important to you too.

In the 26th chapter of Mosiah, Mormon makes mention of a rising generation; *"Now it came to pass that there were many of the rising generation that could not understand the words of king Benjamin, being little children at the time he spake unto his people; and they did not believe the tradition of their fathers."* In the 1st chapter of 3rd Nephi Mormon also speaks of the rising generation; *"And there was also a cause of much sorrow among the Lamanites; for behold, they had many children who did grow up and began to wax strong in years, that they became for themselves, and were led away by some who were Zoramites, by their lyngs and their flattering words, to join those Gadianton robbers. And thus were the Lamanites afflicted also, and began to decrease as to their faith and righteousness, because of the wickedness of the rising generation."* In the book of Alma we read of another rising generation. These 2060 sons of Helaman *"...were all young men, and they were exceedingly valiant for courage, and also for strength and activity; but behold, this was not all— they were men who were true at all times in whatsoever thing they were entrusted. Yea, they were men of truth and soberness, for they had been taught to keep the commandments of God and to walk uprightly before him....they had been taught by their mothers, that if they did not doubt, God would deliver them. And they rehearsed unto me the words of their mothers, saying: We do not doubt our mothers knew it....behold those two thousand and sixty were firm and undaunted. Yea, and they did obey and observe to perform every word of command with exactness; yea, and even according to their faith it was done unto them; and I did remember the words which they said unto me that their mothers had taught them."*

Each of us is a contributing member of a rising generation with an unavoidable responsibility to the one that follows. The discharge of that responsibility is greatly influenced by the generation that precedes us. We have reason to believe that each of these generations was taught the truths of the gospel. However, the son's of Helaman said something that is tremendously important for us to ponder as we consider our rising generation. They said that they **did not doubt that their mothers knew it.**

The generation at the time of King Mosiah was small children when King Benjamin spoke to his people and they could not understand his words. How many small children of any generation understand the words? I think we all know that children are learning long before the words have meaning. They learn by observation. My cousin learned this in the grocery store one day. He approached the check out with his small child in his arm. When he was close enough and before he could do anything about it, the child grabbed the cashier's microphone and the entire store heard, "I would like to bear my testimony." He was too young to know what a testimony was. He was merely repeating behavior he had observed in the people he knew and trusted and loved. Each of us is a teacher. The things we say and do unavoidably represent our personal philosophies and ideals. By our speech and conduct, the way of life we have chosen is promoted within the sphere of our influence. In my early years I never gave it much thought, but now I reflect with love and gratitude as I have come to know that my parents were always teaching. Directly east of our house stood a house that looked like the abandoned homes you see along the freeway in remote parts of the country. It was always just The Old House and I was surprised that people would actually come and live in it. Most of the people left as suddenly as they arrived, but one family stayed for a while; long enough for us to become acquainted. Their needs soon became obvious to my parents and for the sake of the family, especially the small children, my parents stepped in. More than once the children were bathed, clothed and fed in our home. We took food and stocked their cupboards. The Old House is gone now, but the lessons of charity I was shown there will always be a part of me.

The scriptures make very clear our responsibility to the rising generation. The Lord said that *inasmuch as parents have children in Zion, they are to teach them to understand the doctrines of repentance, faith in Christ the Son of the living God, and of baptism and the gift of the Holy Ghost...and to pray and to walk uprightly before the Lord.* The prophet Lehi taught us of our responsibility and accountability to our children when he blessed his grandchildren: *"...I know that if ye are brought up in the way should go ye will not depart from it. Wherefore, if ye are cursed, behold, I leave my blessing upon you, that the cursing may be taken from you and be answered upon the heads of your parents."* The Lord reiterated this in revelation to Joseph Smith when He said, *"...children are redeemed from the foundation of the world through mine Only Begotten; Wherefore, they cannot sin, for power is not given unto Satan to tempt little children, until they begin to become accountable before me; For it is given unto them even as I will, according to mine own pleasure,* [why] *that great things may be required at the hands of their parents."*

The rising generation looks to us for more than they know. What they receive from us may not always be what we imagine or hope, but will always be consistent with what we offer. They will learn and receive most readily the things that we ourselves have made a part of us. If what we profess and hope for our children is more than we ourselves are willing to live it is likely that yet another generation will come to themselves and not believe the traditions of their fathers.

Financial responsibility and accountability often appear to be principles far easier to preach than to practice. In order to offer this in a way acceptable and tenable we must above all else be mindful to make the law of tithing a natural part of our way of life. While the world at large knows a great deal of poverty and want, the world around us is generally quite affluent, and in our affluence it is often easy to express our love for our children by simply giving them the things they want, while withholding those things may actually express it more deeply. Financially my parents were never wealthy and yet I never knew it and never thought about it enough to care. They taught me thrift without calling it that. We did not have a lot of things, but only because we did not need them. They showed me how to be happy and content, never allowing things I did not have to influence my feelings about the blessings I did have.

To this day my father has never held a credit card. His idea of being able to afford something has always been based on need and never the affordability of payments. If he did not have the money, he waited until he did. Again, without knowing it I was learning how to get by and be happy in the process. I remember when skate boards were first introduced. I wanted one, but I don't remember ever asking my parents if I could get one. I think I knew that it just wasn't necessary. But, I still wanted a skate board. After some time of waiting and watching others on their new boards I decided I was going to have one. I found an old 2 x 4 and cut it to what I thought was the right length. I found an old roller skate (not today's in-line roller blades, but the ones with two wheels in front and two in back– adjustable to fit different shoe sizes) and took it apart. By screwing the front wheels to the front of my 2 x 4 and the back wheels to the back, I had a skate board. It served me long enough for the fad to loose its novelty.

The gospel of Jesus Christ is a pearl of great price and embraces all those things we most desire, not only for ourselves but for all those we hold dear. These are the things with which we should shower them and endow them. The following poem describes the contrasting view of two who look back on the generation following them.

As I look back on sorrow's road,

I see others who stumble too.
And with heavy heart must admit,
My steps were all they knew.

I now look back with grateful eyes,
On paths that brought me joy,
And rejoice in those I love,
As my steps they employ. W. T. Svedin

It is my hope and prayer that we will all be able to look into the hearts of our own rising generation and find joy in knowing that they are following in the steps of our worthy example.

****

Self-Reliance

Self-reliance is a subject of grave importance, made obvious by the fact that it has been talked about much longer than any one of us has been alive. Indeed it is crucial to the Lord's plan of happiness for us and is simply a part of the gospel of which we testify.

In the priesthood session of April conference Bishop Keith B. McMullin introduced two new pamphlets entitled, "All Is Safely Gathered In." Keith B. McMullin, Lay Up in Store, Ensign, May 2007 One devoted to 'family home storage' and the other to 'family finances.' Regarding home storage the First Presidency said, "Our Heavenly Father created this beautiful earth, with all its abundance, for our benefit and use. His purpose is to provide for our needs as we walk in faith and obedience. He has lovingly commanded us to 'prepare every needful thing' so that, should adversity come, we may care for ourselves and our neighbors and support bishops as they care for others...We ask that you be wise as you store food and water and build your savings. Do not go to extremes; it is not prudent, for example, to go into debt to establish your food storage all at once. With careful planning, you can, over time, establish a home storage supply and a financial reserve." "All Is Safely Gathered In: Family Home Storage," All Is Safely Gathered In: Family Home Storage, (2007)

Regarding family finances the First Presidency counsels: "Latter-day Saints have been counseled for many years to prepare for adversity by having a little money set aside. Doing so adds immeasurably to security and well-being. Every family has a responsibility to provide for its own needs to the extent possible. We encourage you...to prepare for adversity by looking to the condition of your finances. We urge you to be modest in your expenditures; discipline yourselves in your purchases to avoid debt. Pay off debt as quickly as you can, and free yourselves from this bondage. Save a little money regularly to gradually build a financial reserve."

Bishop McMullin began his talk with a very interesting statement. He said, "Each [of us] can, because of our Savior Jesus Christ, inherit the celestial order of life..." Keith B. McMullin, Lay Up in Store, Ensign, May 2007 The implication is that there are other orders of life but, because of the Savior, the celestial order is within our means and ability to achieve. I have pondered this as related to his subject of self-reliance and our responsibility to 'lay up in store,' and was prompted to read again chapters three and four of 3rd Nephi. Here we read about the righteous Nephites and Lamanites and their struggle against the Gadianton robbers. Under the inspired leadership of Lachoneus and Gidgiddoni the people were able to prepare and gather enough provisions to sustain themselves for seven years. Their self-reliance became their defense and eventually enabled them to defeat the robbers who had no means of their own support. "...it was impossible for the robbers to...have any effect upon the Nephites, because of their much provision which they had laid up in store." 3 Ne 4:18

This account clearly illustrates what self-reliance can do for us individually and collectively. This story makes it obvious why we should strive to become self-reliant and why the Lord places so much emphasis upon it. The enemies in our lives will probably never be so well defined and obvious but our preparations, those things we lay up in store, will just as surely be our defense and will determine our victory.

Our self-reliance is fundamental to 'the celestial order of life.' This does not mean that one who receives assistance cannot achieve it. The people of Lachoneus numbered in the tens of thousands. It is not reasonable to assume that every person contributed equally in their preparations. Surely some were in a position to contribute a great deal while others had little and were assisted. The redemption of the collective was a result of individuals doing all that was in their means to do.

It has been my observation that there are those who have been able to accumulate much of this world's goods and yet they come short of the kind of self-reliance I believe the Lord wants for us. The self-reliance that will prepare us to inherit the celestial order of life entails more than the physical requirements of life. This self-reliance actually acknowledges and rejoices in a dependence upon our Savior, Jesus Christ. This is the self-reliance with which Nephi spoke, "I am encompassed about, because of the temptations and the sins which do so easily beset me. And when I desire to rejoice, my heart groaneth because of my sins; nevertheless, I know in whom I have trusted. My God hath been my support; he hath led me through mine afflictions in the wilderness;...He hath filled me with his love...He hath confounded mine enemies...Behold he hath heard my cry by day, and he hath given me knowledge by vision in the nighttime...O then, if I have seen so great things, if the Lord in his condescension unto the children of men hath visited men in so much mercy, why should my heart weep and my soul linger in the valley of sorrow, and my flesh waste away, and my strength slacken...why should I yield to sin...why should I give way to temptations, that the evil one have place in my heart...Awake, my soul! No longer droop in sin. Rejoice, O my heart, and give place no more for the enemy of my soul...O Lord, I will praise thee forever; yea, my soul will rejoice in thee, my God, and the rock of my salvation." (2 Ne. 4:18-30)

I believe we under estimate the principle of self-reliance and its power to exalt us if we view it as merely a principle of independence. No one wants to be a burden to others and so we work hard to provide for ourselves and our families. Many hours are devoted to jobs in order to provide for ourselves the necessities and good things of this life. However, if we are not careful, our quest for these things can become more of a threat to us than the lack of them ever would be. As we devote ourselves to the celestial order, according to Bishop McMullin, "we turn from excess to that which edifies, for 'that which doth not edify is not of God.' If dealings or involvements or pursuits or schedules detract from putting God first, we must pare back and unencumber our lives." _{Keith B. McMullin, Lay Up in Store, Ensign, May 2007}

The unknown looms as a possibility and may even be a cause of fear in our lives. We cannot prepare specifically for the unknown, but as we follow the counsel of inspired Church leaders and prepare ourselves in a general way, as counseled, fear is dispelled. These preparations make more bearable the personal calamities that many of us have or will experience. Over the years Jan and I have been grateful on more than one occasion that we had prepared for circumstances that would have otherwise threatened our well being. We have noticed, that because of our obedience, we have been preserved in those times to a greater degree than we ourselves had prepared. In our lives, the scripture has been fulfilled wherein the Lord said, "I will multiply blessings upon the house of my servant...inasmuch as he is faithful, even a multiplicity of blessings." D&C 104:46

As we strive for self-reliance there is something we should 'lay up in store' that will actually make the burden lighter. In all our effort let us cultivate and develop the ability to be happy and grateful. One whose heart is filled with gratitude requires far less beyond the necessities to sustain him. Filled with gratitude our appreciation is not impaired by a fruitless focus on the things we do not have and happiness prevails. John A. Widstoe said, "The first lesson in the art of happiness is to do without. Whoever lifts his affections above earthly things expands in spirit and begins to grow." John A. Widtsoe, Evidences and Reconciliations, p.283

With so many obvious reasons to strive for self-reliance we must not overlook the most fundamental. The Lord wants us to be free. Free to demonstrate our true devotion. Free to worship. Free to serve. Free to experience the kind of happiness He intends for us. We must not allow the love and devotion to God within us to become buried by indulgences and lives made too busy. That which we serve and which receives our devotion will eventually rule over us. We must do all that we can to free ourselves of debt and/or circumstances that demand of us the devotion we would reserve for the Lord. The Lord wants us to be free to experience life rather than labor in servitude to it.

I close with the words of our Savior, "With promise immutable and unchangeable, that inasmuch as those whom I commanded were faithful they should be blessed with a multiplicity of blessings." D&C 104:2

****

Testimony

I have had the blessing of sharing my testimony on many occasions as you have. I have felt the spirit bear witness and confirm my testimony in my heart as you have. What is the significance of a testimony to a member of the Church of Jesus Christ of Latter Day Saints? Elder Holland said that, "Christ has asked demanding and difficult discipleship from the members of His Church. He strengthens us for the task and He is patient with our halting efforts, but ultimately–sometime, somewhere–we have to measure up. Although that will not be easy, certainly not convenient, it will bring light to the darkest corner of our world and it will bring 'life more abundantly.' In our necessary moments of self-denial, it will help to know He went that same way before." Jeffrey R. Holland, However Long and Hard the Road, p.26

As we strive to know what it means to be a disciple of Christ and as we struggle through the demands and challenges of life it is testimony that brings stability to the uncertainty of it all. As we look for the balance that brings satisfaction and fulfillment our testimonies are defined by the course we choose. For the faithful disciple of Christ it is his testimony, be it simple or seasoned in years, that allows him to see clearly in a contradictory world. His testimony grows as it gives him direction. On the other hand, others find the ideas embraced in testimony a complicating factor in their lives as these ideas come in direct conflict with the real thoughts and intents of their heart. For many of these, what might have been the beginnings of testimony is dashed by the reality that their hearts cannot sustain it. The apostle John tells us that following the miraculous feeding of 5000, "...those men, when they had seen the miracle that Jesus did, said, This is of a truth that prophet that should come into the world." John 6:14 It would seem that these had received a witness and were bearing testimony. However, later these people sought Jesus and when they found him, "Jesus answered them and said, Verily, verily, I say unto you, Ye seek me, not because ye saw the miracles, but because ye did eat of the loaves, and were filled." John 6:26 Jesus then proceeded to give His 'Bread of Life' sermon. "Many therefore...when they had heard this, said, This is an hard saying; who can hear it? When Jesus knew in himself that his disciples murmured at it, he said unto them, Doth this offend thee?...And he said, therefore said I unto you, that no man can come unto me, except he doeth the will of my Father who hath sent me. From that time many of his disciples went back, and walked no more with him." (John 6)

This was a defining moment for more than 5000 people. While many disavowed themselves others declared, "...to whom shall we go? Thou has the words of eternal life. And we believe and are sure that thou art that Christ, the Son of the living God." John 6:68

Matthew, Mark and Luke record a defining moment in the life of one identified by Luke as a ruler and by Matthew as simply a young man. Jesus had left His home in Galilee and taught as he traveled in the coasts of Judea beyond Jordan, meaning to the east of the borders of Judea. This is where little children were brought to Him. "And He took them up in his arms, put his hands on them, and blessed them." Mark continues, "And when he [Jesus] was gone forth into the way, there came one running, and kneeled to him, and asked, Good Master, what shall I do that I may inherit eternal life?" (Mark 10) There was nothing casual or insincere about this young man's approach and his question seems to be equally sincere. He had acknowledged the Savior. However, when his acknowledgment came to the point of definition it was not enough to rise to the sustaining power of testimony. Jesus told him that his discipleship would require more than the obligatory observance of the commandments. He said, "...One thing lackest thou: go thy way, sell whatsoever thou hast, and give to the poor, and thou shalt have treasure in heaven: and come, take up the cross and follow me. And he was sad at that saying, and went away grieved: for he had great possessions." Mark 10:21

This rich young ruler seemed to know who Jesus was, and if that were all we knew of this story we might be inclined to say he had a testimony. However, because he could not do as the Savior said, it is obvious to all that he did not, or it was at least one of insufficient substance. This also illustrates that there is more to testimony than merely knowing. Knowledge alone has not the power to produce or sustain the substance of true testimony. Bruce R. McConkie said, "If the sole source of one's knowledge or assurance of the truth of the Lord's work comes from reason, or logic, or persuasive argument that cannot be controverted, it is not a testimony of the gospel. In its nature a testimony consists of knowledge that comes by revelation, 'for the testimony of Jesus is the spirit of prophecy'..." Bruce R. McConkie, Mormon Doctrine, 2d ed., p.785 Where testimony is concerned it appears that the source of our knowledge is of greater importance than is the knowledge itself. Early in His ministry as the Savior taught in Capernaum, "...There was in their synagogue a man with an unclean spirit; and he cried out, Saying, Let us alone; what have we to do with thee thou Jesus of Nazareth? Art thou come to destroy us? I know thee who thou art, the Holy One of God. And Jesus rebuked him, saying, Hold thy peace,..." Mark 1:23-25 Similar incidents are recorded with the same rebuke. Theirs was a witness the Savior did not need nor would He solicit. Theirs was a witness of knowledge void of testimony.

In the world there are many who willingly acknowledge God and His Son while the conduct of their lives voids the testimony in their witness and renders it belief only. Even among members of the Church we see those who would claim testimony even as the conduct of their lives comes short of the beliefs they declare. While testimony may be the result of our beliefs they will never rise to such unless we live in harmony with them. The Lord said, "...My doctrine is not mine, but his that sent me. If any man will do his will, he shall know of the doctrine..." John 7:16

As I have studied and pondered the doctrine of testimony I have looked more closely at my own. By the criteria we have discussed, do I have a testimony? Some of you may be asking the same question. Have I received personal revelation? Can I? The Lord has promised, "...to every man is given a gift by the Spirit of God....To some is given by the Holy Ghost to know that Jesus Christ is the Son of God, and that he was crucified for the sins of the world....To others is given to believe on their words..." D&C 46:11-14 Let us never limit ourselves or put restrictions on revelation that would put it out of reach. Whenever the Spirit confirms truth in our hearts, whether the vision was ours or that of another, the revelation is the same and we may claim it as the basis of our testimony.

Quoting Elder McConkie again, "Three great truths must be included in every valid testimony: 1. That Jesus Christ is the Son of God and the Savior of the world. 2. That Joseph Smith is the Prophet of God through whom the gospel was restored in this dispensation; and 3. That the Church of Jesus Christ of Later-day Saints is 'the only true and living church upon the face of the whole earth. Embraced within these great revealed assurances are a host of others..." Bruce R. McConkie, Mormon Doctrine, 2d ed., p.487

When the testimony of Christ fills our hearts we are changed. We are compelled to do His will. President Hinckley said, "...When there throbs in the heart of an individual Latter-day Saint a great and vital testimony of the truth of this work, he will be found doing his duty in the Church. He will be found in his sacrament meetings. He will be found in his priesthood meetings. He will be found paying his honest tithes and offerings. He will be found doing his home teaching. He will be found in attendance at the temple as frequently as his circumstances will permit. He will have within him a great desire to share the Gospel with others. He will be found strengthening and lifting his brethren and sisters..." Regional Representatives' seminar, 6 Apr. 1984

I am grateful to be here, to not only talk about testimony, but to rejoice with you in its strength and power. I pray that each of us will be able to boldly declare with Alma, "...Do ye not suppose that I know of these things myself? Behold, I testify unto you that I do know that these things whereof I have spoken are true. And how do ye suppose that I know of their surety? Behold, I say unto you they are made known unto me by the Holy Spirit of God. Behold, I have fasted and prayed many days that I might know these things of myself. And now I do know of myself that they are true; for the Lord God hath made them manifest to me by his Holy Spirit; and this is the spirit of revelation which is in me." Alma 5:45-46

****

Testimony Meetings

At the Hand of Their Fathers

THE LORD'S LOVE and concern for little children is clearly stated in the scriptures. Just as clear, is the position the Lord takes regarding those who offend, or cause even just one of these 'little ones' to stumble. The Lord is not talking about skinned knees and bruised shins. What he is warning us against is playing a role in a child's stumbling on the path that would lead him home; of impeding rather than encouraging progress toward the Lord's presence. The formative years are so important to the child that the Lord has denied Satan any direct access or influence during those years. The innocence and vulnerability of children seems to be obvious reasons for this protection and yet the Lord gives quite a different explanation. He said, "...for power is not given unto Satan to tempt little children, until they begin to become accountable before me; ....*that great things may be required at the hand of their fathers.*" D&C 29:47-48 We have a tendency to read this scripture and thank the Lord for what he did for the children; to protect them from the merciless influence of Satan when they are most vulnerable and that is a great blessing to them, but only if we, the [parents], do the great things for which the provision was intended. Essentially, the Lord has put parents in a position of influence and if they don't actively steer the children toward God, Satan has his victory without the effort.

Of course, children don't know anything about this and they really don't need to; the provision was given for the parents and they are the ones that will be accountable for that special period of time. Children are spongy hard drives looking for data to soak up and save to their data banks. They watch and listen, even when we would swear they are doing neither and their observations are saved, even though they don't know what to do with the data. The input is just too much for them to process, but later they will analyze the data and act upon what they have stored. Our children will be adults before we see the results of how we handled the time that was given to us. Then we will begin to see the great things the Lord referred to in the characteristics present or missing in their personality.

It would be nice if it was just that cut and dried and it might be if parents were the only influence in the lives of their children. But, the truth, sometimes tragic truth is that unpredictable and adverse data sources are everywhere and there is no shield or filter that will keep it all out. Consequently, the great things we planned and prepared for may not happen the way we thought they should, but we are promised that if we provide the proper example, our children will come back to it.

Sometimes, in our effort to help our children achieve, we intentionally and unintentionally give them responsibilities that are difficult and encourage them to stretch beyond their present abilities. This is just good parenting as long as the stretching is within their reach. This is referring to the intentional challenges. The unintentional ones are a different story. Small children, who are neglected and essentially left to fend for themselves, while parents pursue addictions or other interests, are thrown into a role they are simply not prepared for. This is an extreme and obvious example of misplaced responsibility, but sadly it is happening more than we would care to admit.

Another example of an unintentional shift of responsibility is seen in our Fast and Testimony meetings. I call it unintentional because parents simply don't know what is happening. We see increasing numbers of small children going to the microphone to 'bear their testimony.' Generally speaking, parents smile with pride at this tender moment, but what is really happening? First of all, little children don't know what a testimony is and hearing each other parrot adorable words will never teach or instill one in their heart. Second, the children are not receiving the kind of input parents should be providing during those formative years. Instead, the data they are given tells them that going to the microphone is something that children, not adults, do.

Parents should be maximizing the Satan-free advantage they have been given by teaching their little children the meaning of testimony. A testimony is a statement of personal knowledge regarding the truth of a particular event or idea; such as Joseph Smith's vision and the idea that he is a prophet; that the gospel has been restored, the Book of Mormon is the word of God, the atonement is real and viable and that God and His Son live. How can little children possible know and bear witness of these things? Repeating words of gratitude for parents and siblings is nice, but does not, indeed cannot, do for them what pure and powerful testimony shared by parents would do.

I have been around long enough to see what happens to the children who habitually, and with the approving smiles of parents, go to the microphone and recite the words they have heard and said so many times. Without exception, when they outgrow that cute and adorable stage, they stop going to the pulpit. At that point they begin to notice that "bearing testimony" is something children do and they no longer feel the desire or need to continue. Even after learning what a testimony is and actually beginning to develop one, they join the ranks of those who never or seldom share what they know.

The picture I have just painted is not entirely accurate. We do have adults going to the microphone to share their hearts, but generally it is after all the children have been given time to recite their words. Sadly, many of the adult expressions are filled with gratitude for various blessings and we remain starved for the sustaining power of real testimony.

There are many who genuinely think it is adorable to watch the little children; to hear them express their sweet [testimonies]. I would not think to debate how adorable they are. That is not the point. The real question is; are they really bearing testimony?

Some say that it is good for the children, that it helps them overcome the fear of speaking; does it? From what I've seen, when children begin to become aware of themselves, they no longer want to be the center of attention (at least not in a sacrament meeting) and the "cute" factor no longer applies; more mature emotions begin to replace the childish ones and the young boy or girl has no desire to repeat words in front of a congregation just to be noticed.

Our children would be better served and we would accomplish greater things for them, by teaching them what it means to have a testimony and how such testimony is shared. Their need to mimic adults can be satisfied in a family home evening, in a primary class or sharing time. Watching their parents stand in a testimony meeting and hearing them boldly declare their personal witness that Jesus is the Christ, that God lives and Joseph Smith is the prophet of the restoration, will instill in them the faith and assurance that such knowledge is possible. With that assurance, their desire to know will inspire them to seek and gain their own sustaining testimony. Truly, a great thing will be done at the hand of their fathers.

****

THOU MAYEST CHOOSE FOR THYSELF

WITH HIS INITIAL INSTRUCTIONS to Adam and Eve, the Lord established the purpose and pattern of mortal life. Having presented to them the choices that were theirs, He also explained the consequences involved and then said, *"nevertheless, thou mayest choose for thyself for it is given unto thee…"* (Moses 3:17)

This single sentence outlines clearly and succinctly our purpose, our privilege, our opportunity in life; to choose for ourselves the path of our eternal lives. The Lord has done everything He possible can, while still preserving our agency, to define the path that leads to His Kingdom and the mansions prepared for its heirs. Throughout the history of mankind, the Lord has declared His will and counsel so that His children would have no trouble reconciling their lives to conform to the laws and ordinances of His Kingdom, should that be their desire. He has also declared, *"…the arm of the Lord shall be revealed; and the day cometh that they who will not hear the voice of the Lord, neither the voice of his servants, neither give heed to the words of the prophets and apostles, shall be cut off from among the people."* (D&C 1:14)

Superficially, this declaration may seem harsh, but what marvelous mercy it reveals. It was Satan's plan that would have condemned mankind to universal compliance. The laws of the Lord are clearly defined and He has made it equally clear that only those who learn to do His will [the will of the Father] shall enter into His Kingdom, but again, as he stated, *"… thou mayest choose for thyself."*

The Lord has made his position clear; *"What I the Lord have spoken, I have spoken, and I excuse not myself; and though the heavens and earth pass away, my word shall not pass away, but shall all be fulfilled whether by mine own voice or by the voice of my servants, it is the same."* (D&C 1:38) The laws of God have and will come under the scrutiny of men, but there are no arguments that can alter their efficacy. In the process of attempting to do so, the law itself takes a back seat to more fundamental questions; questions posed by Jesus himself: *"What think ye of Christ..."* *"Whom do men say that I the Son of Man am...."* (Mat. 22:42, 16:13) The way we respond to His laws as declared by his *own voice or by the voice of his servants*, is our answer to these questions.

The proponents of same gender marriage need not be offended when the Lord clarifies the consequences of their choice, but should be grateful, as we all should, that we may choose for ourselves. God's response to our choices is never discriminatory, but always in perfect compliance with eternal law. If our choices and actions separate us from His Kingdom, we should be grateful that the Lord allows us to write our own laws of happiness rather than condemning us to a place where there are laws we cannot abide. Bitterness and resentment toward the Church and the leaders who clarify the laws that opponents have rejected is counterproductive. They cannot find happiness in their protests and the Lord's Church cannot pretend to offer it when their life choices are in contradiction. The Lord has made His will clear, nevertheless [we] may choose for ourselves, for it is given unto [us].

****

THE TRUTH ABOUT TRUTH

\truth\ :the real facts about something : the things that are true : the quality or state of being true : a statement or idea that is true or accepted as true

\tru\ : agreeing with the facts : not false : real or genuine : having all the expected or necessary qualities of a specified type of person or thing

Some philosophers view the concept of truth as basic, and unable to be explained in any terms that are more easily understood than the concept of truth itself. Commonly, truth is viewed as the correspondence of language or thought to an independent reality, in what is sometimes called the correspondence theory of truth. Pragmatists like C.S. Pierce take Truth to have some manner of essential relation to human practices for inquiring into and discovering Truth, with Pierce himself holding that Truth is what human inquiry would find out on a matter, if our practice of inquiry were taken as far as it could profitably go: "The opinion which is fated to be ultimately agreed to by all who investigate, is what we mean by the truth…"[4]

Various theories and views of truth continue to be debated among scholars, philosophers, and theologians.[5] Language and words are a means by which humans convey information to one another and the method used to determine what is a "truth" is termed a criterion of truth.

There are differing claims on such questions as what constitutes truth: what things are truthbearers capable of being true or false; how to define and identify truth; the roles that faith-based and empirically based knowledge play; and whether truth is subjective or objective, relative or absolute. https://en.wikipedia.org/wiki/Truth

"…and for this cause came I into the world, that I should bear witness unto the truth. Every one that is of the truth heareth my voice. **Pilate saith unto him, What is truth?…** John 18:37-38 emphasis added

THE CONCEPT OF TRUTH has been debated for a very long time. It seems like people in general can be quite indifferent about it and yet at the same time they expect it of others. Nevertheless, the world keeps looking for it. Some adamantly claim they have a firm grasp of it, while their critics make the same claim. The world's accepted definition of truth suggests that it is flexible and therefore illusive and that opinion can create it, which in turn suggests that opinion could also quash it. We expect people to speak the truth; not some idea or opinion about it, but the actual truth. So, what is it?

The Lord spoke succinctly regarding truth; *And truth is knowledge of things as they are, and as they were, and as they are to come;* D&C 93:24 But, the world as a whole does not see it that way. If truth is as flexible and variable as some would suggest, then what is the real value of it? Is it any wonder that the world is unable to recognize it?

In order to find actual truth, one must admit that it exists in the first place and that it is an absolute. People may have opinions about truth, but that does not constitute new truth. Sorting out truth amid endless rhetoric is not always easy because we have our own opinions. In a crowded hall a professor delivers his weekly dissertation. One student whispers to his neighbor, "what a great teacher," to which the neighbor rolls his eyes and replies, "he's not that great." Two opinions, but the truth that remains is irrefutable; he is a teacher.

A search for truth begins with an idea, however rudimentary it may be. If we consider the idea to be true our search will be for more ideas and opinions that substantiate it. Of course if we deem it to be false our search will be for anything that will discredit it.

Efforts designed to merely discredit other ideas and opinions seldom if ever will lead to the discovery of truth and a search that presupposes one's own idea to be truth is likely to be just as tainted, unless of course, the idea is actually the truth. Where truth is concerned, mortal man is capable of nothing more than discovery. Those who attempt to make or create their own truth don't understand the irony or the gravity of what they do.

What then, or who, is the source of truth? *Jesus saith unto him, I am the way, **the truth**, and the life: no man cometh unto the Father, but by me.* John 14:6 *For you shall live by every word that proceedeth forth from the mouth of God. For **the word of the Lord is truth**...* D&C 84:45

God is the source of truth. *All truth is independent in that sphere in which God has placed it, ...* D&C 93:30 God has given us the principles that lead to a happy life and the means by which we can secure our salvation in the world to come. These are the foundational truths (laws) that govern our lives. There is a part of our nature that knows and accepts these laws. To one degree or another we apply them to our lives. C. S. Lewis said that it is in our nature to be guided by these laws. He called them the "Law of Right and Wrong." He said, "Whenever you find a man who says he does not believe in the real Right and Wrong, you will find the same man going back on this a moment later. He may break his promise to you, but if you try breaking one to him he will be complaining 'it's not fare'..." C. S. Lewis, Mere Christianity, p. 19

Since the beginning of time people have been adapting their own moral laws because for one reason or another they don't like the laws of God; God's laws simply don't do it for them. However, the laws (truth) of God cannot be altered or nullified by an opinion or even a consensus of opinion. Less than 300 years after the resurrection of Jesus, a council convened in Nicea and formulated the foundational 'truths' of Christianity. Then, roughly sixty years later, another council convened in Constantinople for the purpose of modifying the original Nicene Creed. You may argue that they were

147

only clarifying truths laid forth in the Bible. That is a judgment that must be left to the individual, but I would challenge the truth seeker to set aside the consensus of Nicea and Constantinople and read the Bible without their preconceptions and judge how closely they mirror the truth. Various Christian denominations have further modified those Creeds and have come to their own consensus about 'truth.'

Over the centuries thoughtful men and women have come to the conclusion that the general consensus regarding truth was flawed. Protestant groups split away in an effort to come closer to what they deemed to be true. Some broke away with the hope that the truth that had been lost would one day be revealed or restored.

A friend recently asked me how we can know the truth. This is a wonderful question. It says at least two things about my friend. One; that he acknowledges that there is truth to be learned and two; he wants to know how it can be had. This is the same question that prompted a fourteen year old boy to approach God. *In the midst of this war of words and tumult of opinions, I often said to myself: What is to be done? Who of all these parties are right; or, are they all wrong together? If any one of them be right, which is it, and how shall I know it?* Joseph Smith History 1:10 Young Joseph Smith had a burning desire to know the truth. *While I was laboring under the extreme difficulties caused by the contests of these parties of religionists, I was one day reading the Epistle of James, first chapter and fifth verse, which reads: If any of you lack wisdom, let him ask of God, that giveth to all men liberally, and upbraideth not; and it shall be given him. Never did any passage of scripture come with more power to the heart of man than this did at this time to mine. It seemed to enter with great force into every feeling of my heart. I reflected on it again and again, knowing that if any person needed wisdom from God, I did; for how to act I did not know, and unless I could get more wisdom than I then had, I would never know; for the teachers of religion of the different sects understood the same passages of scripture so differently as to destroy all confidence in settling the question by an appeal to the Bible. At length I came to the conclusion that I must either remain in darkness and confusion, or else I must do as James directs, that is, ask of God....* JSH 1:11-13

Joseph Smith went into the woods to a familiar spot where he knew he would be alone and where he would be able to receive an answer to his prayer. Inspired by the Spirit, Joseph knew in his heart that God would answer him, but I doubt that he could have anticipated what followed. He said, *I saw a pillar of light exactly over my head, above the brightness of the sun, which descended gradually until it fell upon me. ...When the light rested upon me I saw two Personages, whose brightness and glory defy all description, standing above me in the air. One of them spake unto me, calling me by name and said, pointing to the other–This is My Beloved Son. Hear Him*! JS-H 1:16-17

Can you imagine what the boy Joseph must have felt to come face to face with God and Jesus Christ? He simply wanted to know which church possessed the truth and he learned so much more. *I was answered that I must join none of them, for they were all wrong; and the Personage who addressed me said that all their creeds were an abomination in his sight; that those professors were all corrupt; that: "they draw near to me with their lips, but their hearts are far from me, they teach for doctrines the commandments of men, having a form of godliness, but they deny the power thereof."* JS-H 1:19

Joseph Smith saw and learned for himself the nature of the Father and the Son; separate and distinct individuals. He learned that the Church of Jesus Christ was not on the earth, but that he would be the instrument by which it would be restored with authority and complete with the truth from God.

In the years that followed, the prophet Joseph Smith received and translated the Book of Mormon and received the Aaronic and Melchizedek Priesthood along with all the keys of the priesthood. Through Joseph Smith the gospel of Jesus Christ was restored to the earth in its fullness. The question of how we can know the truth was answered specifically in the Book of Mormon: *And when ye shall receive these things, I would exhort you that ye would ask God, the Eternal Father, in the name of Christ, if these things are not true; and if ye shall ask with a sincere heart, with real intent, having faith in Christ, he will manifest the truth of it unto you, by the power of the Holy Ghost.* ***And by the power of the Holy Ghost ye may know the truth of all things****.* Moroni 10:4-5

The truth is here and available to all who will acknowledge it. The same friend that asked me about knowing the truth also asked me if I am seeking truth or simply trying to prove my point. Well, the thing about truth is that it does not need me or anyone else. It stands independent and unchanged regardless of how it is viewed.

Just as in days past, men and women have taken the gospel of Jesus Christ into committee and have come up with countless adaptations of truth that in their minds supersedes the doctrines of Christ and are far more munificent in their scope. With some we cannot doubt their sincerity, but with others it is difficult not to wonder about their motives. I wonder; can a person abandon or diminish God's law without abandoning or diminishing God himself to some degree?

Again, the truth about truth is that it remains in force regardless of how mankind views it. Other philosophies are adopted for a variety of reasons, often in an attempt to give sanction to a preferred life style. The popular thought that all philosophies are true is a contradiction and implies that there is no wrong and therefore, no liability. A personal adaptation of truth may actually offer a measure and moment of relief or satisfaction and even a sense of victory, but the truth will ultimately require accountability of every soul that has or will enter this world. Each of us should seriously consider the philosophy, the truths, that guide our lives because this is essentially what we will be asked to present to the Lord when He asks for an accounting.

I testify, by the power of the Holy Ghost, that Joseph Smith is the prophet of the restoration; that through him, God has revealed and restored the truth in its fullness. Since the calling and ordination of the prophet Joseph Smith there has been an unbroken succession prophets directing the affairs of God's Church, the Church of Jesus Christ of Latter Day Saints.

****

THOU SHALT NOT TAKE THE NAME OF THE LORD THY GOD IN VAIN

Exodus Chapter 20:7, *Thou shalt not take the name of the LORD thy God in vain*…

WHAT DOES IT mean to take the name of the Lord in vain? I have been taught all my life, and it appears to be the general consensus that the third commandment tells us that we cannot profane the name of God and remain guiltless.

-Avoid profanity. It is all around you in school. Young people seem to pride themselves on using filthy and obscene language as well as indulging in profanity, taking the name of our Lord in vain. It becomes a vicious habit… President Gordon B. Hinckley, Living Worthy of the Girl You Will Someday Marry, Ensign (CR), May 1998, p.49

-As a normal part of everyday language, many people take the name of God in vain. Among our youth, vulgar and crude terms seem to come easily as they describe their feelings. Bishop H. David Burton, Standing Tall, Ensign (CR), November 2001, p.65

-I am frequently offended by hearing people in public discourse and on television so casually violate the commandment "Thou shalt not take the name of the Lord thy God in vain. President James E. Faust, "Them That Honour Me I Will Honour", Ensign (CR), May 2001, p.45

-No matter how many people in our society are involved, none are justified in being dishonest, lying, cheating, using profanity, especially taking the Lord's name in vain… President James E. Faust, Choices, Ensign (CR), May 2004, p.51

PROFANE: 1. To treat something sacred with abuse, irreverence or contempt. 2. To debase by a wrong, unworthy or vulgar use.

According to the definition of profanity and its application to God's third commandment, it is not difficult to see and to agree that, of the Ten Commandments, this is the one that is most frequently violated. References to deity in our language have become so common that clearly there is an equally common disregard for the deity rudely misrepresented. Such profanity adds no meaning or substances to any point being made. Those who speak so irreverently, reveal to all their non-existent relationship with their creator. Speaking of authors and playwrights, Spencer W. Kimball said, "Why do they take in their unholy lips and run through their sacrilegious pens the names of their own Creator, the holy names of their Redeemer? Why do they ignore his positive command, 'And ye shall not swear by my name falsely, neither shalt thou profane the name of thy God...'" (Leviticus 19:12.).   Spencer W. Kimball, The Teachings of Spencer W. Kimball, edited by Edward L. Kimball, p.199 He adds, "Profanity displays poverty of language.... We wonder why those of coarse and profane conversation, even if they refuse obedience to God's will, are so stunted mentally that they let their capacity to communicate grow more and more narrow. Language is like music; we rejoice in beauty, range, and quality in both, and we are demeaned by the repetition of a few sour notes." Spencer W. Kimball, The Teachings of Spencer W. Kimball, edited by Edward L. Kimball, p.199

Profanity is the effort of a feeble brain to express itself forcibly.
President Spencer W. Kimball, God Will Not Be Mocked, Ensign (CR), November 1974, p.4

Volumes have been spoken and penned on the subject of profanity. In the minds of those who care, there is no question about how the Lord feels about this subject. He is offended, as are those who know and love him, when His name is profaned.

Having said all of this, may I suggest another meaning behind the third commandment? Please note that the Lord said, "Thou shalt not [take] the name of the Lord..." and not [use]. Is it possible that 'taking' his name might mean something different or more than the way we use or speak it? Let's look at a few scriptures about 'taking' the name of the Lord: "And moreover, I say unto you,

153

that there shall be *no other name given* nor any other way nor means whereby salvation can come unto the children of men, only in and through the name of Christ, the Lord Omnipotent." Mosiah 3:17 Wherefore, my beloved brethren…if ye shall follow the Son, with full purpose of heart… repenting of your sins, witnessing unto the Father that ye are willing *to take upon you the name of Christ, by baptism* 2 Ne 31:13 "…contend no more against the Holy Ghost, but that ye receive it, and *take upon you the name of Christ;…*" Alma 34:38 "Have they not read the scriptures, which say *ye must take upon you the name of Christ*, which is my name? For by this name shall ye be called at the last day; 3 Ne 27:5 *Take upon you the name of Christ*, and speak the truth in soberness. D&C 18:21

While the word of the Lord makes it clear how he feels about the use of his name, it is equally clear that the Lord wants us to '**take his name** upon us." When King Benjamin stood to address his people, he said, "And moreover, I shall give this people a *name*, that thereby they may be distinguished above all the people which the Lord God hath brought out of the land of Jerusalem…" Mosiah 1:11 At the conclusion of his address, King Benjamin proclaims, "…I would that ye should *take upon you* the name of Christ…whosoever doeth this shall be found at the right hand of God, for he shall know the name by which his called: for he shall be called by the name of *Christ…this is the name that I said I should give unto you* that never should be blotted out…" Mosiah 5:8-11

Christians all over the world are known as such because they have taken upon themselves the name of Christ. As members of the Church of Jesus Christ of Latter Day Saints, we have possibly a greater understanding of what that means because it is explained so well for us in the Book of Mormon.

While in the spirit world, in preparation for our mortal experience, we entered into the great covenant of the Atonement and in so doing, took upon us the name of Christ. By entering into the covenant of baptism in this life, we renew our covenant to take and honor His name. Each week, in Sacrament Meeting, we have the sacred privilege of remembering our commitment and renewing the Atonement Covenant by participating in the ordinance of the Sacrament. There is comfort, strength and power in the words of the sacramental prayers:

"O God, the Eternal Father, we ask thee in the name of thy Son, Jesus Christ, to bless and sanctify this bread to the souls of all those who partake of it; that they may eat in remembrance of the body of thy Son, and witness unto thee, O God, the Eternal Father, that they are *willing to take upon them the name of thy Son,* and always remember him, and keep his commandments which he hath given them, that they may always have his Spirit to be with them. Amen." Moro 4:3

"O God, the Eternal Father, we ask thee, in the name of thy Son, Jesus Christ, to bless and sanctify this wine to the souls of all those who drink of it, that they may do it in remembrance of the blood of thy Son, which was shed for them; that they may witness unto thee, O God, the Eternal Father, *that they do always remember him*, that they may have his Spirit to be with them. Amen." Moro 5:2

With no attempt to judge, I watch members of the Church habitually come to Sacrament Meeting late, interrupting or missing the ordinance of the Sacrament. And what about the roughly 50% who never come? Have they taken the name of Christ in vain? In remembering the covenant I have made, I am compelled to examine myself and ask if there is any vanity in the way I have taken His name.

Thou shalt not take the name of the lord thy god in vain has so much more meaning and implication than simply the way the Lord's name is used in our language and conversation. The way we take His name is the essence of our claim to Christianity.

****

155

Tithing

Perhaps you have noticed as I have that there are those who seem to be compelled or driven to do all they can to know the Lord and to serve Him. We marvel at president Hinckley, his counselors, and general authorities. Similarly there are those here among us who demonstrate a willingness to accept, without reservation, every principle of the gospel and diligently keep the covenants they have made regarding them. On the other hand there are those who have made the same covenants and yet seem to be indifferent toward them. When asked, these may express a testimony of the gospel but in their expression is little commitment or accountability. Without that inner conviction, the witness and testimony of others and even their own acknowledgment, holds little relevance for them. Nevertheless, we stand as witnesses and boldly testify in the hope that something will arouse their spirit and inspire in them a desire for the things of eternity. Until that happens, their ability to keep the commandments and honor their covenants will be limited to an intellectual and personal analysis of gospel principles.

I am convinced that the principles of the gospel were given as much to define us as they are to refine us. Each principle affords us the opportunity to make a statement regarding ourselves, while at the same time making of us the sum of that statement. Since it is our purpose to demonstrate our devotion to the Lord and prove our worthiness and our desire to have glory added upon us in eternity, each principle of the gospel holds a dual blessing in our lives. As we keep each principle, we are naturally endowed by its associated blessings. In addition, these principles afford us the means and blessing of expressing the nature, depth and sincerity of our love for and devotion to our Lord and Savior.

My purpose here is to examine the principle of tithing. Regarding the doctrine of tithing Bruce R. McConkie said, "One tenth of the interest or increase of each member of the Church is payable as tithing into the tithing funds of the Church each year. Salaries, wages, gifts, bequests, inheritances and the increase of flocks, herds, and crops, and all income of whatever nature are subject to the law of tithing....Payment of an honest tithing is essential to the attainment of those great blessings which the Lord has in store for his faithful saints." (Mormon Doctrine p.796-797) Elder McConkie goes on to say that, "Strictly speaking there is no such thing as a part tithing. Tithing is a tenth, and unless a person contributes the tenth, he has only made a contribution to the tithing funds of the Church." (p. 798)

Every principle or law of the gospel entitles us to specific blessings which cannot be denied or withheld when we "abide the law which was appointed for that blessing." (D&C 132:5) With regard to the law of tithing the Lord has said, "...I will...open you the windows of heaven, and pour you out a blessing, that there shall not be room enough to receive it. And I will rebuke the devourer for your sakes, and he shall not destroy the fruit of your ground; neither shall your vine cast her fruit before the time in the field,..." (Mal. 3:10-11)

The Lord has literally promised us eternity for merely giving back a portion of what He has given us. Within the limits of mortal view we sometimes consider what He asks to be a sacrifice. Satan would have us believe that the payment tithing is a generous gesture on our part. He knows that if he can persuade us to do that, then he may also be able to convince us that it is negotiable and all together optional. The danger of reducing tithing to a matter of generosity is illustrated in a fictitious letter between two equally fictitious devils. I quote in part, "As I said, generosity is a topic of conversation far more than actual practice. Present conditions almost always prohibit it and yet many will claim its virtue on the basis of what they intend to do. 'When I win the lottery' or 'When the company starts seeing greater profits.'...If you want to know if he is truly of a generous nature, help him achieve a little prosperity and see what he does with it. It is a curious irony and delightfully true that generosity is often stopped cold by prosperity. Most humans find it quite easy to share, even in a most grand fashion, those things they do not have. It becomes quite another story when prosperity knocks on the door." W. T. Svedin, The Reluctant Devils, Temptation 101, p. 55

If the payment of tithing were based on our own generous ability to pay, we would forever question if or when we qualify for its blessings. If we make it a matter of money and wait until we feel we can afford it, it is not likely we ever will. But, since money is not the real issue every member of the Church, regardless of financial status, is made equal in his ability to participate and receive the blessings promised. Whether we have a little or a lot it is a matter of how we choose to invest it. If our faith and testimony is broad enough to include the realities and the blessings of eternity, then tithing becomes a sound investment. If our vision is limited to this world and its goods, tithing will never be more than something we occasionally think we ought to do. As far as my personal salvation is concerned, the Lord is not all that interested in the money I have come by. He has said, "...for I, the Lord, require the hearts of the children of men." (D&C 64:22) Because it is our hearts that interest Him, He was able to say of the widow, who had contributed less than a half penny, "...this poor widow hath cast more in, than all they which have cast into the treasury; For all they did cast in of their abundance; but she of her want did cast in all that she had, even all her living." (Mark 12:43-44) In addition to her money she had given all that she had, her love, her devotion, her heart. How grateful I am that the Lord has given me this very simple means of telling Him that my heart is His.

In the 25th chapter of Genesis we read about Jacob and Esau. "And Esau said to Jacob, Feed me, I pray thee...for I am faint...And Jacob said, Sell me this day thy birthright. And Esau said, behold, I am at the point to die: and what profit shall this birthright do to me?

Then Jacob gave Esau bread and pottage of lentiles; and he did eat and drink, and rose up, and went his way; thus Esau despised his birthright." (30-34) This is a very interesting narrative. How sad it is that Esau had not learned to appreciate his birthright. At a time when it should have been more sacred than ever before, there were other considerations of greater value to him. He despised his birthright and could not bear to be denied the physical, much less surrender his heart to retain the promise. By the condition of his heart, Esau had lost his birthright long before he formally surrendered his right to it. We too have a birthright; a right to the blessings of heaven. The Lord has promised to open Heaven's Window and pour them out upon us. However, there are those who effectively close the window because they cannot or will not keep the law of tithing. Other considerations are of greater importance to them. Their actions echo the words of Esau, "what profit shall this birthright do to me?" and for today's equivalent of bread and pottage of lentils, they too despise their birthright.

Of course these blessings of which we speak are not merely bought and sold for a price. We do not pay our tithing in an attempt to buy blessings. We pay our tithing to demonstrate to the Lord that there are no worldly considerations in our lives that take precedence over the eternal blessings He has promised. We pay our tithing to show that we really do believe that He is God and that we have faith in Him.

I contrast the story of Esau with one of my great grandpa Barton and his testimony of the blessings of tithing. Grandpa took his wife and young family and settled in Price. There he started a business and struggled to make it work. He had not been as active in the Church as he should have been and was not paying his tithing. The patriarch in the stake blessed him and promised that if he would pay a full and honest tithe, his business would prosper, he would be able to provide for his family and neither he nor any of his children would ever want for the necessities of life. He considered the promise, but he was $100 in debt and just didn't know how he could afford it. The next year, he found himself in debt $200 and the year after that, $300. The fourth year he thought maybe he better give the promise a try. He began to pay his tithing and he found out that the Lord operates on principles with formulas we do not know or understand; principles by which Elijah was able to promise the widow of Zarephath that "...The barrel of meal shall not waste, neither shall the cruse of oil fail, until the day that the Lord sendeth rain upon the earth." (1 Kings 17:14) His business did begin to prosper and in time he was doing very well. In the process his testimony grew as did his love for the Lord. One day he had set aside a rather large sum of money to be paid as tithing and was briefly tempted by the thought of what he could do by investing the money. He quickly repented of the thought and paid his tithing. He told the Lord that if money and prosperity would cause him to forget Him, he would rather be poor. Unlike Esau, grandpa knew that if he lost his relationship with the Lord, there would be precious little compensatory profit in any amount of money. Not long after that his best team of horses died and his business began to fail. He took his family to Nevada where he had purchased a dry farm (emphasis on dry). He and his family struggled but faithfully paid their tithing. One morning following breakfast grandpa commented on what a good meal it was. Grandma was grateful, but she informed the family that there was no more food in the house. I'm sure this was not a complete surprise. With that grandpa recalled the promise given by the patriarch in Price and the family went to the Lord in prayer. As they closed their prayer they heard a horse coming toward the house. It was their neighbor, a well-to-do rancher who had come to buy the family cow. With the money from the sale of the cow cupboards and pantry were gratefully restocked. Later the rancher asked my grandfather if he wanted to buy the cow back. He did not know why he felt compelled to buy a cow he did not need. The dry farm never really did very well but grandpa was able to get a good job with the railroad and never again was without employment.

Even through the depression years he and all of his children were never without employment and life's necessities.

I am grateful for parents and a family that has learned and taught the blessings of tithing by keeping the law. Because of their example my testimony of tithing developed early and has been a blessing all of my life. I am grateful for faithful parents everywhere who teach their children. I will always remember a beautiful little three year old who was excited to pay her tithing. I was serving as bishop. During sacrament meeting I looked down at this precious little girl, seated on her mother's lap on the front row. With an ear-to-ear smile she held up a tithing envelope and whispered, "this is for you bishop." She could hardly contain herself during the meeting and at its conclusion she rushed up onto the stand. What a blessing it was to be able to receive what was given in the purest faith and love of a child. Later as I pondered this I realized that I had been privileged to witness something far greater than just a tender moment. I had witnessed the faithfulness of good parents whose home was filled with love for the Lord. By instruction and example they were teaching their family of the joys of faithfully paying tithing, that there are no earthly possessions of greater value than our devotion to the Lord. For them the windows of heaven were opened wide.

The Lord wants all of His children to be happy and certainly he wants all who will, to be able to receive and enjoy the blessings of eternal life. However, he will never impose His wishes upon us. If we are to return to Him it will only be upon our wishes to do so. All of the laws and ordinances of the gospel are designed not only as preparation for eternal life, but are also our means of showing the Lord the depth and extent of our desire. The law of tithing, possibly more than any other law of the gospel, gives us the means of clearly showing the Lord that the world and its goods have no claim on us, but that our desire, our hope, and our devotion rests in the Lord and the eternal blessings He has promised.

Treasures in Heaven

The Lord has counseled us to seek first the Kingdom of Heaven and to lay up treasures in heaven. I would like to talk about our treasures as the substance of our defense and refuge.

In speaking with his son Corianton, Alma talks in length of the plan of salvation. In the 42nd chapter he refers to it first as 'the plan of salvation', then 'the great plan of happiness, the plan of redemption,' and then again as 'the plan of mercy.' He explains that it is by this plan that "...God bringeth about his eternal purposes, which were prepared from the foundation of the world." (Alma 42:5,8,11,13,15,26) The repeated use of the word "Plan" is worthy of note and carries with it important implications for each of us. Our introduction to this plan, as Alma said, "before the foundation of the world," gave cause for shouts of joy, and surely came as a great deal more than an announcement. Dr. Hugh Nibley said, *"Though the plan from first to last is entirely God's own, he discusses it with others, 'consulting with the souls of the righteous before deciding to create the world,' not because he needs their advice, but because the plan concerns them and requires their maximum participation in it."* (Time and the Timeless p.51) A plan of this nature involving the agency of free-thinking individuals had to include its participants, if not in the making then in full disclosure. Certainly it was not our plan; nevertheless it became ours by individual endorsement. The agency of those who would not be party to the plan was respected. They, just as those today who will not acknowledge the will of the Lord, remain as if there were no plan.

Because He has told us, we know that the glory of God rests in the salvation of His children. Because this has always been His purpose, His work in our behalf began long before the first mortal breath was ever taken. What God freely offered there constitutes the pearl of great price offered again here. He gave us the details of His plan for our salvation, and to the extent we personally received them, they became our treasures there. We knew of the atonement of Christ and that He was to be the Only Begotten Son of our Father in Heaven. We not only knew of the Savior's role in the plan, we knew Him and were personally grateful to Him. We knew and sanctioned the plan for mortality's introduction. We knew there would be challenges for us to face and of their purpose and necessity in the definition of our character. We had opportunity to learn and know of the commandments and ordinances that would safeguard our salvation and the promise of eternal life. Imagine the magnitude of the work that was and is involved in the instruction of God's children as they prepare to come to earth. This great work surely introduced us to the noble and great who would play key roles in this life. By our conduct and devotion to the plan we were chosen to experience our mortality in these last days. Each of the elements of our Father's plan are treasures in heaven, offered and promised there, to be secured by our devotion to them here. Imagine the treasures that were available to us; treasures of knowledge, treasures of associations and covenants. What greater treasure is there than to know that those associations were meant to be eternal and indeed were promised. I wonder sometimes if I was personally acquainted with my wife Jan. If she was not one of my treasures there, she has become my greatest treasure here. Without her I could not imagine happiness in the next life and our promise of eternal life is a treasure without price.

Quoting Dr. Nibley again *"In coming to earth each* [person] *leaves his particular treasure, or his share of the Treasure, behind him in heaven, safely kept in trust ('under God's throne') awaiting his return. One has here below the opportunity of enhancing one's treasure in heaven by meritorious actions, and also the risk of losing it entirely by neglecting it in his search for earthly treasure. Hence the passionate appeals to men to remember their tremendous stake on the other side and 'not to defraud themselves of the glory that awaits them' by seeking the things of the world. To make the 'treasure' test a fair one, the two treasures are placed before us on an equal footing, ...their two natures being mingled in exactly equal portions in every human being. To neutralize what would otherwise be the overpowering appeal of the heavenly treasure, the memory of its former glories had been erased from the mind of man,...In this state, whatever choice is made represents the true heart and mind of the one who makes it. What conditions the Elect to make the right choice is no unfair advantage of instruction...but a besetting nostalgia, a constant vague yearning for one's distant treasure and happy heavenly home."* (Time and the Timeless p.54)

I remember a discussion I had with a young man some time ago. He had not been home long from his mission when he decided he should clean out his room. He explained that he had many boxes of treasures he had collected from his high school days and had carefully stored them away prior to going on his mission. But as he went through them, he found that now they were only things and had no real value to him anymore. While they reminded him of some fond memories, even the memories had lost much of their significance as new things, people, and experience had replaced them. Now he had new treasures. Fortunately the old treasures were of little real significance compared to the treasures that were now commanding his devotion. Aside from my amazement that a young man voluntarily cleaned and organized his room, I thought, surely there must be a lesson here. I asked myself what happened to those things, those treasures that were deliberately and carefully stored away. They remained exactly as they had always been and yet they lost their value. I began to realize that regardless of inherent monetary, spiritual, or sentimental worth there is no value to us personally in treasures unless and until we make them such by placing that value in them.

Some of the treasures we adopt are a direct reflection on our physical and/or spiritual maturity. Some of them are of little consequence and easily discarded as we mature. As we go through life discovering and discarding treasures, ultimately the trove we cherish and to which we devote ourselves here will determine the relevance and value of those we tucked away for safekeeping in that time and place now forgotten.

Because of the influence our treasures have over us it is critical that we make a conscious choice of what they will be. Regardless of what they are they will isolate us from all else that would pose a threat to them. Worldly treasures naturally and jealously repel the heavenly and vice versa. The two may struggle against each other, but the struggle cannot last. One will win out, creating its own enmity toward the other. One might ask, "At this very moment what are the most important treasures in my life?" Hopefully the answer will include such things as spouse, children, home, temple covenants, Church, etc. Then I would ask, "What occupied my time in the past four to six weeks?" "How did I spend or invest my money in the last six to twelve months?" Has my time, money and talents been directed at those treasures that the spirit has born witness at this moment are my most important considerations. Possessing the good things of this world is not a bad thing. In fact, they may actually enable us to obtain and use more readily the heavenly gifts we seek. However, as Neal A. Maxwell has said, *"When we draw other things too close, placing them first, we obscure our vision of heaven."* (Of One Heart p.19) If our treasures establish themselves as something other than a means of furthering our eternal purposes they become counterproductive in our quest for "all that the Father has."

Our treasures reveal themselves and our character as we devote ourselves to them. Those worldly are often self-serving and indulged for the sake of personal pleasures. Those of an eternal nature are not complete without the inclusion of our family and friends. The latter give reason for broken hearts and tears when those we love will not share the treasure while there are no such tears with the former. How many of those who will not attend sacrament meeting because their treasure forbids it are broken hearted over those who do? When Lehi partook of the Love of God represented by the fruit of the Tree in his dream "...it filled [his] soul with exceeding great joy; wherefore, [he] began to be desirous that [his] family should partake of it also..." However, those whose treasure was found in the large and spacious building had no such feelings, but were filled with contempt and they "...were in the attitude of mocking and pointing their fingers towards those who had come at and were partaking of the fruit." (1 Ne. 8:12, 27) When the sons of Mosiah were converted and the gospel became a treasure to them, "they were desirous that salvation should be declared to every creature, for they could not bear that any human soul should perish;" (Mosiah 28:3) In Moses 7 we read that Satan laughed while heaven wept.

As we seek and identify those things that are important to us here and now we will be as near or removed from our treasures in heaven as we choose to be. As we make our homes, the temple, and the Church our treasures they become for us a defense and a refuge from a world that seems bent on denying all that is sacred. They will insulate us from the world and will qualify us for the great promises reserved for the faithful. They will be a place and means of continual revelation where, "God shall give unto you knowledge by his Holy Spirit, yea, by the unspeakable gift of the Holy Ghost, that has not been revealed since the world was until now; which our forefathers have awaited with anxious expectation...a time to come in the which nothing shall be withheld,...All thrones and dominions, principalities and powers, shall be revealed and set forth upon all who have endured valiantly for the gospel of Jesus Christ...How long can rolling waters remain impure? What power shall stay the heavens? As well might man stretch forth his puny arm to stop the Missouri river in its decreed course, or to turn it up stream, as to hinder the Almighty from pouring down knowledge from heaven upon the heads of the Latter-day Saints." D&C 121

The revelation of these great gifts presupposes a desire for such revelation. These things are true and eternal. Each and all of us has equal claim to them. God will not, indeed he cannot impose them upon us. However, He has said, "I deign to reveal unto my church things which have been kept hid from before the foundation of the world..." D&C 124 To those faithful, desiring such revelation, the Lord said, "To them will I reveal all mysteries [or treasures], yea, all the hidden [treasures] of my kingdom from days of old, and for ages to come, will I make known unto them the good pleasure of my will concerning all things pertaining to my kingdom." D&C 76

As we establish our Homes, the Temple, and Church as our personal repository and sanctuary of our heavenly gifts our hearts will swell and echo the testimony of Enoch, "Thou has made me, and given unto me a right to thy throne, and not of myself, but through thy grace..." (Moses 7:29) We will feel the safety, confidence and assurance in the Lord's promise; "...great tribulations shall be among the children of men, but my people will I preserve." (Moses 7:61)

****

167

Voice of the Lord

In the temple Thursday evening President Jaussi and I talked briefly about the one thing the members of our stake need to hear and concluded that there isn't just one thing. However, as I've pondered that I have been impressed that there is one thing each of us must know; that God's love, His perfect love is universal. It is my pray and great desire that everyone will feel that love and will be filled continually.

Last September Jan and I drove to Phoenix for our grandson's baptism. Along the way we listened to talks by general authorities and as I listened, I pondered what I might say in the talk I was to give at the baptismal service. I became aware of my feelings and of the many impressions coming to my mind. That made me notice how many times the speakers would say things like, "I had a feeling" or "I was impressed." Since then I have thought a lot about the impressions we receive and I feel impressed that I should talk about that tonight. I am grateful to be able to share this time with you and I hope and pray that each of us will indeed feel those things the spirit will tell us individually.

We were asked to prepare for our conference by, among other things, observing the hand of the Lord in our lives and recording those tender mercies in a journal. I have found the words of President Eyring to be true in my life. "As I would cast my mind over the day, I would see evidence of what God had done for one of us that I had not recognized in the busy moments of the day. As that happened, and it happened often, I realized that trying to remember had allowed God to show me what he had done." (O Remember, Remember; Ensign November 2007)

You may have noticed, as I have, that many or most of the mercies we experience come in the form of or the result of feelings or impressions. Two weeks ago, in Fast and Testimony meeting, a sister stood to share her testimony. She is a convert to the Church, not accustomed to public speaking. It was difficult for her, but she expressed herself well and I was proud of her. I watched her take her seat again and as soon as she was seated a cute little three year old ran down the aisle and sat on her lap. The delight on this sister's face made me smile, but I also wondered how or when this relationship had developed. Following our meetings I visited this sister in her home and learned, as Paul Harvey would say, "the rest of the story." Sharing her testimony in front of the entire ward made this sister so nervous that it left her with a terrible headache. The pain was severe and she was about to leave the meeting, but a little girl came and sat on her lap and talked to her, calming her nerves and the headache subsided. After the testimony meeting the little girl's mother told this sister that when she sat down her daughter said, "I need to go see my friend." "What friend," whispered the mother? "Right over there," said the little angel and she ran to her friend. I've seen this little girl sit with others in the ward with no apparent favorites; she even sat on my lap once. I don't think there was anything random about her choice that day.

Here was a tender mercy; the hand of the Lord extended to a sister in need and in the process we were taught a wonderful lesson by a small child acting upon an impression. Almost always, the blessings we receive in life come as the result of another person's kindness and if you look deeper you will see that those acts were driven by impressions or feelings. This little girl showed us the way; I need to go see my friend, she said, and she ran.

During the past month I have seen the hand of the Lord touching the life of a beautiful young girl. I first met her over ten years ago. I felt something then and wanted to put my arm around her, but at the time she was somewhat of a teen agy teen, and the last thing she needed or wanted was some old guy putting his arm around her. But, still, I felt something; an impression that told me someday. During the years that followed I thought about her often and recently

I had the privilege of placing my hands on her head to give her a priesthood blessing of strength, comfort and reassurance. I asked her what she felt during the blessing. She said she felt hope and I thought what a wonderful description of the Comforters influence. By the power of the priesthood I was able to see in her what, to that point, had only been impressions. In the weeks that followed the blessing, she endured terrible circumstances with every bit of the strength she was promised. In the face of conditions that would more naturally be met with self-pity, I heard love and concern expressed for her family. I saw empathy for others who suffered and gratitude that helped smiles wipe away the tears. She has been a wonderful example of faith and courage and I am proud of her as I know the Lord is. I could not love her more if she were my own daughter; in part because I know that God loves her. His love shines in her beautiful smile.

Some impressions might be so commonplace they are dismissed as quickly as they come. Recently I got caught in a traffic jam on the freeway. I was frustrated and mentally kicked myself because I had had a feeling that I should have taken the exit I had just passed. On another day I found myself at the Maverik, in my truck with a battery as dead as a door nail and reminding myself that I had had a feeling I should grab my cell phone before leaving the house. My guess is that each of you has had similar experiences. These are inconvenient and aggravating, but essentially inconsequential. There are, however, impressions of real significance and potential, that, when unheeded leave us lamenting, "if only I had listened."

Some time ago a young man came to visit me in my office; there was something familiar about him and when he saw my name on my business card his eyes lit up. Roughly twenty years earlier he was one of the first of many missionaries to live in my father's basement. We shared some memories and he asked about my father. At the time my father was in a care facility; he said he would like to visit him and I told him my dad would love to see him. A year went by and the young man stopped in again and again he asked about my father. The brightness of fond memories I had previously seen in his eyes faded when I told him of my father's passing. I saw emptiness in his eyes and a shadow on his face. He said he had felt he should visit my dad, but he never did.

As I listened to the talks in October's General Conference I noticed again the many references to spiritual impressions. Craig C. Christensen of the Seventy spoke in the Saturday morning session about "An Unspeakable Gift from God." He told about taking his family to the open house of the Bountiful Temple. His six-year-old son clung to his leg and when asked what was wrong he replied, "what's happening here? I've never felt this way before." Elder Christensen continued, "As we talked, it became clear that what was most inspiring to Ben was not what he saw, *but what he felt*—not the physical beauty around us, but the still, small voice…" Ensign, November 2012

About a month prior to entering the Mission Home in Salt, when there was a mission home in Salt Lake, I had the privilege of being present when Elder Spencer W. Kimball set my cousin apart for her mission to the Netherlands. Roughly seventeen years later I had another experience with Spencer W. Kimball, then President of the Church. President Kimball passed away in November of 1985 and in May that year, through a series of circumstances, I was asked to make some modifications to his special recliner. The stationary arms made it difficult for him to get in and out of the chair. My task was to remove one arm and install an arm that would swing out and give him easier access. I wondered how I was going to do this; how was I going to remove the very large arm structure and not leave a gaping hole where the much smaller pivoting arm would be mounted? I felt a little like Nephi, "not knowing beforehand what I would do," but as I began the project I was able to see how it would be possible. President Kimball's personal bodyguard was an acquaintance of mine and so I made arrangements through him to deliver the chair personally. One of the vice presidents of the company where I worked, who had actually made the arrangements to modify the chair, went with me. We met my friend at the service elevator in the basement of the Hotel Utah. As the elevator went higher, so did my anticipation. The thought of meeting the prophet in his home made wishes and dreams come alive. We were escorted into the apartment to see where the chair would be placed. We entered a rather large, well-furnished room, but there was no sign of the prophet. He was in another room, too ill to greet us or to be greeted. We placed the chair and were able to stand for a moment in the quiet and reverence that permeated the room. I could feel it. Like Elder Christensen's little boy, it was not what I could see that impressed me, but what I felt. While I could not see him, I knew that I was in the presence of the Lord's Anointed, a prophet of God.

I think it is important for us to understand that impressions can, and do, come from several sources. Those we have been discussing are from the Lord. These are always reliable and designed for our happiness. Another source, less reliable, is our own reasoning. A third is Satan. Feelings prompted by him are always shallow in the sense that they focus on our vanity, but if entertained can be debilitating. Satan's influence is strongest when we are unsure of ourselves, not fully conscious of the impressions the Lord is giving us. God bless parents who have the vision their children have not yet gained. I remember times of uncertainty, when my own self image and sense of worth was under attack. I am forever grateful for parents who loved me when I was not loveable and treated me according to what they saw in me. Without fully knowing it, I relied on their feelings and impressions before I was able to sort out my own.

Whether the guidance of the Holy Ghost or the whispered warning of a guardian angel, the key is to listen to our impressions and obey. One of my favorite scriptures stories is found in the second chapter of Luke. A few brief verses tell us of a just and devout man by the name of Simeon. "It was revealed [to] him by the Holy Ghost, that he should not see death, before he had seen the

Lord's Christ." Luke 2:26 The day Mary and Joseph brought the infant Jesus to the Temple Simeon was prompted; he had a feeling he should be there. I am fairly certain that Simeon did not know why he was prompted to be in the temple that day, but because he followed his prompting the Lord was able to grant his lifelong desire and, we are able to see what he would have missed had he not. Rarely will we know in advance the reasons for our impressions beyond the general good that may result.

Several months ago I had the impression that I should go to the temple. Since going to the temple is not unusual for me, I began to wonder why I was anticipating this visit so much. I thought about Simeon and followed his example. I sat in the chapel and listened to the reverent music and then I began to be filled with the spirit. I experienced for myself what Joseph Smith described when he said, " the eyes of our understanding were opened." I was taught about the eternal nature of the atonement and my role in it. I was taught about my own eternal nature and much more. I am grateful that I listened and went to the temple that day.

We all have impressions. It is important that we live worthily; not just to be able to receive them, but possibly more importantly to be able to recognize them and then follow the prompting.

I would like to tell you about my stupid bicycle. I'll skip the details and go right to the point. I was only about seven years old and was testing my skill on a brand new bike. I didn't like it when the older kids would race full speed at me and then veer away at the last minute. It scared me, and they knew it; that's why they did it. One day, when I was returning from one of my trips to the head of the street, I saw the three girls who lived four houses to the north. I guess I thought it was time for me to show that I could ride like the big kids. The girls were just walking home and minding their own business when I pointed the front tire straight at them. Something inside was saying, don't do it, but I didn't listen; I pumped harder. I think you can guess what happened next, but I'll tell it anyway. I waited too long to make my move. The handle bars froze and refused to turn. By that time the breaks could only slow me down a little before impact. One of the girls went down the same time I did. Fortunately, the brakes had slowed me some and there were no serious injuries. I was angry at myself and then I realized that stupid bicycle was to blame. I picked up a stick and proceeded to teach the retched thing a lesson. I whaled on it hard enough to teach it a thing or two. When I realized I was being watched, suddenly the bicycle wasn't nearly as stupid as it had been. Grandpa said something like, "You can't blame things or others for your actions." I never did try that stunt again, but it would have been so much better if I had listened to the prompting that would have prevented the whole thing.

There may be times when we would like to blame the stupid bicycles in our lives for our troubles and for the spiritual abandonment we might feel. With our focus so misdirected we might wonder why God has forsaken us, when, in reality we are simply too busy pounding on our bicycle to hear. The spirit is reluctant to talk to one who is not listening.

Feelings are the repository of life's tenderness as well as the pain that seems to be an unavoidable part of living. God bless those who consider the feelings of others above their own and strive to ease the pain and preserve the tenderness.

I feel that I need to say a few things about another subject that has great bearing on our ability to receive the spiritual guidance we've been talking about. That subject is Pride. C. S. Lewis called Pride the Great Sin and described it as self-conceit. This is one of a very few things I would debate with him, but I won't burden you with that. I will simply say that I would call Pride Satan's universal antidote for all the virtues and describe it as a consuming love of self. Of course this is had in degrees and so Pride is always personalized and manifests itself in degrees. In small doses, Pride inhibits our ability to have and recognize the kind of feelings we've been talking about. In larger doses it makes us entirely insensitive to them and promotes its own. In the grasp of Pride we react to things and people in terms of how our lives will be disrupted rather than our ability to help them pass through theirs with less difficulty. Under its influence we are prone to cast a stone rather than extend a hand to wipe a tear.

C.S. Lewis sites Humility as Pride's opposite. I would suggest, however, that Pride's opposite is Charity; the pure love of Christ; the kind of love that puts us outside of ourselves, enabling us to love ourselves and others the way Christ loves us. Humility is a distinguishing attribute of one who is filled with Charity. Such individuals are those that the Lord promises to lead by the hand and give them answers to their prayers.

Each one of us is entitled to and receives impressions. Whether profound personal manifestation or the quiet suggestion that we should do our home and visiting teaching we are under the obligation that comes with the prompting. When the rich young man asked, *"...what good thing shall I do, that I may have eternal life..."* Jesus answered, *"...if thou wilt enter into life, keep the commandments."* When the young man proudly admitted he had kept the commandments from his youth and wanted to know what more he must do, Jesus suggested, *"...**If thou wilt be perfect**, go and sell that thou has, and give to the poor, and thou shalt have treasure in heaven: and come follow me."* Matt 19:16-22 The suggestion proved to be too much for the young man and he walked away.

In the pre-earth councils in heaven the Lord outlined His Great Plan of Happiness for us. We would leave our existence there for an experience outside of his presence. He said, *"...we will make an earth whereon these may dwell; And we will prove them herewith, to see if they will do all things whatsoever the Lord their God shall command them;* Abr 3:24-25 I'm sure that many of you, like the rich young man, could say, *"All these things have I kept from my youth up"* but how do we do with the suggestions or impressions personalized to assist and guide us to our perfection? Is a commandment more binding than an impression when the impression comes from the Lord? These promptings are customized mercies, given not just for our good, but for our perfection. They are the extension of the Lord's hand by which he will lead us if we will take hold and follow him.

I testify that the Lord is very aware and mindful of each of us. He said, *"...I, the Lord am merciful and gracious unto those who fear me, and delight to honor those who serve me in righteousness...to them will I make known...the good pleasure of my will concerning all things...for by my spirit will I enlighten them..."* D&C 76:5-10

I testify that God lives and that Jesus Christ is our Redeemer. Of all the impressions and feelings we might have, I pray that the one that we will feel most deeply is that God's love is real and it is specific to each of us. The Lord, through his tender mercy is our Redeemer today. Struggle and even heartache are a part of life, but we are redeemed daily from these by His matchless love and guiding hand. It is my prayer that each of us will feel deeply that love and cherish the impressions that testify of it.

Scripture Study

- READ: Reading is the obvious first step.
    - We believe the Bible to be the word of God as far as it is translated correctly. We also believe the Book of Mormon to be the word of God. D&C 91...*whoso readeth it...spirit manifesteth thruth.* Initially, a quick novel-read of the scriptures gives us a sense of time and place; orientation of an overall story.
    - Bible translation: Consider the miracle of it and be mindful of how vulnerable our understanding of the truth can be by virtue of lost or perverted content.
        - LOSSES—CORUPTION IN TRANSLATION—Sincere but misguided efforts as well as evil designs have left us with a bible laced and riddled with misrepresentations and perversions of the truth as originally taught and recorded. When something just doesn't sound right or is not consistent with other scripture, we should not be afraid or hesitate to question and trust the still small voice. Trying to understand the principles of the gospel by studying the bible can be a lot like running a very physical obstacle course. Some will handle it better than others, but not without difficulty. A simultaneous study of all the standard works will make the course much easier to navigate.
        - CHALLENGES: Evolutionary change of language—over time words and phrases come to mean something entirely different, such as *I can't believe it.* It used to mean exactly that, but now it might actually mean I do believe it

but it's incredible, amazing or wonderful. A young man used that phrase, quite enthusiastically in his talk just prior to his mission. It was rather humorous because everyone knew what he meant; "The gospel is so true, I can't believe it."

- LOSS OR CHANGE OF MEANING from one language or culture to another—Words and phrases in one language are often meaningless or total nonsense when translated to another language. I remember trying to find dry ice while serving my mission in Sweden. We got some interesting looks from people who had no idea how there could be such a thing as ice that is dry. We found the dry ice, but only after we learned that it is actually called carbon dioxide ice, which actually makes a little more sense.

- CULTURAL DIFFERENCES: John 2:4 *"Woman" "The noun of address, "Woman," as applied by a son to his mother may sound to our ears somewhat harsh, if not disrespectful; but its use was really an expression of opposite import."* James E. Talmage, Jesus the Christ: A Study of the Messiah and His Mission According to Holy Scriptures Both Ancient and Modern, p.136 We should bear in mind that the basic nature of men and women is and always has been essentially the same. The words and phrases used to express emotions my change over time and across cultural lines, but the meaning and sentiment remains the same. If we forget this and use only the words provided us, I think we can easily misunderstand and misjudge individuals and their message.

- CONTEXT; We need to read the scriptures, particularly the Bible, as a whole. Using selected verses to establish doctrine has the opposite result unless those verses agree with the whole. For example; a popular 'Christian doctrine' is that man is saved by grace and not works, taken from Eph. 2:8-9 *For by grace are ye saved through faith; and that not of yourselves: [it is] the gift of God: Not of works, lest any man should boast.* But, the interpretation is not supported by the very next verse. *For we are his workmanship, created in Christ Jesus <u>unto good works, which God hath before ordained that we should walk in them.</u>* James makes the relationship between faith [grace] and works very clear; *But be ye doers of the word, and not hearers only, deceiving your own selves...What doth it profit...though a man say he hath faith, and have not works?...faith, if it hath not works, is dead, being alone.* James 1:22, 2:10-18 Even in the Book of Mormon select verses can be found that, on their own, undermine the gospel Alma 31:16 *Holy God... we believe that thou hast elected us to be thy holy children; and also thou hast made it known unto us that there shall be no Christ.* Selected reading is done by those more interested in establishing their doctrine rather than knowing the Doctrine of Christ.

o Understand scriptural usage of words:

- HEART: There are over 1600 references to 'heart' in the scriptures with few of them referring to a physical organ. As we read we recognize this word refers to our inner soul, center of emotion and conviction, center of our prayers, holding place for our treasures, spiritual receptacle and dwelling place of the Holy Ghost.—we begin to understand what the scriptures mean when it says that men's hearts shall fail them. Men and women in good health all around us have hearts that fail them.

- REST: The word 'rest' is used at least 614 times in the scriptures. The Sabbath day is supposed to be a day of rest, but I'm sure a lot of mothers would actually take exception to that idea. In Matthew the Savior said "Come unto me...I will give you *rest*" and to Joseph Smith he explained, "...which *rest* is the fullness of my glory." This helps us to understand that the Sabbath was not necessarily meant to be a day of physical reprieve, but might more appropriately be seen as a day of spiritual exertion. It gives us an idea of what is and isn't appropriate for the Sabbath day.

- GRACE: Used freely throughout the scriptures, but widely misunderstood in the world's application. Generally the word is thought to mean a free, unearned gift. But, the scriptural definition of grace gives it substance and impact; 'enabling power.' When we read this wherever we see the word, grace, we feel the power of the message sink deep into our hearts. For example, *"My grace is sufficient…" "My [enabling power] is sufficient.* A favorite verse of mine with application to us all is *1 Cor. 15:9-10 9 For I am the least of the apostles, that am not meet to be called an apostle, because I persecuted the church of God. But by the grace of God I am what I am: and his grace which [was bestowed] upon me was not in vain; but I laboured more abundantly than they all: yet not I, but the grace of God which was with me.* Fully aware of his past as we are of our weaknesses, Paul takes strength and courage in the enabling power. See also *Moroni 10:32 Yea, come unto Christ, and be perfected in him, and deny yourselves of all ungodliness; and if ye shall deny yourselves of all ungodliness, and love God with all your might, mind and strength, then is his grace sufficient for you, that by his grace ye may be perfect in Christ; and if by the grace of God ye are perfect in Christ, ye can in nowise deny the power of God.*

- SEARCH:
  - Reading is not enough—Reading by the spirit we find that there is more. Throughout the Bible and Book of Mormon the question is asked repeatedly, "Have you read the scriptures." The injunctions we read regarding our study use the word SEARCH.
    - Joseph Smith did more than appeal to the Bible; he read, prayed, pondered and continued to ponder. He listened to the prompting of the spirit during the pondering part of his prayers.

183

- John 5—Speaking to the Jews (ranking and ruling class) who had read the scriptures, Jesus said, "Search the scriptures; for in them ye think ye have eternal life…." These were the same ones who had sent the Pharisees to see if John was the Christ. They had read the scriptures and knew of the promised Messiah. Had they understood the scriptures they would have known Jesus was the one Moses spoke of.
  - Foot notes and inspired translation:
    - I love the translations and explanations Joseph Smith gave us: John 1, John 2:4, John 4:24, John 20:17 are good examples of clarifications made and meaning added.
  - Ponder: Pondering is the stage of study when inspiration and understanding begin. Pondering comes after reading, is included in our searching and propels us into the light of understanding; it opens the door to revelation. *"Could you gaze into heaven five minutes, you would know more than you would by reading all that ever was written on the subject."* Joseph Smith Pondering is the searching time, when we begin to gaze into heaven with questions in our heart. Pondering is our invitation to the Lord to enter into a dialogue and as we listen He responds with the answers to our question and to all the questions it implied.
- Reading—Searching—Pondering
  - Ask—What is being said, what does this mean
  - Ask—How does this apply to me
  - Ask—Is there more
  - Pondering the scriptures is the most essential part of our study. The scriptures themselves

are only a place to start, a catalyst of sorts. There is a vast wealth of knowledge and understanding which the Lord has promised to reveal to us. Reading the scriptures is like opening the door to an eternal spiritual reservoir of wisdom. Searching the scriptures is the equivalent of identifying the questions; the things we want to know. Pondering is stepping through the door and immersing ourselves in that spiritual reservoir.

- Luke 18: 35-43 A blind man is healed. This is more than just a nice story; it is also a metaphor with application. Reading this story, some of the questions we might ask: Are we not all spiritually blind to some degree? Can we not all be made to see more clearly into the things of eternity? What does it mean to glorify God?

And that from a child thou hast known the holy scriptures, which are able to make thee wise unto salvation through faith which is in Christ Jesus. All scripture [is] given by inspiration of God, and [is] profitable for doctrine, for reproof, for correction, for instruction in righteousness: 2 Tim 3:15-16

It is important to know about numbers as figures of speech. In the days of ancient Israel, as now, numbers were used to convey a meaning quite removed from its numerical value. For example, today we might express our gratitude by saying "thanks a million" or, as in Sweden, "a thousand thanks." We often hear a parent's frustration in his or her appeal to a child; "I've told you a thousand (or a hundred, or a million) times…" No one ever believes the comment is an actual summation of the number of times the child has been told; it is simply understood that, in this context, the numbers mean, many or multiple times. The use of numbers to convey alternate meanings is often a subtle thing. Today, the number 24 might be used to mean a day and the number 7 might represent a week. These two numbers used together have come to mean something quite different than the sum of 31. 24/7 is a recent addition to modern numerology and means simply, every hour of every day, or all of the time. We should not be surprised to find the same sort of thing in the scriptures. Just as now, in our language, numbers were not always used as numbers, and particularly in Hebrew, where numbers have specific meanings and were used extensively for those meanings. For example: 1 Cor 14:19 "Yet in the church I had rather speak five words with my understanding, that [by my voice] I might teach others also, than ten thousand words in an [unknown] tongue." 1 Sam 17:40 "And he took his staff in his hand, and chose him five smooth stones out of the brook, and put them in a shepherd's bag which he had, even in a scrip; and his sling [was] in his hand: and he drew near to the Philistine." (Emphasis added) Why did Paul say "five words" and not something like "a few words" or simply "words?" Why was Samuel particular about the number of stones David picked from the riverbed; why not "a handful" or merely "some?" I suppose it is entirely possible that the number five meant exactly that, but consider these verses with the associated meaning of the number five. Five meant grace or God's goodness. The number 1000 was the Father's Glory. Paul was saying that he would rather speak 5 words of God's goodness, if they are understood, than ten thousand words of His glory if they cannot be understood. David's stones were more than rocks; they were the grace of God, His goodness to deliver Israel from the invading Philistines. Considering the descriptive meaning of numbers deepens the meaning of these and many other verses.

Consider a new view that is opened to us when we apply trial, probation, purification and testing to the number, 40: Gen 7:4 For yet seven days, and I will cause it to rain upon the earth forty days and forty nights; and every living substance that I have made will I destroy from off the face of the earth.

Gen 8:6 And it came to pass at the end of forty days, that Noah opened the window of the ark which he had made:

Ex 16:35 And the children of Israel did eat manna forty years, until they came to a land inhabited; they did eat manna, until they came unto the borders of the land of Canaan.

Ex 24:18 And Moses went into the midst of the cloud, and gat him up into the mount: and Moses was in the mount forty days and forty nights.

1 Sam. 17:16 And the Philistine drew near morning and evening, and presented himself forty days.

Matt 4:2 And when he had fasted forty days and forty nights, he was afterward an hungered.

Acts 1:3 To whom also he [showed] himself alive after his passion by many infallible proofs, being seen of them forty days, and speaking of the things pertaining to the kingdom of God:

Acts 7:30 And when forty years were expired, there appeared to him in the wilderness of mount Sinai an angel of the Lord in a flame of fire in a bush.

In our spoken and written language today, we know by usage when a number is a number and when it is being used for a more descriptive purpose. It was the same in the ancient language and text. It seems clear that the number forty was often used in reference to an undetermined period of time; a time of trial, testing and of purification, rather than a specific number. It is interesting to note, in the story of the flood that the rain began to fall on a specific day of a specific month, but no day or month is mentioned when the rain stopped. The duration of the rain is referred to as a number of days and nights, 40. Again, the Ark came to rest on Ararat on a specific day of a specific month, while there is no mention of day or month on which Noah and his family disembarked. The days they were required to wait on the ark were simply 40. It seems unlikely, to me at least, that the duration of the rain and of Noah's confinement on the ark would both be exactly 40 days, unless 40 meant something more than merely a number. If we look at the meaning of the number 40, a time of testing and purification, a different, more enlightened understanding presents itself.

One more example: In the book of Revelations John writes, "Fear none of those things which thou shalt suffer: behold, the devil shall cast some of you into prison, that ye may be tried; and ye shall have tribulation ten days: be thou faithful unto death, and I will give thee a crown of life." Writing to the saints, specifically the [servant] of Smyrna, John compassionately tells him that he is aware of his work and tribulation and poverty. What a comfort it must have been to this servant to hear that his tribulation would last only ten days. Tribulation would be much easier to endure if we knew the duration, particularly if it was only ten days. But, is that what John meant, or did he use the number 10 to describe the days of tribulation, i.e. days of responsibility and of testimony? Note that John admonishes faithfulness until death. While that is sound and wise counsel, how difficult would it be, if our tribulation were limited to only ten days? Would it be likely that we would effectively learn the lessons of life, if our lives were essentially void of tribulation? Perhaps the most effective teacher we will ever know is the one called experience, but to take tribulation out of the curriculum is to tie the hands and mute the voice of this great teacher. Tribulation is the classroom of most of life's advanced courses. (See the list of numbers and their meaning, compiled by W. E. Filmer in his booklet "God Counts".)

The number "1" in ancient Hebrew held the same meaning as is commonly used today and yet, in the Christian world its usage is misinterpreted more often than not. Then and now the number "1" meant unity. Then, just as now, oneness is achieved by two or many when they come to agreement and unanimity. When Jesus said, "I and my Father are one," John 10:30 he was not misunderstood and in fact, the Jews were offended that he would assume a oneness with God, not that he had claimed to be the personification of God, but that he would make himself equal. (see John 10:30 (24-38), 5:18)

188

No.	Meaning
1	Unity; New beginnings
2	Union; Division; Witnessing
10	Testimony; Law and responsibility
18	Bondage
19	Faith
20	Redemption
21	Exceeding sinfulness of sin
22	Light
40	Trials; Probation; Testings
144	The Spirit guided life
1000	Divine completeness and Fathers glory
144,000	Those numbered of Israel

Preparing to Walk Where Jesus Walked
Study Notes:

I include here some of the study notes and thoughts I've collected in my personal study of the life of Jesus. They are not included as authoritative evidence, but merely as thoughts in a process and effort to understand in preparation to walk where Jesus walked. They may seem somewhat fragmented and might be repetitious; they are notes, not edited as a treatise, but hopefully will still be food for thought.....

THE ACTUAL BIRTH DATE of Jesus has been and remains a matter of debate. In the end it makes no difference, although the timing of his birth helps to add clarity to other events. Here we will discuss three theories and some of the logic behind them.

THEORY #1: There are few who think to challenge December 25th as Christmas day, or the day Jesus was born, except among those of the LDS faith. Owing to the first verse of section 20 of the Doctrine and Covenants, Latter Day Saints have held that the birth of Christ occurred exactly 1,830 years prior to the organization of the Church on April 6, 1830. Therefore, April 6, 1 BC, is the actual birth date of the Savior, and I am sure that there are those within the LDS faith who would be surprised, if not offended, that anyone would take exception to what appears to be a direct revelation. James E. Talmage, in Jesus the Christ, sights this verse as evidence of the actual birth date of the Savior.

There is something sentimental and poetic about fixing the birth and resurrection of the Savior at or near the date of the restoration and organization of His Church in this dispensation. However, it is the least favorable of the three theories when other factors are considered. Placing the birth date in April puts the

Annunciation in the month of July, two months after Passover and two months prior to the Feast of the Tabernacles, leaving Mary with a bit of a problem. What rational reasons for visiting Elisabeth would she have been able to offer, that would not have been met with, "wait six weeks when we go for the Feast?" I would not suggest that the Lord is limited in His abilities, but everything about Jesus' birth was orchestrated by His exalted father. There were no details too small or that were overlooked. Mary had found favor in His eyes and certainly in His love for her, he would have done all He could to eliminate any possible embarrassment. The timing of the birth would have been such as to make a visit to Elisabeth and Bethlehem a natural course of events.

THEORY #2 There are others, such as J. Rueben Clark and Bruce R. McConkie, who take exception to an April 6 birth. "Steven C. Harper, a BYU assistant professor of church history and a volume editor of the Joseph Smith Papers, said in a phone interview that some people, including Talmage, have read this verse [D&C 20:1] as if it is the Lord speaking and revealing precisely that Christ was born 1,830 years before that day and that the revelation was given on April 6, 1830. The recent discovery of the Book of Commandments and Revelations manuscript of D&C 20, however, showed that the verse was actually an introductory head note written by early church historian and scribe John Whitmer—something he did for many of the revelations, (THE BOOK OF JOHN WHITMER, KEPT BY COMMANDMENT; John Whitmer, Book of John Whitmer, Byu Archives and Manuscripts, Writings of Early Latter-day Saints, p.1 I shall proceed to continue this record, being commanded of the Lord and Savior Jesus Christ, to write the things that transpire in this Church (inasmuch as they come to my knowledge,) in these last days. It is now June the twelfth, one thousand eight hundred and thirty one years, since the coming of our Lord and Savior in the flesh.)

Harper said. 'So those are separate from the texts that Joseph produces by revelation.' The manuscript, published as part of the Joseph Smith Papers, also shows that the revelation was given on April 10—not April 6. So although it references the organization of the church a few days earlier, the revelation—which topically has nothing to do with the birth date of Christ—and its introductory verses 'shouldn't be read as if it is a revelation of the birth date of Jesus Christ.' Harper said, 'The interpretation that has been most popular over time is very much subject to question; that's all I'm saying.'" (Michael De Groote, Deseret News, Dec. 24, 2010) "President J. Reuben Clark, Jr., in Our Lord of the Gospels, a scholarly and thoughtful work, says in his preface that many scholars 'fix the date of the Savior's birth at the end of 5 B.C., or the beginning or early part of 4 B.C.' He then quotes the explanation of Doctrine and Covenants 20:1 as found in the Commentary, notes that it has been omitted in a later edition, and says: 'I am not proposing any date as the true date. But in order to be as helpful to students as I could, I have taken as the date of the Savior's birth the date now accepted by many scholars,-late 5 B.C., or early 4 B.C, because Bible Commentaries and the writings of scholars are frequently keyed upon that chronology and because I believe that so to do will facilitate and make easier the work of those studying the life and works of the Savior from sources using this accepted chronology.' This is the course being followed in this present work, which means, for instance, that Gabriel came to Zacharias in October of 6 B.C.; that he came to Mary in March or April of 5 B.C.; that John was born in June of 5 B. C.; and that Jesus was born in December 5 B.C., or from January to April in 4 B. C." (Bruce R. McConkie, The Mortal Messiah: From Bethlehem to Calvary, 4 vols., 1:, p.504) References are made by Luke to the sixth month in reference to the birth of John and in connection with the Annunciation to Mary. Here we need to take a look at ancient and modern calendars for the names and numbering of the months of the year.

Among other things, theory #2 offers Luke 1:26 as the starting point to fix the date of Jesus' birth. "And in the sixth month the angel Gabriel was sent from God unto a city of Galilee named Nazareth." The calculation is simple enough. Add nine months to the month of March (the sixth month of the year) and Jesus was born in the month of the December. However, this idea is based on assumptions made out of context and without foundation. A closer look at verse 26 and the preceding two verses shows that Luke was not referring to the calendar, but instead to the month of Elisabeth's pregnancy. "And after those days his wife Elisabeth conceived, and hid herself five months…And in the sixth month the angel Gabriel…" (Luke 1:24-26) It appears from these verses that Gabriel's Annunciation to Mary occurred during the sixth month of her cousin's pregnancy. This is later confirmed by the angel, "And, behold, thy cousin Elisabeth, she hath also conceived a son in her old age: and this is the sixth month with her, who was called barren." (Luke 1:36)

Assuming, for a moment, that Luke was actually referring to the sixth month, there is something else to consider. The sixth month of the calendar at the time of Christ was March/April, however, the sixth month of religious calendar was actually August/September (which would put the birth date some time in June/July.

I really don't have a problem with the idea that Jesus was actually born on the traditional Christmas day. In fact, I like it. However, we should always resist the natural tendency to adopt an idea and then set out to validate it. I think religion in general has shown us that almost any idea can be supported by the Bible, if that is our only intent.

Theory #3: This theory also takes its basis from statements regarding John's birth. Luke tells us that following Zacharias' revelation in the temple, and "…as soon as the days of his ministration were accomplished, he departed to his own house. And after those days his wife Elisabeth conceived, and hid herself five months…" (Luke 1:23-24) With that information, it is a simple matter to add 9 months for the birth of John, or to add 6 months for the Annunciation to Mary and then another 9 months for the birth of Jesus. Simple enough, but when were the days of Zacharias' ministration accomplished? This is a very interesting idea and study. I refer now to a paper by Michael Scheifler and refer the reader to: http://biblelight.net (What day was Jesus born?)

Conclusion

So, if you have followed the above reasoning, based on the scriptural evidence, a case can apparently be made that Jesus Christ was born on the 15th day of the month of Tishri, on the first day of the Feast of Tabernacles, which corresponds to the September - October timeframe of our present calendar!

I LIKE THEORIES 2 AND 3 because each of them places the very important events relating to the birth of Jesus during the time of the Feasts, making trips to Jerusalem and Bethlehem a natural course of events. A December birth places the Annunciation (and trip to see Elisabeth) during the time of the Feast of the Passover. A September/October birth places the Annunciation at the time of the Feast of Dedication. I know there are those who would say that too much is being made of these feast times; that God has the ability, and would have delivered Mary when and where she needed to be. I would never presume to dispute the power of God, but I would add that God, more often than not, uses what is natural to bring about his purposes. It will also be shown later how very important these feasts, and the associated pilgrimages were in the beginning days and weeks of both John's and Jesus' ministries.

Some argue that a December birth is ruled out by the fact that there were shepherds watching their sheep, at night, in the surrounding hills of Bethlehem. There might be some merit to this observation if we were talking about some other location, but we must remember that Bethlehem is only 2300 feet above sea level and is bounded on the west by the Mediterranean Sea (only about 35 miles away) and by the Dead Sea, roughly 15 miles to the east. It is on roughly the same latitude as Tucson Arizona. All this combined makes the climate in Bethlehem very warm in the summer months and quite mild the rest of the year, with winters being cool, but pleasant. (average low temperature in December in the mid 40's, only about seven degrees colder than the month of April) It should also be remembered that, of necessity, shepherds tend their flocks every month of the year, regardless of the weather.

The Star

Suppose for a moment that the other worlds we are contemplating are found in our neighbor galaxy, Andromeda. (I suggest this merely as food for thought) Suppose further that the star was placed midpoint between us and them. The star would have had to been placed in its appointed course untold eons ago and would have had to arrive at its appointed position over a million years ago so that its light would have ample time to reach our earth at precisely the right time to coincide with Jesus' birth. There had to have been something else unique about this star. A star, large or small in its own natural course, if visible to those on earth, would have been just another star. Possibly the star had always been a part of the night sky, but small and undetected until it went super nova, casting brilliant light for several days or weeks as it burned out its existence in declaration of the Lord's birth. Again, if there was a super nova, it had to have occurred probably thousands of years earlier in order to be visible as a new star on that night. The chances of a new star appearing randomly at that point and at that time are so remote as to remove all doubt that it was nothing less than the act of an all powerful being as part of a predetermined course of events. The Star of Bethlehem declares the Father and the Son.

The Star of Bethlehem is often depicted as conspicuously large, and with a conduit of light streaming down to light the manger scene below. While the symbolism is beautiful and essentially correct, the new star did not literally point to Bethlehem. The star, in every other way, was essentially just another star and it went entirely unnoticed by most of the people on earth.

Why a star? Why not a worldwide aurora borealis at midday, with shouts of acclamation from heaven? Why didn't God announce the birth of His Son, an event eternally important to everyone, with a voice to shake the souls of heaven and earth? As already discussed, the sign may not have been specific to this earth and if so had to be universal in nature. More importantly the sign of the Savior's birth was really not intended for everyone. That may seem a strange thing to say, but the sign of Jesus' birth had to be given in such a way as to safeguard the agency of man and was given so that those who had eyes to see would know. Speaking of Jesus, the apostle John said, "He came unto his own, and his own received him not." (John 1:11) King Benjamin prophesied of Jesus' 124 years prior to his coming; "And lo, he cometh unto his own, that salvation might come unto the children of men even through faith on his name; and even after all this they shall consider him a man, and say that he hath a devil, and shall scourge him, and shall crucify him." (Mosiah 3:9) Amulek taught, "And he shall come into the world to redeem his people; and he shall take upon him the transgressions of those who believe on his name; and these are they that shall have eternal life, and salvation cometh to none else." (Alma 11:40)

Jesus will come one day in undeniable power and glory, but had he come then in that manner agency would have been compromised. Everyone would have had no real choice but to accept him, even if it was contrary to their nature to do so. Their mortal probation would have been rendered ineffectual in revealing their true nature. The sign had to be one that would be visible to only those looking for it.

There are those who prefer to think of God as one capable of magic and therefore could have simply ordered the appearance of a new star. I would never presume to limit the power and abilities of God, but I rather believe that God works within the laws of universal science and physics. Suppose he did order the appearance of the star by some magic; he still would have had to have done that in advance however many years necessary for the light of the star to arrive at the precise time to accomplish its purpose; over a million years if Andromeda was involved, but as little as fifty to one hundred thousand years if the worlds sharing the star are confined to our galaxy. It remains a wondrous sign all the same, of the birth of Jesus and of the majesty of God.

Shepherds

An angel accompanied by a heavenly host proclaimed to shepherds, "...unto you is born this day in the city of David a Savior, which is Christ the Lord." (Luke 2:11) This may seem a contradiction to the above paragraph, but really is not. The manifestation witnessed by the shepherds appears to be personal and isolated. This was undoubtedly a witness and confirmation granted to men who had proven themselves to be worthy of such a manifestation; who had shown sufficient faith and desire to merit such a witness. Alma prophesied that "it shall be made known unto just and holy men, by the mouth of angels, at the time of his coming..." Alma 13:26 Seldom does the Lord or his representatives grant spiritual manifestations that are not first solicited. It is doubtful that these good shepherds had anticipated a vision of this magnitude and they were at first taken aback and frightened. Their initial apprehension was quickly overcome by the words and glorious presence of the heavenly messenger. "Unto you is born this day..." It is interesting to note that the angel said, "Unto you" and not unto the world or unto all men. While Jesus' life and mission was an offering available to all men, only those looking for him would or will be beneficiaries. The angel told the shepherds they would find the babe wrapped in swaddling clothes and lying in a manger. If more detail was given regarding the location of the birth, we do not know about it. Apparently it was required of the shepherds to search. Although the shepherds are often portrayed on a hill top overlooking

Bethlehem, the scriptures give us no basis for that assumption. In fact, the narrative by Luke might be read to indicate they were not in the immediate vicinity. We read, "...there were in the same country shepherds abiding in the field..." Here there is no indication that they were close by, but there is a hint of some separation. When the angel left them they quickly concluded, "...let us now go even unto Bethlehem, and see this thing which is come to pass..." In the same country might have reference to the surrounding hills and fields of Bethlehem, but might also simply mean they were in Judea and therefore had to travel to Bethlehem. Regardless of their proximity, the shepherds immediately left what they were doing and "...came with haste, and found Mary, and Joseph, and the babe lying in a manger." (Luke 2:16)

The shepherds played an important role in laying the groundwork for the ministry of Jesus that would begin some 30 years later. The manifestation they received gave them a sure witness of the divinity of the baby in the manger, a witness they were able to share. These humble men added their witness to that of the star, fulfilling the law of witnesses. They were able to establish the truth and reality of the birth of the Messiah, "...they made known abroad the saying which was told them concerning this child." (Luke 2:17) "And all they that heard it [marveled] at those things which were told them by the shepherds." (Luke 2:18) The witness of humble shepherds became the topic of conversation and inspired a great anticipation in the hearts of seekers as far away as Northern Galilee.

After the birth of Jesus, the first mention of his youth is the on the occasion of his circumcision at the age of eight days. In compliance with custom and the law of the Lord, Joseph and Mary took Jesus to the temple in Jerusalem "...to present Him to the Lord;" (Luke 2:22) we can only speculate as to who might have accompanied young Joseph and Mary. For such a significant event, family members such as Zacharias and Elisabeth would likely have been there. One might envision a small and intimate group, limited to family and a few close friends. However, it is just as likely that the temple was crowded with hopeful people, anxious to see the Christ Child who had become the subject of great interest. Many others, including Joseph's family, might have been in Jerusalem for the Feast of The Dedication and could have been in the temple.

For all those that might have been there, one is specifically identified, one who had come to the temple that day having been prompted by the spirit to be there. Simeon was now an old man, but he had received a spiritual witness that before leaving this life he would be able to see the Savior. Simeon was a good man and lived a life worthy of the promise he had received. It would be nice to know more about this very devout man. How long did he carry the promise in his heart and was he able to confide in others? If he shared the witness he had received, it was undoubtedly met with skepticism by some and appreciated by few. (Today there are those who express the feeling that they will be privileged to see the coming of the Lord as promised in the last days. A common response to this is that we have been in the last days for a very long time and that event cannot happen any time soon. People have a tendency to protect themselves from disappointment by dismissing the possibilities, thinking that nothing really good, and especially not that, ever happens to me.)

When Simeon saw the infant Jesus, the spirit bore witness to him that this was he for whom he had waited "...he took him up in his arms, and blessed God, and said, Lord, now lettest thou thy servant depart in peace, according to thy word: For mine eyes have seen thy salvation, which thou hast prepared before the face of all people." (Luke 2:28-31)

I have tried to imagine the emotion that filled the heart of this wonderful man, when, at last, after a life of waiting, he saw the Lord. I know that what he felt will also fill my heart when I am witness to the great Coming that has, for so long, been foretold and anticipated. I share the feelings of the prophet Alma, "And now we only wait to hear the joyful news declared unto us by the mouth of angels, of his coming; for the time cometh, we know not how soon. Would to God that it might be in my day; but let it be sooner or later, in it I will rejoice." (Alma 13:25)

There was another stalwart in the temple that day, who is also mentioned by name, a prophetess by the name of Anna. She too recognized the Redeemer. Just as with Simeon, the goodness of this great woman is a matter of contemplation where the scriptures do not elaborate. The Appellation of the prophetess speaks volumes of her, as does her obvious love for the child Jesus. "And she coming in that instant gave thanks likewise unto the Lord, and spake of him to all them that looked for redemption in Jerusalem." (Luke 2:38)

It is noteworthy that Anna, pursuant to her witness in the temple, spoke to all them that looked for redemption and not simply to all those at Jerusalem. Luke makes a significant point here. All through the Savior's ministry there would be many who would interact with him and yet fail to recognize him because they would not be looking for the redemption of their soul. Jesus had come under the very nose of Herod. He should have known and yet he knew nothing. Jesus remained undetected by Herod because he and his circle of friends and supporters did not include those who were looking for Him. In spite of Herod and those like him, the coming of the Messiah was being celebrated in Judea and an infectious anticipation began to spread throughout Israel.

The scripture just sited tells us that Anna's declaration was to "all who looked for redemption." This statement may have reference to all those who were of a disposition to look beyond the everyday cares of life with a concern for their eternal welfare. It may also be speaking of those who were present at the temple and in Jerusalem, literally looking for the Christ. If the latter be the case, who would have been there looking for redemption? Of course, one can only speculate, but it is interesting to consider the possibilities, which admittedly might be more poetic than prophetic. Whichever it might be, the possibilities are best appreciated if we consider first the timing of Jesus' birth.

Wise Men

The "wise" men who came from the east to pay homage to the newly born King of the Jews are often depicted as visitors to the manger scene, however, this could not have been the case; their visit had to have been weeks, if not months, later. Their sighting of the star was followed by days or weeks, possibly months of preparation and then by weeks or months of travel. By the time they arrived in Bethlehem, Joseph had long since secured a house for his little family; the wise men from the east found them, not in a stable, but in a house. (Mat.2:11)

The story of the wise men is an interesting one, and illustrates the differences in men's hearts regarding the Christ. I think we have a tendency to misread this narrative and in so doing miss a portion of the important lessons being illustrated. Matthew is the only gospel writer that mentions wise men. "Now when Jesus was born in Bethlehem…there came wise men from the east…" Mat. 2:1 Tradition has made some assumptions about these men; that because costly gifts are mentioned they were men of means and because there were three gifts, there were three wise men. Tradition has even given them names which are not mentioned in the bible. They have become known as "the wise men" as if this was a title they bore rather than simply men who were wise. We might safely assume that these men were of means, not so much for the gifts they carried, but for the fact that they were able to make such a journey. We may also safely assume that there were more than three. To undertake such a journey, servants and family likely would have been included in the company. Others would have made the journey for the same reason the wise men did and for the practical reason of safety in numbers. These men from the east were, at the very least, informed, if not scholarly. They were also likely Christians in the sense that they too looked for the coming of their Christ; not just a king of the Jews. They were wise because they were not merely informed, but were of sufficient faith to act upon the knowledge they possessed. With their knowledge they traveled to a distant land in search of the promised Messiah. Those who act upon the knowledge they have been given are indeed wise.

Those who were looking for Christ saw the star and rejoiced in the heavenly sign. Those who were indifferent or incredulous simply did not see. When the men from the east came to Judea, they went to Jerusalem and to the court of Herod. This begs the question, why did they not go straight to Bethlehem? These men knew that the star was the sign of the birth of the "King of the Jews" and it is reasonable to assume that they would have also known that Bethlehem was to be the birthplace. Was their visit merely one of courtesy? With great effort and purpose they had come to worship the Messiah of the Jews. It would have been logical for the men from the east to assume that one as important as the promised Messiah would have been found in the courts of royalty. By the time they arrived in Judea they knew that they were not looking for a new born infant. Who should know best the whereabouts of one so important, and so they went to Herod. They did not ask where Jesus was born, they simply asked, "Where is the child that is born, the Messiah of the Jews?" (JST Mat. 2:2) Whether or not the men from the east knew about Bethlehem prior to their interview with Herod is of little importance. What is made obvious is that Herod did not know and until then, he was completely disinterested. Jewish scripture was replete with prophecies regarding the coming of the Messiah and yet Herod had to summon his chief priests and scribes for answers. Only then did Herod begin to take an interest in what was already being talked about all through Judea and spreading into Galilee. Because of disbelief, Herod either did not see the star or he simply dismissed it. He had to ask the wise men when the star had appeared. Apparently even his priests and scribes were just as ignorant as he was.

Receiving nothing more than they already knew, the wise men continued their journey to Bethlehem, where Jesus' birth, by that time was more or less common knowledge. It is reasonable to suppose that the residents of Bethlehem spoke openly of the fulfillment of the prophecy. The visitors from the east would have had little difficulty finding many who would direct them to the house and child they sought. "And when they were come into the house, they saw the young child with Mary his mother, and fell down, and worshiped him..." (Mat. 2:11)

Herod had hoped to learn from the wise men the identity and location of Jesus, not to worship as he had claimed, but to deal with a threat. When Herod realized that the wise men (they having been warned in a dream) were not returning with the information he wanted, he devised his terrible and infamous plan. Uncertain of the time that had elapsed, to be safe, he ordered every male child of Bethlehem, to the age of two, be killed. Even Herod, in terrible irony, gives a witness of sorts, of the Messiah. In his actions is found the admission that the long foretold birth of the Savior of the world was a reality. But, instead of seeking out his Savior and King with the intent of worshiping Him, his evil heart was bent on the destruction of his own salvation.

The long awaited Messiah came to earth under the humblest of circumstances without fanfare, but the miracle was not, nor was it intended to be a secret. The shepherds responded with haste to the manifestation and witness they had received. Others would add their witness and then good men and women from the east came bearing gifts as witness that the King of the Jews had come. Jesus the Christ, King of all creation, had taken upon himself mortality. As news of his birth spread, all those he would later refer to as "his sheep" rejoiced. From that time forward, expectations and anticipation began to mount in the hearts of men. Some looked earnestly for the

Son of God while others looked jealously for one posing a threat to traditions they considered more dear than their redeemer.

Can any of us fully appreciate the humble circumstances surrounding Jesus' birth? We can only wonder how long Mary and Joseph sheltered their son in the stable. We don't know where Zacharias and Elisabeth lived, but we can safely surmise that it was not in Bethlehem. Had they been there, Joseph would have undoubtedly gone directly to their home.

For those willing to consider the idea that Jesus was actually born in December, the significance of Luke's explanatory statement regarding the prophetess, Anna's declaration, comes to life. During the month of December, Jerusalem would have been teeming with pilgrims, faithful Jews, from all parts of Israel, who had come to observe the Feast of the Dedication, known today as Hanukah. Many of these would have been there solely for the traditional observance of the feast, but then, others would have seen the sign of Jesus' birth and would be "looking." Among those, might have been men from Galilee, such as Jona(s), the father of Peter and Andrew, and Zebedee, the father of James and John. It is just as probable as it is improbable that all of these seekers would have been in the temple at the time of Simeon's and Anna's declarations. But, regardless of the presence or absence, the word of those prophetic declarations could not have been contained. It would have spread like fire among those "looking," and would have been the beginning of 30 years of anticipation, culminating in Bethebara, where John was baptizing. (Luke 3:15, John 1:41, 45).

Can we even begin to imagine the thrill and joy that must have surged through the hearts of these faithful men and their families at the news of the birth of the Messiah? We can only guess that Peter, Andrew, James and John, as well as others, might have been old enough to have actually seen the star. But even if they didn't, countless conversations, with their fathers, on the shores of the Sea of Galilee would have been dominated by what was seen that sacred night and noised about in Bethlehem and Jerusalem.

With so little said about Jesus' early formative years we may safely conclude, at the very least, that the gospel writers deemed them common and ordinary; not worthy of mention, other than to say that he "increased in wisdom and stature, and in favour with God and man." (Luke 2:52) With only this header on the pages of his youth we are free to fill them as we will. With the DNA of Deity and the latent nature he had achieved in the eternities, he came as all others do, into an imperfect, mortal world. He became subject to temptation, as any other. He did not come with the unfair advantage of favoritism, but with the capacities and character he had developed and which made Him God the Son, and qualified Him for the role to which He was foreordained.

We are told that Jesus' first years were spent in Bethlehem and then, for his safety from those who sought to kill him, in Egypt. By the time Joseph and Mary returned to Galilee, Jesus was a toddler, or young boy. From Egypt, Joseph took his family directly to Nazareth, where Jesus became known and respected as the carpenter's son.

We know by revelation that Jesus was "chosen from the beginning" to be the Savior of mankind. He was the first born of God's spirit children, and by his obedience became God, the Son. He entered upon his mortal experience as the Only Begotten of the Father. There are those who are offended by the idea that he might have been anything less than the God we now revere, that he might have actually been mortal in mortality. Some years ago, in a Sunday School class, the instructor posed a question; "why did Jesus deliberately ignore the hypocritical accusations and questions of the Pharisees, when they had brought a woman to him, caught in the act of adultery." When I suggested that he might have been soliciting the guidance of the spirit, an older gentleman, rather indignantly, replied, "He was God, the Son; he didn't need guidance." As a visitor to the ward and class, I chose not to press the issue. I wonder if we honor Christ, or merely misunderstand when we think of him coming to earth as God, void of any dependence, by virtue of his parentage. The scriptures certainly do not teach us this. "Forasmuch then as the children are partakers of flesh and blood, he also himself likewise took part of the same…For verily he took not on him the nature of angels; but he took on him the seed of Abraham. Wherefore in all things it behooved him to be made like unto his brethren, that he might be a merciful and faithful high priest in things pertaining to God, to make reconciliation for the sins of the people. For in that he himself hath suffered being tempted, he is able to succor them that are tempted." (Heb. 2:14, 16-18) Paul continues, in the fifth chapter, "Though he were a son, yet learned he obedience by the things he suffered." (Heb. 5:8) We have additional insight from the writings of John, found in the 93rd section of the Doctrine and Covenants; "And I, John, bear record that I beheld his glory, as the glory of the Only Begotten of the father, full of grace and truth, even the spirit of truth, which came and dwelt in the flesh, and dwelt among us. And I, John, saw that he received not of the fullness at the first, but received grace for grace; and he received not of the fullness at first, but continued from grace to grace, until he received a fullness;" (D&C 93:11-13) Clearly, we can conclude that, in spite of Jesus' parentage, he had assumed mortality and as a mortal, he faced the same challenges of life common to every other child of God. He came to this life, foreordained to save the children of God or at least offer salvation to all, but he also came to work out his own salvation. For his own sake, he did not come with unfair advantages or exemptions. His agency was never compromised by premature revelation or the unsolicited intervention of heaven.

In short, I cannot believe that Jesus was denied the blessing and privilege of simply being a boy. It is not hard for me to see his mother smiling at his innocent questions, nor does it diminish in any way, my love for him, to think that, as a child, he may have left his clothes lying about. My confidence in him as the God of heaven and

206

earth is not shaken in the least by the idea that, as an apprentice carpenter, he may have cut a board too short or possibly forgot to cut it in the first place. On the other hand, I am also convinced that, because of the nature he developed in preparation for mortality, he needed far fewer of life experiences, than the rest of us, to learn the lessons in them. It is not my wish to make the Lord appear to be less than he was or is, but knowing that he did indeed experience the normality of life like any other, makes him more approachable. He understands life, not just because he is God, but because he lived it. Scriptural accounts of Jesus' life exclude the lighter side and are limited to only the seriousness of the important events of his ministry. Because we do not read about the everyday things of his life we sometimes overlook the idea that there was a lot of life that he lived and enjoyed. He was, after all, a boy who became a man and we do him no discredit to think of him as such. We know that he wept with his friends, but I am sure that he was able to laugh with them as well.

Some of life's greatest lessons are learned in the association and interaction of pretended realities in childhood games. Learning to win and lose gracefully is a vital part of growing up and Jesus learned well the social arts. He learned how to relate to everyone. He knew how to love at every level and age. Children were drawn to him because he knew how to love them. He immersed himself in life. The spirit inside the boy, Jesus, surely would have heightened his perception and appreciation for life. Such awareness would have had the same effects on his ability to find the wonder and happiness in life as it surely did the seriousness of it.

Other than his birth in Bethlehem, proclamations in the temple and exile in Egypt, the only mention of Jesus' youth is of his audience, at the age of twelve, with the doctors in the temple at Jerusalem. This is a very interesting narrative, as much for what it does not say, as for what it does. For example, we are told only that he was found "in the temple, sitting in the midst of the doctors, and they were hearing him, and asking him questions." (Luke 2:46) This begs the questions, "why would a boy of twelve leave his family and friends to go to the temple," and "why would the doctors give audience to a boy?"

It should also be remembered that it was just twelve years earlier, in that temple, that Simeon and Anna proclaimed Jesus to be the infant Messiah and prophesied of him. Many of those who were present, to hear the prophetic witnesses, likely would have been among the learned men who now gave ear, as the boy, according to custom, became a man. It is not unreasonable to picture Zacharias among the doctors and those who "looked for their redemption." Many would have become acquainted with Joseph and Mary and watched with great interest, the Messiah, one year older with each Passover visit to Jerusalem. To them, Jesus was more than a curiosity and remarkable boy. Many of these learned men knew who He was and so, even though they had not yet seen the wonder of miracles or witnessed a resurrection, they would, indeed, listen to this boy. It should be no surprise that in spite of what they knew, they "were astonished at his understanding and answers." (Luke 2:47)

Luke tells us that Joseph and Mary went to Jerusalem every year to keep the Passover. It is not hard for me to picture, on these and other occasions, the young Jesus running and playing with his cousin John, just six months his elder. While the scriptures say nothing of such meetings, it is more than just reasonable to suppose that, like any other families, Joseph and Mary would spend time with their extended family. Mary and Elizabeth knew how important it was for their sons to develop and maintain a close relationship. Why else would the angel have told Mary of Elizabeth's pregnancy and why else would Mary have felt compelled to go, with haste, to be with her. John was very much a part of Jesus' life, even in childhood.

Without taking too many liberties, a look at Jewish life at the time of Christ will help us visualize the boy, Jesus, during those years not mentioned by the gospel writers. It will also give us a basic understanding of the customs and motivations that prepared Jesus for his life mission and prepared others for association with him in key roles during and after his ministry.

Education—Rabbi—Disciple

The education of Jewish children was the responsibility of the father, but shared in the home by the mother. This presents the premise for interesting discussions. Joseph was not the father of Jesus; however he was far from resentful of that fact. Joseph undoubtedly assumed the role, where Jesus was concerned, right along with his other children. It is apparent that Mary and Joseph told Jesus at an early age of his parentage. In his younger years Jesus was an apt student at the feet of Joseph. As he grew, "in favor with God," and became more aware of his relationship with the Almighty, he sought the solitude of the mountains and was taught by his Father, not neglecting the traditional educational opportunities.

The lessons and instruction taught in the home were the principles and ideals of the Torah, as the father had been taught by his father and Rabbi. The boys were also taught the family trade. At ages 4 to 5 boys and girls were deemed ready for Beth Sefer, elementary school. Some scholars contend that the girls did not have an equal opportunity with the boys for formal education, while others say they studied side by side; whatever the case, each community hired a teacher and respectfully called him Rabbi. The Rabbi taught in the Synagogue, but he held no particular office there, other than teacher. The Torah, first five books of the Old Testament, was the text. The children learned reading and writing by copying and reciting verses from the Torah. Memorization was emphasized and, as remarkable it may sound, by the time the students completed their elementary studies, many of them had actually committed to memory the entire Torah.

At age 12 the girls became Bat Mitzvah and the boys, Bar Mitzvah at age 13; which means they became daughters/sons of the commandment and were considered adults in many ways. There is no record of Bar/Bat Mitzvah ceremonies as has become the custom today; however, this was a significant time in the life of a Jew. As a son or daughter of the commandment the Jewish youth assumed responsibilities with the adults of the community. Among other things, boys were allowed to take an active part in the events of the Passover; to converse with the other men and scholars.

At the age of Bar Mitzvah many of the better students elected to continue their education, again under the tutelage of the Rabbi in Beth Midrash, secondary school. This phase of education was pursued along with additional roles and responsibilities in the home and family business and, depending on the goals of the student, continued beyond his teenage years. At some point in this phase of education some would choose to be a Talmid, a disciple-student. This gifted student sought out one of the most celebrated Rabbis and would make application to be his disciple. While a disciple is one who follows, the Talmid is more than that. The Talmid was more than a student; he wanted more than to simply know what the Rabbi knew, he wanted to think and act as the Rabbi did. The Talmid wanted more than to merely follow the Rabbi; he wanted to be able to do the things he saw the Rabbi do and be like him in every way. The Talmidim literally followed the Rabbi wherever he went, for months at a time, observing his mannerisms and actions and listening intently to everything he said. The hope of the Talmid and the design of the Rabbi was for the Talmid to become, in every possible way, the image of the Rabbi. For this reason the Rabbi chose his Talmidim, either directly or indirectly by accepting or denying the application of the Talmid based on his confidence in the abilities of the applicant to become like him. A close study of Jesus' ministry shows that Jesus invited everyone to follow him and that he never directly denied or dismissed a single person. However, there were many who solicited him and then found discipleship too difficult and ultimately fell away. (see Mark 10:17-22, John 6)
The Stages of Life in Education

The basic stages of one's life are listed in the Mishnah Avot 5:21 which gives some idea of how the ancient individual was educated. Many of these date from ancient times. We see them applying to the life of Yeshua [Jesus] as detailed in the gospels. At age five one is ready for the study of Scripture. We are told that the children were taught first from the Book of Leviticus for ritual purity and how to approach God by sacrifice and then from the Book of Psalms concerning the nature of God, before they went on to other things. Possibly this is what Yeshua meant when He referred to people's coming to Him as a child (Matthew 18:2-4) in child -like purity. At the age of ten one was fit for the study of the words of the Oral Law, and at the age of thirteen one was old enough to fulfill the commandments. Some scholars believe it was the Oral Law which the ancient boys were questioned about on the steps of the Temple, as in the case of Yeshua (Luke 2). At the age of fifteen one was ready to study of the sages, at the age of eighteen, for marriage, and at the age of twenty, for pursuing a vocation. Yeshua is called both the son of Joseph the carpenter and Yeshua the carpenter (Book of Mark). Obviously, Joseph had followed this pattern and taught his son his vocation. At the age of thirty one entered the full vigor of his ministry. It was at this point in Yeshua's life that we see Him entering the full ministry. At age forty one reached a place where he had understanding, and at age fifty the individual was worthy to counsel others. It is in this setting that the Biblical injunction for the older (age fifty) men to counsel the younger men and the older women to counsel the younger. (Jewish Education in Ancient Times by Dr. Ron Moseley)

A few (very few) of the most outstanding Beth Midrash students sought permission to study with a famous rabbi often leaving home to travel with him for a lengthy period of time. These students were called talmidim (talmid, s.) in Hebrew, which is translated disciple. There is much more to a talmid than what we call student. A student wants to know what the teacher knows for the grade, to complete the class or the degree or even out of respect for the teacher. A talmid wants to like the teacher, that is to become what the teacher is. That meant that students were passionately devoted to their rabbi and noted everything he did or said. This meant the rabbi?talmid relationship was a very intense and personal system of education. As the rabbi lived and taught his understanding of the Scripture his students (talmidim) listened and watched and imitated so as to become like him. Eventually they would become teachers passing on a lifestyle to their talmidim. As a result, Galilee was a place of intense study of Scripture. People were knowledgeable about its content and the various applications made by their tradition. They were determined to live by it and to pass their faith and knowledge and lifestyle on to their children. It was into this world that Jesus came as a child and eventually a rabbi.

Being like the rabbi is the major focus of the life of talmidim. They listen and question, they respond when questioned, they follow without knowing where the rabbi is taking them knowing that the rabbi has good reason for bringing them to the right place for his teaching to make the most sense. In the story recorded in *Matthew 16*, Jesus walked nearly thirty miles one way to be in Caesarea Philippi for a lesson that fit the location perfectly. Surely he talked with them along the way but the whole trip seems to have been geared for one lesson that takes less than ten minutes to give (*Matt. 16:13?28*).

When the teacher believed that his talmidim were prepared to be like him he would commission them to become disciple makers. He was saying ?As far as is possible you are like me. Now go and seek others who will imitate you. Because you are like me, when they imitate you they will be like me. This practice certainly lies behind Jesus great commission (*Matt. 28:18?20*). While in one sense no one can be like Jesus in his divine nature, or in his perfect human nature, when taught by the Rabbi, empowered and blessed by the Spirit of God, imitating Jesus becomes a possibility.

The mission of the disciples was to seek others who would imitate them and therefore become like Jesus. That strategy, blessed by God's Spirit would bear amazing fruit especially in the Gentile world.

It also helps to understand the teaching of Paul who sought to make disciples. He invited Herod Agrippa and the Roman governor to become like him (*Acts 26:28?29*). He taught the young churches to imitate him and others who were like Jesus (*1 Cor. 4:15-16, 11:1*; *1 Thess. 1:6-7, 2:14*; *2 Thess. 3:7?9*; *1 Tim. 4:12*. The writer to the Hebrews had the same mission (*Heb. 6:12, 13:7*). (Ray Vander Laan, Author-theologian, founder of "That the World May Know Ministries" He received an undergraduate degree in 1973 from *Dordt College*. In 1976 he received a *Masters of Divinity* degree from *Westminster Theological Seminary*. He continued graduate studies in Jewish Studies at *Yeshiva University* in New York, *Hebrew University of Jerusalem* and *Trinity International University*)

The Rabbi-Talmid relationship was an important element in Jewish culture. The Talmid took his credentials from the Rabbi that instructed him and the Rabbi received his acclaim, in a sense living on, through his Talmidim. We see this idea and philosophy in an exchange between Jesus and the Jews, recorded in John 7:15-18; "And the Jews marveled, saying, How knoweth this man letters, having never learned? Jesus answered them, and said, My doctrine is not mine, but his that sent me. If any man will do his will, he shall know of the doctrine, whether it be of God, or [whether] I speak of myself. He that speaketh of himself seeketh his own glory: but he that seeketh his glory that sent him, the same is true, and no unrighteousness is in him."

In these verses Jesus presents himself as the Talmid, but the Jews marvel because, as far as they know, Jesus had not followed a Rabbi and they didn't know the source of his great knowledge. Many simply were not prepared or willing to accept his divine Sonship.

This important relationship is illustrated again in Jesus' response when Phillip asked to be shown the Father. "Jesus saith unto him, Have I been so long time with you, and yet hast thou not known me, Philip? He that hath seen me hath seen the Father; and how sayest thou [then], Shew us the Father? Believest thou not that I am in the Father, and the Father in me? the words that I speak unto you I speak not of myself: but the Father that dwelleth in me, he doeth the works. Believe me that I [am] in the Father, and the Father in me: or else believe me for the very works' sake. Verily, verily, I say unto you, He that believeth on me, the works that I do shall he do also; and greater [works] than these shall he do; because I go unto my Father." John 14:9-12

The principles of the Rabbi/Talmid relationship are further illustrated by the commission of the Seventy. Jesus ordained them, and commissioned them to do the things they had seen him do and said, "He that heareth you heareth me; and he that despiseth you despiseth me; and he that despiseth me despiseth him that sent me." Luke 10:16 (1-16)

Years of Preparation

Luke's reference to Jesus 'temple visit and scholarly exchange at the age of 12 is scriptural evidence that, as a boy, he had been taught of and knew his Father. At that tender age he knew, in part at least, his life's mission.

While not mentioned, we may safely conclude that Jesus, all through his youth and pre-ministry years, visited Jerusalem at least once a year and likely two or three times. In addition to the Passover Feast, there was also the Feast of Tabernacles and the Feast of the Dedication. During these visits, Jesus and his family sought lodging with extended family and/or friends. These occasions introduced Jesus to humble seekers from surrounding areas such as Bethlehem and Bethany. Many of these acquaintances, possibly including Lazarus and his sisters, Mary and Martha, became loyal and lifelong friends. These frequent and regular visits gave Jesus and his cousin, John, the opportunity to grow up together and develop a bond of love and devotion. Both John and Jesus were taught by their parents of each other and the respective roles to which they had been born. Of all the bonds between two men, could there ever be one stronger than the one between John and Jesus?

Eighteen years of Jesus' life are left blank. Since we know that the gospel writers did not witness the events in Jesus' life prior to his ministry, we might wonder why Mary and others said nothing of those eighteen years. Why didn't Jesus relate at least some events to Matthew and John? (Mark and Luke both wrote after the death of Jesus. Their narratives were commissioned by Paul and Peter, and naturally focused primarily on the Savior's ministry.) Jesus' interaction with Matthew and John would have had the same emphasis on the ministry, leaving his private life unmentioned, not secret or even guarded; simply not pertinent.

The blank pages of Jesus' life have been filled with speculations ranging from spiteful to insightful, by the uninformed as well as those who have made a study of his life. I know of nothing conclusive regarding those years, and so I look at them from a point of view that renders them natural and normal for a Jewish boy approaching and entering manhood. For all we do not know, we are assured that Jesus was indeed a man, subject to life and the demands of living it. From what we read of his later life and ministry, we have an image and idea of him in those years of preparation. He was a student of life, giving full attention to every aspect of it. He loved and had a great respect for nature and all forms of life. He was physically strong, but gentle. He was quiet, but commanded the confidence of self awareness. He was true to all that is good. He was all that we read about long before his character and attributes were revealed by the events described by the gospel writers. He was devoted to his family and worked for their support. Some suggest that Joseph is not mentioned by the writers because he had died prior to the commencement of Jesus' ministry; Jesus was the head of the family and primary care giver. He looked after his mother and provided for her. Jesus spent a great deal of time in meditation, being taught from on high and developing a close relationship with his Father.

Even in the most introspective moments of deep reflection, I cannot imagine the emotions that must have dominated the mind and soul of the youthful Messiah. At times we may feel to lament what seems to be the weight of the world crushing down upon us; burdens we would walk away from, if only we could. Try if you will, to feel what he must have felt, in his moments of solitude, as he pondered the burden he would carry; the burden, and the pain of the sins of all mankind.

At the age of twelve, Jesus knew that he had a responsibility to "be about his father's business." How much he knew of what that meant, we cannot know. In addition to being an apprentice carpenter, he was a student of the scriptures. Not a student as one of us, but as one with a unique perspective. At some point his devotion and dutiful study must have revealed a familiarity that only he could know and feel. The words he studied were his own; words that he, as Jehovah, gave to the prophets. Now, as the mortal Son of God, he became subject to his own words and to the plan of salvation along with all of God's children. He too came to be proven; to see if he would do all that he was commanded to do. Here we might be tempted to debate the advantages he might have had as a literal son of God in the flesh. However, to entrain such a notion is to deny the perfections of God. While Jesus is the only begotten of the Father in the flesh, his father is our father as well. With perfect love for all of his children, God could not give to one what he would not give to all. God could not deny Jesus the right to agency any more than he would deny any of his children. We know by our own observations and experience, that the gifts and qualities of men and women are not a foregone heritage of their children, nor can parents, with any degree of success, simply impose them upon their children. In time the children may or may not emulate the character of their parents. Children will mimic their parents and in time, define themselves by the course they choose, whether in compliance or defiance of the examples bestowed upon them. The misuse of agency on the part of parents and others may compromise the agency of the children, and influence the child's understanding and use of his agency, but ultimately the child will use his agency to define and prove himself. God could not and did not impose himself upon his son but, at a very early age, Jesus proved himself; he "gained favor with God" and was taught by him. By age 30, the commencement of his ministry, he was fully aware of his mission and had long since embraced it..

Even in the scarcity of details of his early life, there is ample written to conclude that Jesus and his family were devout Jews. They held in high regard the traditions and customs of their faith and their country. Social tradition said that at age 13 a boy began to be responsible and assumed many of the rights and responsibilities of an adult. Age 18 was considered the age of marriage (references in the Talmud put the proper age of marriage at the ages of 16 to 24), age 20, the age of one's chosen vocation and 30, the age of one's life work. Jewish children had three teachers; first the mother, until the child was weaned; second, the father, until puberty. The Torah, with all its "Mitzvah" (laws), was the third and final teacher.

We have already seen that, by age 12, Jesus was very much aware of his parentage, and spoke frankly of his Father to Mary and to Joseph. Being a father myself, and feeling very keenly what is expected of me (see D&C 29:48), my thoughts go to Joseph. I am certain that he did everything in his power to give every opportunity to Jesus, along with his children, to glean from life all that it has to offer. While Jesus was not ordinary in the way he dealt with life, we have no reason to think that he did not experience all that was normal and traditional for his time and culture. This includes a vocation and marriage.

Orson Hyde had quite a lot to say about the marriage of Jesus (see Journal of Discourses, 26 vols., 2:, p.80-83) According to Elder

Hyde, Jesus was married to both Mary and Martha and that the occasion of the wedding feast at Cana was Jesus' marriage. Personally, I don't know how or why Elder Hyde came to that conclusion. I have no problem with the idea that Mary or Martha, or even both of them, might have been married to Jesus, but why would he not be married long before his ministry began. As has already been discussed, Jesus had many years of opportunity to know and become close to Lazarus and his sisters. The concern shown by Jesus' mother at the Cana wedding, suggests the wedding was for a family member. However, Jesus was well past the usual age of marriage and he did have brothers and sisters.

"Did the Savior of the world consider it his duty to fulfill all righteousness? And if the Savior of the world found it his duty to fulfill all righteousness to obey a command of far less importance than that of multiplying his race, would he not find it his duty to join with the race of the faithful ones in replenishing the earth?"-Orson Hyde, Journal of Discourses, volume II, page 79.

Elder Hyde's observation is perceptive and one might further read from Jesus' statement to John that the ordinance of marriage had already occurred and his baptism was to fulfill, or complete the necessary ordinances of salvation. Elder Hyde continues, "Next let us inquire whether there are any intimations in the Scriptures concerning the wives of Jesus. One thing is certain: that there were several holy women who greatly loved Jesus, such as Mary and Martha, her sister, and Mary Magdalene; Jesus greatly loved them and associated with them much; and when he arose from the dead, instead of first showing himself to his chosen witnesses, the apostles, he appeared first to these women, or at least to one of them, namely, Mary Magdalene. Now it would be very natural for a husband in the resurrection to appear first to his own dear wives, and afterwards show himself to his other friends. If all the acts of Jesus were written, we no doubt should learn that these beloved women were his wives. Indeed, the Psalmist David prophesies in particular concerning the wives of the Son of God. 'Kings' daughters were among thine honorable wives; upon thy right hand did stand the Queen in a vesture of gold of Ophir."-Apostle Orson Pratt in The Seer, page 159. B. H. Roberts, Defense of the Faith and the Saints, 2 vols., 2:, p.272

Prophecy:

From the beginning of time, the children of God have been taught to look forward to the coming of the Lord. Old Testament prophets spoke and prophesied of the Messiah's birth and mortal ministry; New and Old Testament prophets spoke of his coming in the last days. The ancient Jews knew and cherished the words of the prophets. Collectively they looked for the coming of the Messiah. But, just as we see today, individually, there was a wide array of beliefs that determined the nature and extent of their anticipation. Those not apathetic regarding the prophecies viewed the Lord's coming according to the object of their individual faith. Some looked for political salvation, while others, with greater understanding and grasp of the scriptures, looked for the salvation and redemption of their souls.

The Jews were likely the most religious people, as a whole, in the entire world. They took great pride in their genealogical ties to Abraham and the Fathers. The idea of a promised Messiah coming through the royal lines of Israel was only natural to them. However, their devotion to Abraham and the Law of Moses proved to be an insurmountable barrier between them and the living Christ. Nevertheless, their knowledge of the prophets pointed their minds to the coming of the Messiah, however misguided their devotion was.

Birth of John:

The birth of John marked the beginning of the fulfillment of the great promises and visions of the prophets. His birth was a sign to those who looked, that the day foretold was at hand. The birth and mission of John was no secret. Zacharias spoke openly and prophetically about his son and of the promised Messiah. See Luke 1:69-79

The pregnancy of Elisabeth and subsequent birth of John were nothing less than miraculous, and when Zacharias declared the divine mission his son would accomplish, the miracle of John became a topic of great interest and was discussed throughout all of Judea (Luke 1:65). Undoubtedly this news spread far beyond Judea. Among the faithful, the words of the prophets had been an integral part of their lives and now hope swelled in the hearts of humble men and women in Judea and spread north throughout Galilee. They knew that in thirteen years John would become a man, a Bar Mitzvah, in twenty years he would choose his vocation, and in thirty years he would be ready to begin his ministry. Because of the coming of John, people began to look for the Messiah.

The Star:
 The new star, or Star of Bethlehem, was the sign to all the world that the Son of God, the Savior of all creation, had been born. If such a sign could go unnoticed, it would be by those whose apathy blinded them to things beyond their own materialistic devotions. The Bible mentions only a few who saw and responded to the heavenly sign. However, the Book of Mormon describes widespread anticipation and acknowledgement of the sign of Jesus' birth. While the Bible does not mention the same recognition, it is reasonable to assume that the sign of the star was received by a great many with joy and even rejoicing. Certainly it was talked about all through Palestine. Among the faithful it would be discussed between friends and in homes. Children grew up, hearing about the Star of Bethlehem. The promise of the Messiah made them ever watchful.

Pilgrimages brought the faithful together at Jerusalem for the Passover, the Feast of the Tabernacle, and Feast of the Dedication. These journeys were likely dominated by discussions of the Star and its implications. Year after year the discussions continued, perhaps waning at times, but still reaching and involving additional hopefuls, as well as skeptics, creating a general sense of anticipation, (Luke 3:15)

Shepherds:
As has been discussed, shepherds of Judea were chosen and given a witness of the divine birth of the Messiah. There testimony solidified that of the Star and generated an anticipation among the people of Israel. They were, in a sense, proxy for all who look, and still look, for the promised Messiah. The words of the angel to them, penetrate humble hearts and are consolation to all who seek the Lord, "unto *YOU* is born this day…"

Simeon and Anna:
The testimony of Simeon and Anna, in the temple, was heard by many faithful seekers, those "who looked for redemption." The identity of the Messiah was no secret. Those in the temple that day who were not already acquainted with Joseph and Mary soon were. The faithful, those who Jesus would later refer to as 'his sheep,' offered the hospitality of their homes and lifelong bonds were almost instantly established. Subsequent pilgrimages to the temple at Jerusalem were eagerly awaited and talked about.

Wise Men:
Men (and women) came from the east; a distance that required dedication, preparation and determination. They came to pay homage to the King of the Jews. While they came in response to the star they had seen, their journey was one of several months. Their arrival in the small town of Bethlehem was a curiosity to the locals; that a company from the Far East also saw the star. Their presence renewed conversations of the royal birth and the anticipation of the promised Messiah.

Herod's Infamy:

It is difficult to imagine the depravity that would cause a man to do what Herod did, but history has shown that men and societies are capable of even the most horrific atrocities. The murder of the baby boys of Bethlehem etched the name of Herod into the dark tablets of infamy and no doubt secured a place for him in the darkest corner of Hell. Ironically, in his attempt to eliminate a rival, Herod unwittingly announced the Lord's birth to a population that might have otherwise remained in ignorance. News of his savagery traveled far beyond Bethlehem and Jerusalem. Even skeptics and the indifferent were compelled to wonder, what could motivate such cruelty. A new King of the Jews had come and while Herod could not accept it, his response declared it and generated a sense of anticipation among many who would have otherwise remained in their self-serving oblivion.

Temple Visits:
Regular Passover visits to the temple in Jerusalem by Joseph and Mary included Jesus. Those who were privileged to be in the temple when Jesus was presented according to law looked and longed for those visits. They witnessed the growth of a boy and with each visit, marveled at the level of maturity he achieved.

Ministry of John:
After the many signs of the Lord's coming there followed formal and informal discussions of the implications and ramifications. The years of waiting and watching reduced much of the discussion to rumor and wonder. Nevertheless, there were many still hopeful and still looking for the promises to be fulfilled. Perhaps there were more than a few whose anticipation heightened with the realization that it had been 30 years since the star appeared; the baby would be a man, of the age to begin his life's work, the age when he could be recognized as a Rabbi and begin his ministry. John, being older than Jesus, had begun his ministry six months earlier, as foretold, to

prepare the way for the Messiah. Many, including both the hopeful and skeptical, traveled long distances to see and hear this new Rabbi, thinking that perhaps he might be the Messiah.

The Prophet at Bethebara

John's ministry was centered in Judea, in the general vicinity of Jerusalem. The scriptures tell us that he was baptizing in Bethebara. The exact location of that site is not known today, but is thought to be in the general vicinity of Jericho, roughly ten to fifteen miles north of the Dead Sea. For six months, John had been teaching the gospel of repentance and of baptism, preparing for the arrival of Jesus. He began his ministry about the time of the Passover which also marked his 30th birthday.

With so little written of John, the religious, and not so religious, community has taken liberties in widely varied speculations about his life and training for his ministry. Speaking of John, Luke tells us, "...the child grew, and waxed strong in spirit, and was in the deserts till the day of his [showing] unto Israel." (Luke 1:80) With the exception of this statement and another in modern revelation, the scriptures are silent regarding the youth and early training of John. In September of 1832, the prophet Joseph Smith received a 'revelation on priesthood' in which we learn more of John's youth; "...he was baptized while he was yet in his childhood, and was ordained by the angel of God at the time he was eight days old..." (D&C 84:28) We are not given the name of the angel, but we know of several Old Testament prophets who had been translated, retaining their ability to officiate in such an ordinance. This was an important event in John's life, even though he was too young to know it at the time. It was also a sacred occasion for Zacharias and Elisabeth, reaffirming to them the great commission to which their son had been called and ordained. It is more than reasonable to visualize an intimate scene, attended by close family members, such as Mary. Such an affirmation would have been a great strength to the expecting mother of the Messiah. At a very early age, John was taught of his calling and ordination. The extent of the training and tutelage of John is not included in our scriptures, but he knew who he was and he devoted himself to becoming what he had been foreordained to be.

By the time we hear of John again, he is a man, seemingly living in the wilderness, wearing a coat of camel hair and eating honey and locusts. Casual and superficial glances at the scriptures have painted John as an eccentric, honored and despised, loved and feared and mocked and revered by men. It is a flawed assumption on our part, that because the scriptures say he was in the wilderness, wore camel hair and ate locusts that this was all he ever did. It is not likely that years of wilderness isolation would have prepared him for the respect he received of some and for his ability to confront the hypocritical Pharisees as he did. The same surface perusals make Jesus a stranger to John when, at last, they meet at the waters of the Jordan. Such notions and inconsistencies fade in the light of logic. John came of parents who were true, and who were devoted to righteousness. They were well aware of his divine commission and their parental responsibilities. As devout Jews they would not have neglected their duties to prepare him for his life's work. Zacharias and Elisabeth were more diligent than most, because they knew more about their son than others did of theirs. They taught him from the scriptures and by age 5, as was typical for a Jewish boy, he was prepared for Beth Sefer (elementary school), taught by a local rabbi in the Synagogue. This phase of education focused on the oral Torah, and here, many students, certainly John, memorized much, if not all of it. At age 13 he became Bar Mitzvah (son of the commandment) and continued his studies in Beth Midrash (secondary school), also taught by the rabbi, which focused on the written Torah and the oral interpretations. We have no reason to think that John was not a normal Jewish boy, who became a normal man, in every sense. The only thing that was really different about him, over any other boy, was that, as a boy, he was aware of his life's mission.

Because Luke tells us that John was in the wilderness until the day of his showing, some are tempted to conclude that he led a life of isolation. However, others teach that John had frequent contact with Jesus, actually traveling to Nazareth to make advance preparations, and as a young adult sought a humble life as a shepherd in the so-called "wilderness" hill country of Hebron; not at all the isolating wilderness we often imagine. Still others suggest that Herod the Great killed Zacharias when John was still a small child and Elisabeth, of necessity, fled to the wilderness for her safety and that of John, where she raised him in preparation for his mission in life. Undoubtedly he spent a great deal of time there, as did Jesus, in private spiritual retreat. His devotion to his calling is evidenced by the simplicity of his life, requiring little more than the honey and locusts the wilderness provided him during periods of meditation and instruction. As a devout Jew, John was well acquainted with customs and traditions. He observed the Feasts and made the associated pilgrimages. This, along with his formal education, made him aware of the Pharisees and the Sadducees and their hypocrisy. As a devout Jew, John placed great importance in family life and we have no reason to think that he did not have a family of his own. He would not have abandoned them in favor of wilderness solitude. The fact that multitudes sought him out, listened to him and believed his teaching, is evidence of a life and life style not just acceptable, but exemplary. Ideas of a strange ascetic life in the wilderness do not hold up in the light of his calling as the prophet ordained to prepare the way of the Lord.

Because of the knowledge they possessed, Elisabeth and Mary made every possible effort to allow John and Jesus to grow up together. Once a year, at the time of the Passover feast, Mary and Joseph brought Jesus to Jerusalem. The most likely place for them to stay was with their family, Elisabeth and Zacharias. This and other occasions gave John and Jesus precious days together affording them time to play together, to talk with each other, and to look ahead. As adults, Jesus and John would continue their traditional reunions in anticipation and preparation. John's thirtieth birthday, which marked the beginning of his ministry coincided with the Passover. This Passover meeting was more than typical for them. Here they would make plans to meet again in six months. They were well acquainted with the entire region and talked about Bethebara and what their next meeting held for each other.

There is even less written of John's pre-ministry life than there is of Jesus'. Assumptions based on the few existing verses are unfounded at best and often simply absurd. Six months prior to Jesus' arrival in Judea, John had begun his ministry. Many came to see and hear this new Rabbi and very quickly John had a following. Some traveled great distances to see if he might, in fact, be the promised Messiah, but many were there because they already knew him. His father, Zacharias, had made it very clear that his son would be the forerunner of the Christ. Many came to be baptized, recognizing both their need for it and John's authority to perform it. Any idea or notion that John was a strange man immerging out of the wilderness is dismissed by the very fact that he was a prophet of God. He came from a family respected in the community and in the faith. As a devout Jew, he had been well educated. He held the Mosaic Law in the highest regard and conformed to it, which meant he would have been married at the appropriate age. Like all Jews, he had a strong desire to have children and bring them up in the faith. He was respected in his own right and was recognized, even by the Pharisees, as one authorized to teach and to baptize. They asked him why he baptized, but never challenged his authority. Following John's imprisonment, Jesus spoke most highly of him: "...Jesus began to say unto the multitudes concerning John, What went ye out into the wilderness to see? A reed shaken in the wind? But what went ye out for to see? A man clothed in soft raiment?...But went ye out to see? A prophet? Yea, I say unto you, and more than a prophet. For this is he, of whom it is written, Behold, I send my messenger before thy face, which shall prepare thy way before thee.

Verily I say unto you, Among them that are born of women there hath not risen a greater than John the Baptist:..." (Mat. 11:7-11)

John's personal preparations and his associations with Jesus, prepared him for the day when Jesus would approach him for baptism. For roughly six months John taught and prepared the people for the coming of the Lord. He made it very clear that his was a preparatory work. Listen to his words again, "I indeed baptize you with water unto repentance: but he that cometh after me is mightier than I, whose shoes I am not worthy to bear: he shall baptize you with the Holy Ghost, and [with] fire:" Mat. 3:11 "...when the Jews sent priests and Levites from Jerusalem, to ask him; Who art thou?...he confessed, and denied not that he was Elias; but confessed, saying; I am not the Christ. And they asked him, saying; How then art thou Elias? And he said, I am not that Elias who was to restore all things. And they asked him, saying, Art thou that prophet? And he answered, No. Then said they unto him, Who art thou? that we may give an answer to them that sent us. What sayest thou of thyself? He said, I am the voice of one crying in the wilderness, Make straight the way of the Lord, as saith the prophet Esaias." JST John 1:20-24 (Isaiah 40:3)
John's answer to the priests and Levites could not have been clearer. They, and the Pharisees who sent them, were well acquainted with the prophesies of Isaiah. John had declared himself to be that prophet foretold, who would prepare the way for the Messiah. When they challenged him, asking why he performed baptism if he was not the Christ, he bore witness of Jesus; that he would baptize "...with fire, and with the Holy Ghost." JST John1:28 Matthew's record indicates that the Pharisees and Sadducees themselves came on at least one occasion to witness the baptisms of John. He was bold in his response to their presence and denounced their self-serving claims as children of Abraham, "O generation of vipers, who hath warned you to flee from the wrath to come? Bring forth therefore fruits meet for repentance:" Mat. 3:7-8

When John saw Jesus approaching, there was no question or hesitation on his part, as suggested by some. He boldly and exultantly declared, "Behold, the Lamb of God, who taketh away the sin of the world!" The day they had been waiting and preparing for had come; the beginning of the ministry of Jesus the Christ. John and Jesus had embraced each other many times before, but their embrace, this day, was one of joy and triumph. While we may safely and logically make assumptions, the scriptures give us no indication of witnesses to this great and momentous occasion. The heavens opened and a voice proclaimed the divinity of the Only Begotten Son of the Father. Mark's record of this appears to be an affirmation to Jesus, "thou art my beloved son…" while Matthew's seems to be addressed to one or more, other than Jesus, "this is my beloved son…" Luke does not mention the baptism. John's record gives us the indication that there were others present at the time of Jesus' arrival and following the baptism. We might safely make the assumption that Jesus did not travel alone and that close companions, family members and close associates, were there to witness this important and sacred ordinance.

The Bible translation we read today is often confusing and misleading, leaving an impression that Jesus and John were, more or less, strangers to one another. However, as has been discussed, this would not have been the case. Among the flawed impression left by translators is the idea that John would forbid Jesus at his request for baptism as recorded in Mat. 3:14. In that same verse we read John's reaffirmation of the baptism, by fire, that he had been teaching and anticipating. Some may contest and debate the idea that John knew in advance that Jesus would request baptism at their meeting; however, I think it most likely that such an important event would have been discussed and anticipated by both Jesus and John. John's message had been one of repentance for the remission of sin. Recognizing the sinless life of Jesus, John would not have forbidden him, but might have humbly questioned the need. In addition, he acknowledged the divinity of Jesus and his own need and subservience. John humbly expressed his desire for the baptism that Jesus offered; the one of fire he had been preparing his disciples to receive. Jesus' response was simple and direct. "Suffer [permit] it to be so now: for thus it becometh us to fulfill all righteousness." Mat. 3:15 There is no rebuke in Jesus' words, but in them is found a reaffirmation of the solemnity of the occasion and of the sacredness of what they, together, were about to do. Jesus acknowledged not only the universal necessity of baptism, but also the authority to perform it and that John held that authority. This was not something that Jesus could do alone. Note that he said "it becometh us" not me, to fulfill all righteousness.

The humble goodness of John and his selfless commitment to his appointment was evidenced following the commencement of Jesus' ministry. He had been preparing his disciples to receive and accept the Christ and accordingly, his discipleship began to diminish, while that of Jesus began to increase. This was brought to his attention and John's answer reveals the love he had for Jesus and his own humble nature; "He that hath the bride is the bridegroom: but the friend of the bridegroom, which standeth and heareth him, rejoiceth greatly because of the bridegroom's voice: this my joy therefore is fulfilled. He must increase, but I must decrease." John 3:29-30

The People Were in Expectation: (Luke 3:15)

Jesus did not begin His formal ministry until He was 30 years of age. According to custom one could not be recognized as a teacher before age 30. John was subject to and would have honored the same tradition and began his ministry approximately six months in advance of Jesus'. Many of those who were in Judea, who knew Zacharias and Elisabeth were still living. They remembered the miraculous birth of the prophet—forerunner of the Messiah and, undoubtedly, they would have shared the experience and the prophecies with their children. The faithful were waiting for these prophecies to begin to unfold. This anticipation was contagious, even among skeptics. "And as the people were in expectation, and all men mused in their hearts of John, whether he were the Christ..." (Luke 3:15) John quickly became popular and many, remembering the sign of the Messiah's coming, came to him, thinking he might actually be the Christ. "...the Jews sent priests and Levites from Jerusalem to ask him, Who art thou?" When John confessed that he was not the Christ some protested, "...Why baptizest thou then, if thou be not that Christ..." (John 1:19-25) John explained, "...I indeed baptize you with water; but one mightier than I cometh...he shall baptize you with the Holy Ghost and with fire:" (Luke 3:16)

The immediate popularity of John speaks something of the condition of the faith and religious climate at the time. Matthew tells us, "Then went out to him Jerusalem, and all Judea, and all the region round about Jordan, And were baptized of him in Jordan, confessing their sins." (Mat. 3:5-6) The people saw in John what was lacking in their synagogues and in their priests. They recognized his authority and their own need for the repentance and baptism he taught. Their presence and compliance was evidence of their regard for this new Rabbi-Prophet and his divine authority.

When the Pharisees and Sadducees also came, John saw in them the pride and arrogance that compelled them to come. Steeped in their traditions, they were more comfortable with the idea of a promised Messiah than they were with the possibility of a living Christ. They had not come in search of truth but in self-righteous curiosity, to examine their opposition. The teachings of John posed a threat to them. What he taught required of them the same as it did of all men, and they had become comfortable in their position as judges, protected and exonerated by their interpretations of the law. They were not ignorant of the truth, but because their hearts were not receptive to it, it threatened to expose them and they could not passively go their way. John was well acquainted with them and their self-serving philosophies. They took great pride in their assumed position and privilege as children of Abraham. John spoke boldly, "Why is it that ye receive not the preaching of him whom God hath sent? If ye receive not this in your hearts, ye receive not me; and if ye receive not me, ye receive not him of whom I am sent to bear record; and for your sins ye have no cloak. Repent, therefore, and bring forth fruits meet for repentance; And think not to say within yourselves, We are the children of Abraham, and we only have power to bring seed unto our father Abraham; for I say unto you that God is able of these stones to raise up children into Abraham." (JST Mat. 3:34-36)

When Jesus came to Bethabara, John had been declaring him for six months. Possibly hundreds, and even thousands, considered themselves disciples of John and yet he spoke frankly of the Christ that would come. John's followers were attracted to him because of the expectation his presence generated and his words captivated them in heightened anticipation. People came to him from regions beyond Jerusalem, many speculating that he might be the Christ. Nearing his 30th birthday, Jesus made his way to Jerusalem to keep the Feast of the Dedication. He shared the road with others from Galilee, also going to the Feast. Many were going specifically to see and hear John.

To fully appreciate this wide spread interest that was bringing so many people to Bethebara, we need only look back thirty years, at the circumstances surrounding the miraculous birth of John. The scriptures tell us that Zacharias and Elisabeth were elderly, but does not tell us exactly how old they were. The miracle attracted no small stir among their family and friends. "Now Elisabeth's full time came that she should be delivered; and she brought forth a son. And her neighbors and her [relatives] heard how the Lord had shewed great mercy upon her; and they rejoiced with her. And it came to pass, that on the eighth day they came to circumcise the child; and they called him Zacharias, after the name of his father. And his mother answered and said, Not [so]; but he shall be called John. And they said unto her, There is none of thy kindred that is called by this name. And they made signs to his father, how he would have him called. And he asked for a writing table, and wrote, saying, His name is John. And they marvelled all. And his mouth was opened immediately, and his tongue [loosed], and he spake, and praised God....Zacharias was filled with the Holy Ghost, and prophesied, saying, Blessed [be] the Lord God of Israel; for he hath visited and redeemed his people, And hath raised up an horn of salvation for us in the house of his servant David... And thou, child, shalt be called the prophet of the Highest: for thou shalt go before the face of the Lord to prepare his ways...And the child grew, and waxed strong in spirit, and was in the deserts till the day of his shewing unto Israel. (Luke 1:57-80)

The miracle of John's birth by itself gave rise to considerable interest. Add to that the prophetic declarations of Zacharias regarding his son, and of the coming Messiah, and you have fuel for conversations that spread throughout all of Judea. Travelers and pilgrims from surrounding regions came to Jerusalem and were drawn into these discussions. Age old prophecies came to life in the birth of John as their fulfillment was made imminent by the words of Zacharias. These discussions were carried back to all parts of Palestine, particularly Galilee, and fueled the ever increasing expectation of the people everywhere. Thirty years later, John was more than the passing curiosity of just one more rabbi. It was much more than curiosity that drew people to him. However, over the course of those thirty years, the prophecies of Zacharias became diluted and confused. People began to question the identity of John, speculating that he might actually be the Christ. "Then went out to him Jerusalem, and all Judaea, and all the region round about Jordan." "And as the people were in expectation, and all men mused in their hearts of John, whether he were the Christ, or not;" Mat. 3:5, Luke 3:15

Understanding this general knowledge and speculation on the part of the people helps us understand the immediate popularity of John and why men from Northern Galilee were among his disciples. It also provides substance to the simple statements of Andrew and Phillip, and helps us to have a sense of the emotion behind them. "...Andrew...first findeth his own brother Simon, and saith unto him, We have found the [Messiah], which is, being interpreted, the Christ…Phillip findeth Nathanael, and saith unto him, we have found him, of whom Moses in the law, and the prophets, did write, Jesus of Nazareth, the son of Joseph." (John 1:40-41, 45)

The hopeful pilgrims came and listened intently to John's message and his declaration that the Messiah was coming. The star that proclaimed Jesus' birth had been talked about for thirty years. For some, their longing and searching intensified, at long last finding expression, echoing the words of Andrew and Phillip, "we have found Him."

Perhaps there were those surprised to see John embrace this carpenter from Nazareth, but there were others present who were not. In all likelihood, Zacharias and Elisabeth had passed away by then, but other family members and friends followed John's training and mission with more than simple curiosity. The meeting and embrace of John and Jesus was the culmination of much anticipation on their part. For them, John's declaration that Jesus was the awaited Messiah, was one of great joy while, for others, it brought a mix of reactions, from surprise and elation, to skepticism and hostility.

Very few knew the significance of what was taking place. In the waters of the Jordan at Bethebara the Kingdom of God began to be established; the fulfillment of all righteous was put into motion and being made available to all mankind. Probably only a select number were privileged to witness the Lord's baptism and hear the declarations of John, although the scriptures give us no indication of witnesses. In my personal walk through those sacred days and places I see tears flowing freely from the eyes of an honored and loving mother. Can we even imagine the joy that coursed through Mary's veins when she heard the voice of God, her son's father, proclaim, "This is my beloved Son, in whom I am well pleased." (Mat. 3:17)

There were others from Galilee who had come for the Feast of the Dedication; disciples of John, they were also looking for the Messiah. John (the beloved), Andrew and Peter were in the area, but apparently not present for the baptism. These men, and many others, had already become disciples of John and were in his company the day following the baptism. When John saw Jesus walking nearby, he pointed him out to his disciples, "…behold the Lamb of God." (John 1:35-36) When Andrew and John heard Jesus speak they followed him. Verses 35 to 51 are filled with the humility and sincerity of true seekers of Christ. In them is expressed the joy of faithful men who, at last, had found the Messiah. All those who have sought and found him can feel the joy and thrill again and again with each reading. Jesus invited Andrew, John, Peter, Philip and Nathanael to follow him. It was a special company of men and women that made their way back to Galilee as Jesus took his first steps into his ministry.

Preparation for the Ministry—
What was the purpose, or mission, of Jesus' life and his ministry? Moses 1:39 quickly comes to mind. The immortality and eternal life of His children is, and always has been the primary interest of the Lord. Understandably, the first thing that comes to mind is the Atonement. The mission of Jesus the Christ might well be summed up in the Atonement and in addition, his ministry was focused on the establishment of the Kingdom of God on the earth. This is what Israel had been waiting and hoping for; to be rid of foreign intruders in their land and to be able to rule with Christ, as God's chosen people. However, the Kingdom Christ came to establish was not a political kingdom, but one of heaven. Because of their expectations many would readily follow him, but ultimately would not be able to accept the doctrines of His Church and Kingdom.

We might reasonably say that Jesus' formal ministry was inaugurated with his baptism. His cousin, John, had accomplished his mission, as Zacharias had foreseen. He had gained a discipleship made up of men and women from all parts of Palestine and invited them to follow Jesus.

The scriptures, as they are written, leave us with some questions regarding the days that immediately followed the baptism. It appears from the accounts of Matthew and Mark that he went straight from his baptism into the wilderness, being lead there by the spirit, to be with God. Luke does not say the wilderness retreat was immediate, but he leaves us to assume that it was the next thing Jesus did after being baptized. John was the only gospel writer that was actually present at the time and, interestingly, he does not mention the wilderness retreat at all. However, he does mention his short visit in the home where Jesus was staying. The day following his baptism, (or so it seems; some statements may or may not indicate an exact chronology) Jesus had personal interactions with several who would later be numbered among the twelve apostles. (John 1) We see here that Jesus began his ministry with a discipleship ready and waiting to follow him. One might ask if he would actually leave these disciples, as well as the family members that had journeyed with him from Galilee, to spend 40 days in solitude. The timing and duration of this wilderness experience comes under question. Considering his family and new discipleship as well as the great amount of work he had to do, it seems unlikely that he would simply leave to be alone for nearly a month and a half.

Forty days and nights of fasting, particularly in a wilderness without shelter, would result in death and yet, the scriptures say Jesus did it. Logic has prompted theories about how such a thing was possible. Perhaps the fast was not total abstinence; maybe he had water to drink and a minimal amount of food. Another thought is that he was the Son of God and therefore endowed with some kind of special power over physical needs. These and other thoughts seem to be fabrications designed to make us feel better about something not logical and otherwise unbelievable.

Statements by John and Matthew might indicate the

possibility that Jesus' wilderness experience and temptations may have taken place several months after his baptism, and not immediately after.

After relating the glorious events associated with Jesus' baptism, Matthew states, "Then was Jesus led up of the Spirit into the wilderness to be with God." (JST Mat. 4:1) In the eleventh verse we find the ordeal is past; "Then the devil leaveth him, and now Jesus knew that John was cast into prison, and he sent angels, and, behold, they came and ministered unto him (John)" (JST Mat. 4:11) Several months after his baptism Jesus is in Capernaum and from there he returns to Jerusalem for the Feast of the Passover. While in Jerusalem Jesus instructs Nicodemus regarding rebirth, of being born of water and spirit. Following this Jesus goes with his disciples into Judea where he, along with John, performs baptisms, "For John was not yet cast into prison." (John 3:24) Matthew's account seems to indicate that the Baptist's imprisonment occurred at the same time as Jesus' wilderness experience and according to John, Jesus was months into his ministry by that time.

I find it interesting that John, the gospel writer most closely associated with Jesus and the only one with him at, or near the time of the baptism, does not mention Jesus' wilderness experience and encounter with Satan. From John's record it appears that Jesus went back to Galilee, or at least set out for Galilee, within just a couple days of his baptism. (John 1:43) This may or may not be of significance, but it seems to me that John would have mentioned Jesus' absence if he, after finally finding Jesus, was required to wait for him for a month and a half. John's silence on this is at least some indication that the popular interpretations of the three accounts may be flawed. I mention Jesus' wilderness experience now, only because it is generally thought that it occurred immediately following the baptism. [*After reviewing my notes on this subject, I have been impressed with another thought. I now think it possible, if not likely, that Jesus did go into the wilderness more or less immediately after his baptism. He may have left his family in John's charge or even Lazarus while he went into the wilderness for a period of refinement (not literally 40 days)spending the remainder a day or two of isolation and meditation. Following his fast and encounter with Satan, he returned to Betherbara. When he returned, John and Andrew were there. Either they had just arrived from Galilee or they simply were not present the day Jesus was baptized. We need not assume that John 1:35 means that John and Andrew were introduced to Jesus on the day following the baptism. Days could have passed, giving Jesus time to go and return, after which, "...the next day after John stood... "]*

Following Jesus' baptism, and what seems to be a general acknowledgement of the Christ, John began to make personal introductions. The following day, or a day, the Baptist identified Jesus for two of his disciples, again as the Lamb of God. One of these disciples was Andrew and the other, while not identified, is believed to be John, the author of the narrative. After hearing Jesus speak Andrew and John followed Him. They were invited to spend the day with Jesus. What had brought these men so many miles from their homes in northern Galilee is made clear when Andrew, without delay, located his brother Peter and said, ..."We have found the Messiah..." (John 1:35-41) The fame of John the Baptist had reached at least to Bethsaida, the home of Andrew and Peter. They had come, as did many others, looking for the Christ and found Him in Judea. Here is where Jesus first met three who would become His apostles and here Peter received the name Cephas "...which is, by interpretation, a seer..." (JST John 1:42)

Within just two or three days of his baptism, Jesus makes preparations to leave Judea. His ministry had begun and already disciples were gathering around him. Some, possibly many, joined him for his return trip to Galilee. Jesus left Bethebara and Judea making his way to his home in Nazareth. The original party that had accompanied him to the Feast of the Dedication and baptism received the addition of disciples who had also come to the feast. They too were returning to their homes in Galilee, but did so with joy in their hearts; they had found their Messiah. So, in late December/early January, a new Rabbi, Jesus the Christ began his ministry on the road to Galilee.

The Ministry—

Following his baptism, Jesus went, more or less, directly to Nazareth. Along the way he took every opportunity to teach in the Synagogues and lay the foundation of his ministry. Because there is no mention of Joseph after the family's temple visit when Jesus was twelve, some speculate that he had already died. Assuming this was the case, as the oldest son, Jesus assumed the primary responsibility for the care of his mother and family. Jesus knew that he would not be well received in Nazareth, but his home was there; family affairs would have to be settled before moving and relocating the family.

In the years prior to his ministry, Jesus prepared himself in every possible way. He traveled and acquainted himself with the region, well beyond the borders of Nazareth. Knowing that Nazareth would not receive him as anything more than the carpenter's son, he knew that he would have to abandon the home of his youth. Following the baptism, Jesus had new companions traveling with him; Andrew, John, Peter, Phillip, Nathanael and others. If Jesus had not already decided upon Capernaum, his new friends, his disciples from northern Galilee were likely influential in his decision to relocate his family there.

Shortly after returning to Nazareth, a wedding feast was held in the city of Cana. While the scriptures do not tell us whose marriage was being celebrated, they do suggest that it was someone close to Mary; she apparently had some responsibility for the care and entertainment of the guests. As has been discussed, there are those who believe this wedding was actually Jesus' wedding; a theory not supported by scripture. Personally I prefer to believe that Jesus was already married and that he was attending the wedding feast held for another family member. Whatever the case, Jesus was there and it is evident that there was already a close relationship between Jesus' family and his disciples; they too were present. It is here, at the Cana wedding that Jesus performed what is recognized as the first of his many miracles.

It is unclear as to how long Jesus remained in Nazareth following his baptism. It appears that it was only a matter of a few months or possibly only weeks. It is probable that the wedding in Cana was part of a longer trip which took him, his family and his disciples to Capernaum.

John tells us that they were not in Capernaum long before the Passover. (see John 2:12-13) From Capernaum Jesus made his way again to Jerusalem for the Feast, roughly four months after his initial visit and baptism.

It should be remembered that John was the only one of the gospel writers that was actually with Jesus from the very beginning of his ministry. Matthew joined the discipleship sometime after the Sermon on the Mount, roughly six months after Jesus had been baptized. Mark and Luke became disciples after the death of Jesus and never had a personal relationship. They wrote and compiled the accounts of others in relation to Jesus' ministry.

For six months, more or less, Jesus traveled throughout Galilee and Judea with his disciples. In Judea, at least some of his disciples received the priesthood and were authorized to perform baptisms. (John 2:22, JST John 4:1-4) Here, in the first months of Jesus' ministry, we begin to see the hearts of men revealed. There were those who were offended that Jesus and his disciples were also baptizing and that people were seeking out Jesus instead of John. (John 3:25-26, 23-36) Some readily accepted John as a prophet and yet they would not accept his message and testimony of Jesus. Even in the presence of Christ they were not willing to acknowledge their Messiah. Tenaciously they clung to the promise of a messiah while denying the living Christ. John testified of Christ and humbly told the people that his purpose was to prepare the way for the Messiah and that Jesus was indeed the one promised. In these early months a line was drawn between the Disciples of Christ and those of Satan. Men and women from all over Palestine had come to Jerusalem for the Passover and there they witnessed the miracles and majesty of Christ.

From there he walked the shores of the Sea of Galilee and selected Peter, Andrew, James and John to be apostles in his church. He took these and other disciples (likely women as well as men) to the mount where he instructed them on how to be his 'Talmidim' (disciples). (see Matt. 5-7)

While Jesus attended to his role as provider for his family, his disciples resumed their livelihoods. He found Peter, James and John, along with Andrew, fishing and mending nets on the shores of the Sea of Galilee and issued to them a formal call to the ministry. It should be noted that these men and possibly others had already joined the discipleship and had been ordained or at least authorized to perform baptisms. (see John 3:22 and JST John 4:1-4) These and other select disciples were taken apart from the multitude, into the mount, in the vicinity of Capernaum, where formal instruction was given. He was training his newly called, and others, soon to be called, members of the Twelve and the Seventy. (Matt. 5-7) Jesus' call to his disciples to follow him and the recorded response "they left their nets" should not be interpreted to mean they abandoned their livelihood, families and former life to devote their entire time and lives to 'following Jesus.' They were devout Jews as was Jesus. Their responsibility to their families was as sacred to them as it was for their new Rabbi. We are all invited to follow the Master and a large part of that includes the way we treat and care for one another, particularly our families. It was a normal and natural thing to find Peter and others fishing after they had been called to the apostleship.

I have often wondered about the story of Mary at the tomb of Jesus. Why would she have not recognized him and think he might be a gardener? Why would Jesus tell her to not touch him because he had not yet ascended to His Father? The scriptures that create these questions offer little to answer them. How fortunate we are to have Joseph Smith's inspired translation of these verses, from which we learn that Jesus did not forbid the loving touch that Mary so desperately needed. The emotion of such a moment surely must have culminated in not just a touch, but a in the embrace of perfect love. Who, among us, have seen a resurrected being? Mary was the first person in the history of this world to see a person resurrected from the realms of the dead. Her last visions of Jesus were of him hanging in agony on the cross and then prepared and wrapped for burial. Jesus stood before her in the newness and miraculous transformation of a priesthood ordinance she knew about, but could not completely understand. Gone were the subtle marks and blemishes of mortal life. Sun bleached hair would have been replaced by perfect strands glistening in the morning sun. Mary had gone to complete some of the burial preparation that haste had prohibited. Can we even begin to imagine her shock and horror when she found only burial clothes? In my mind's eye I see not only love's touch, but a compassionate walk in the Garden with tenderness and love in every step they took together. The coldness in those misinterpreted words melts away in the light of modern revelation and reason. Why would Jesus appear to Mary only to tell her keep her distance because he had some other place to go? If there were some significance or reason that a mortal touch should not occur prior to his ascension to the Father, would he not have simply done that first?

My WALK with Him

Note: When reading the Bible, I think we sometimes make a subconscious mistake by not considering those things not talked about. We need to remember that we are reading about real events that took place in the lives of real people. With only relevant facts included in the narrative, there are a lot of blanks. If we fill in those blanks, the whole is more understandable, but we need to be careful how we do that. A realistic and completed picture makes it easier to walk where Jesus walked. We should not be afraid to imagine the reality of the times, the customs and places where he walked. We should also bear in mind that we actually believe the Bible contains flaws. We should not be afraid to question passages that seem to be strange and out of character and we certainly should not make such passages the basis by which we read and interpret the whole. As I walk with Jesus I try to visualize what the times and people were like and see how closely the scripture describes these very real people and places....

I OFTEN IMAGINE what it might have been like to have lived in the day of the Savior's mortal ministry. I try to put myself there, watching him and listening to his words. I hear his invitation, "follow me," and sadly I see many turn away from him. His invitation is as personal and universally applicable today as it was when he issued it. A study of His life and ministry will, if it is sincere, transport us to those sacred places. We will find ourselves eyewitness to a humble birth in a simple, but hallowed stable. We will watch a boy become a man and then marvel at the miracles that proclaim the divine in him. We will see him do all that he came to do and open the doors of eternity for all mankind.

A study of the life of Jesus begins with questions, the answers to which establish the premise and scope of the study. *Is he the Son of God? Is he the Messiah of the Jews and the Savior of mankind? Did he die and conquer death that all would live again? Is he the great law giver who will judge the earth and its inhabitants?* If we cannot answer these questions in the affirmative, his life is reduced to that of any other man, however remarkable or influential he may have been. The miracles that would otherwise proclaim him become little more than lore. A study on such a premise, while entertaining, holds no power of transformation; we are left enlightened, but empty.

My walk with Jesus is inspired by the sure knowledge that He is the Christ, the Savior of all His creations. As I walk with him, I see him as God of heaven and earth. His is the voice of eternity. He is the First Born, the Chosen One and only begotten of the Father. He is the great Jehovah of the Old Testament and Messiah of the New.

As Jehovah of the Old Testament, Jesus revealed the Father's plan for our salvation which included his birth. Indeed, the gospel was preached to Adam and Eve and "they blessed the name of God, and made all things known unto their sons and their daughters." (Moses 5:12) All the prophets, from Adam to Moses and from Moses to Christ, testified of the future birth and ministry of the Savior of the world. The law of sacrifices, as given to Adam in the Garden of Eden, was given for the singular purpose of preparing the minds and hearts of man for the foreordained atoning sacrifice of the Christ. These sacrifices were to be a "similitude of the sacrifice of the Only Begotten." (Moses 5:7) The Law of Moses was given entirely as a preparation for the higher law and was fulfilled by the higher law Christ established. From the time of Adam to the Birth foretold there was no ignorance regarding the Christ, except in those who preferred ignorance and in those who were innocent victims of their influence. All the believers, the sheep of His fold, looked with faith on miracles yet to come. It is with that same faith we look back on miracles of long ago, miracles that proclaim him. As we study and ponder the life and ministry of Jesus and walk where He walked, the spirit will validate our faith by a witness that will make His ministry a reality in our lives and turn our faith to sustaining power as we choose to follow Him.

As we sincerely walk where Jesus walked "the eyes of our understanding" are opened and we find ourselves eyewitness to His power and authority. We understand that the things He taught and the wonders he performed are personal and as applicable today as they were at the time of his ministry. We are compelled to consider the questions he asked and eventually, each of us will answer. Indifference to His Life and Mission will pacify some, but will not void accountability. The eternal truths that Jesus established remain true and binding regardless of their reception. By those truths all mankind will be blessed or condemned. A casual perusal of His Life will not merit more than an interest in the tears He shed over those who could not see beyond the carpenter of Nazareth.

Zacharias and Elisabeth

MY WALK WITH JESUS begins roughly fifteen months prior to his birth, in the house of Zacharias. The coming of the Messiah had been long anticipated in all of Israel. The faithful watched for the signs of his coming and among those most anxiously watching, were Zacharias and his wife, Elisabeth. He and Elisabeth were good people, "...righteous before God, walking in all the commandments and ordinances of the Lord blameless." (Luke 1:6) Their worthiness was further evidenced by the heavenly manifestation of an angel.

I admire Zacharias and Elisabeth for their enduring faith. As devout Jews, they had a wonderful desire and a sacred regard for family. More than anything, they had looked forward to having children and posterity. They prayed fervently for that blessing, but the passage of time made it apparent that children were not likely. They continued to pray, hoping for a miracle until age made it apparent that it would not be granted in this life. Their devotion to each other was their consolation, as was their dedication to their faith. Zacharias served faithfully in the temple and it was there that an angel appeared, "standing on the right side of the altar of incense." (Luke 1:11) Zacharias was amazed and filled with wonder. The angel quickly put his mind at ease and told him that his prayer had been heard. For a brief moment Zacharias wondered *what prayer? A child!* The thought flashed in his mind, but then, *no, how would that be possible?* "…thy wife Elisabeth shall bear thee a son, and thou shalt call his name John." (Luke 1:13) Having already abandoned his hope, Zacharias was filled with doubt; not in the words of the angel, but in his own physical abilities and that of Elisabeth. He humbly asked the angel how it would be possible. The angel assured him that he had come from the presence of God to bring this miraculous news, that all things are possible with God. Tears of Joy and gratitude ran freely down Zacharias' cheeks as the reality of it all settled in on him. *At our age, how is this possible? Will anyone believe me?*

Zacharias was spared the necessity of explanation and the possible ridicule of thoughtless speculations. Recognizing Zacharias' doubt in his and Elisabeth's ability to do such a thing, the angel told him he would be dumb, unable to speak, until the miracle was complete.

Zacharias was much longer in the temple than his duties normally required. As soon as the people outside saw him, they knew right away that he had seen a vision but, unable to speak, all he was able to do was confirm that he had indeed seen an angel.

For the next five months, Zacharias and Elisabeth secluded themselves as much as possible. They had time to quietly reflect and ponder the honor and responsibility of nurturing their son, John; the one foretold who would prepare the way for the Messiah. Dutifully, Zacharias did all that he could do for his wife, to see to her well being and comfort. They spent many hours alone, immersed in their miracle and in the realization that they were, as far as they knew, the only two people on the earth who knew that the birth of the Messiah was imminent.

Mary

VERY LITTLE is said in the Bible to give us an idea of what brought Mary to the point of becoming the mother of Christ. There is, however, information included in Apocryphal writings. These writings are doubted by some, but considered by many to be just as reliable as the Bible. Accurate or not, they do add insight without compromising the message of canonized scriptures, answering some of the questions created by fragmented accounts in the Bible.

Mary was the daughter of Joachim and Anna, a very righteous couple who were devoted to the Lord. Joachim was a direct descendant of David, giving Mary royal blood. Joachim and Anna wanted nothing more than to be parents but, like Zacharias and Elisabeth were not able to have children. For this they were considered unworthy and were shunned by the community. In their old age they prayed fervently for a miracle. Anna promised the Lord that if they were granted this miracle, the child would be dedicated to His service. Joachim and Anna each received a personal visitation and were granted their miracle. They had a daughter and named her Mary. True to their vow, they took Mary to the temple at age three and committed her to service there. Mary was instructed and became well versed in the Torah. Her parents visited her often, but by the time she was ten, both had died.

When Mary reached the age of marriage, the priests in the temple became concerned about her prospects. Given the sacred regard Jewish custom held for marriage (actually unlawful for a man to remain single past the age of twenty) the high priest Zachariah, a contemporary of Zacharias, petitioned the Lord. He was told to gather worthy men from whom the Lord would choose. The sign of a dove was given, designating Joseph of Nazareth, a man much older than Mary and already married.

Mary became betrothed to Joseph, which meant in the eyes of the law she was his wife. However, there was no cohabitation during the betrothal period, which was customarily a year or more. Joseph took Mary to Nazareth. He provided for her in his house.

During the betrothal period he lived elsewhere as he pursued his carpentry trade.

Mary was a dutiful wife. Her temple training and education gave her maturity beyond her years. Her greatest love and devotion was for the Lord. Near the conclusion of the betrothal period, the same angel that had appeared to Zacharias came to her. "Hail, thou that art highly favored, the Lord is with thee: blessed art thou among women."

In spite of her training in the temple, Mary was not prepared for such a visit and certainly not for the message she received. The angel told her that she had found favor with God and that she was to be the mother of His son. She was confused. She was Joseph's wife, but they had not completed the 'Home Taking' (Likkuhin) which allowed for cohabitation. Like Zacharias, she had a very practical and logical question. She asked the angel how it would be possible, since she was not with her husband. The angel responded tenderly, "...The Holy Ghost shall come upon thee, and the power of the Highest shall overshadow thee:" (Luke 1:35) Filled with wonder, Mary knew that it was true as powerful emotions flooded over her.

The angel told Mary that, as unlikely as it was, her cousin, Elisabeth, was in her sixth month of pregnancy. It was a lot for her to take in. First she was told she was to be the mother of the Son of God and now that her elderly cousin, whom she knew as well as she knew her own mother, would also bear a child. The angel assured her that with God, all things are possible. Humbly, Mary responded, "...be it unto me according to thy word..." (Luke 1:38)

The angel left Mary and, alone with her thoughts, she felt detached from reality. Her life as it had been was over. Her thoughts went to Joseph and then to Elisabeth. She began to miss her mother and wanted desperately to be with Elisabeth. She was the one person who would understand her wonderful blessing. Mary was filled with a sense of urgency; she had to go to Judea, but she was also thinking about Joseph.

Joseph

MARY WAS uneasy, even afraid of how Joseph might react, but she knew that she could not keep this from him. She needed to go to Judea and she also needed his support.

My heart goes out to Joseph. Artificial insemination is common today and a blessing to those unable to conceive normally, but to Joseph, Mary's condition meant only one thing. He was devastated. She tried desperately to explain that she had not been unfaithful. She tried to help him understand the wonderful stewardship they would be able to share. Joseph wanted very much to be able to understand. But it was too fantastic and Mary carried a child that was not his. The thought that she had had a relationship crushed him. He saw no option, and to Mary's dismay, he concluded that he would seek an annulment. However, he still loved her and had compassion for her. He had no wish to shame her publicly. She pleaded with him, but he was determined to "put her away privily." (Mat. 1:19)

The days that followed were torturous for Mary, and for Joseph. Mary poured out her heart to the Lord for her beloved husband while he agonized over what he must do. Joseph could think of nothing else and sleep offered only temporary relief. As he slept, the angel appeared to him in a dream. Joseph was assured of Mary's faithfulness and that everything Mary had said was true and that he should not be afraid to proceed with the 'Likkuhin,' to complete the marriage custom. Joseph was filled with relief and joy when he awoke and rushed to the house where Mary was to share with her the revelation. Elated beyond words they immediately did as the angel had instructed and arranged for the Likkuhin ceremony. "…he took unto him his wife:" (Mat. 1:24) Freed from the burdens of doubt and suspicion, Joseph joined Mary in wonderful anticipation of what lay ahead for them. Together, they made preparations to visit Elisabeth.

Mary and Elisabeth (and Joseph)

BEING RAISED in the temple, Mary had grown up near the home of Zacharias and Elisabeth and had developed a close relationship with her cousin. That relationship was not diminished when miles came between them. Mary's miracle only served to strengthen their bond. She could not wait to share this with her beloved cousin.

Joseph understood Mary's eagerness and that alone would have been reason for him to accompany her to Jerusalem, but he had another reason for going. It was the time of the annual Passover observance and for the faithful that meant a pilgrimage to Jerusalem. Together they made the week long journey of roughly 80 miles.

Zacharias and Elizabeth happily opened their home to their beloved family members. They were happy to see Joseph again, but Elisabeth was particularly pleased to see Mary. The reunion was one marked by tears of joy. As they held each other, Elisabeth was filled with the spirit of revelation. "…And she spoke out with a loud voice, and said, Blessed art thou among women, and blessed is the fruit of thy womb. And whence is this to me, that the mother of my Lord should come to me?..." (Luke 1:41) Enveloped by the spirit in this sacred moment, Mary began to prophecy; "My soul doth magnify the Lord. And my spirit hath rejoiced in God my Savior. For he hath regarded the low estate of his handmaiden: for, behold, from henceforth all generations shall call me blessed. For he that is mighty hath done to me great things; and holy is his name. And his mercy is on them that fear him from generation to generation. He hath [showed] strength with his arm; he hath scattered the proud in the imagination of their hearts. He hath put down the mighty from their seats, and exalted them of low degree. He hath filled the hungry with good things; and the rich he hath sent empty away. He hath [helped] his servant Israel, in remembrance of his mercy; As he spake to our fathers, to Abraham, and to his seed forever." (Luke 1:46-55) Their joy was mingled with a great weight of responsibility, made easier to bear by the bond they shared.

John

ZACHARIAS AND ELISABETH were pleased to learn that Joseph had formally [taken] his wife, Mary. (Mat. 1:20) They spent hours talking (Elisabeth being voice for Zacharias) about their sons and the relationship they would build.

Elisabeth's due date was close, only weeks away. Mary had planned to be with her for the delivery, but Joseph had to return to Nazareth to take care of his business. Mary remained with other family members to be of assistance and to be there for the naming ceremony.

The birth of this special child was of great interest, even beyond immediate family. "And her neighbors and her [relatives] heard how the Lord had [showed] great mercy upon her; and they rejoiced with her." (Luke 1:58) At the appointed time of the baby's circumcision and naming, those assembled "called him Zacharias, after the name of his father." (Luke 1:59) With Zacharias still unable to speak, it was Elisabeth that spoke and explained that their son was to be called John. Mary understood, but there were protests, saying there was no one in the family named John. They looked to Zacharias who, by writing on a tablet, reaffirmed what Elisabeth had said and immediately he was able to speak. He began to give praise to the Lord and to prophecy concerning the Christ and of his own son, John. *"And fear [wonder, amazement, reverence] came on all that dwelt round about them: and all these sayings were noised abroad throughout all the hill country of Judea. And all they that heard them laid them up in their hearts, saying, what manner of child shall this be!..."* (Luke 1:65-66) Even in his infancy, John began to fulfill the mission for which he was born. The word of his birth spread throughout Judea, and even into Galilee, sparking in the hearts of the faithful a great sense of anticipation (Luke 3:15).

Following the naming ceremony, Mary and her company returned to Nazareth. Mary cherished the hours she had spent with Elisabeth, as together they looked ahead into the lives of their sons. Elisabeth had been the center of attention, but it was her time with Mary that she cherished most. Mary pondered deeply the favor and trust she had been given as the mother of the Messiah. She looked forward to returning to Jerusalem, as she knew she must do often so that her Son would know the man ordained to proclaim him.

Mary and Joseph

RELUCTANTLY, ELISABETH SAID her goodbyes and sent Mary away with wonderful anticipation for the birth of the Messiah. On the return trip, Mary pondered deeply the prophecies they had discussed regarding John and Jesus.

Joseph was happy and relieved to have Mary safe again in his home. With less than six months of Mary's pregnancy remaining, they were both filled with a sense of urgency. The Son of God would soon be in their charge. As much as time would permit, they devoted themselves to the study of the scriptures and the prophecies relating to the Messiah.

The anticipation of the birth of a child, especially the first, gives rise to the profoundest elation and to the deepest searches of one's soul. Unlike other married couples, who know only hopes and dreams for their unborn child, Mary and Joseph knew very well the mission of the man their son would become. The scriptures they had studied as children and young adults were about to be fulfilled in their home.

As the time of the birth came near, Joseph and Mary began to be concerned about the trip to Bethlehem to deliver her son. Her expected delivery date was during the time of the Feast of Dedication which meant Joseph had reason to go, but that was hardly reason for Mary to go. Their concerns were laid to rest when Caesar sent out the decree that all should be taxed; they were spared the necessity of explanation as "...all went to be taxed, every one into his own city." (Luke 2:1-3) Both Mary and Joseph were of the lineage of David and so, late in her final trimester, Joseph took Mary those many miles again to Judea; to Bethlehem the city of David.

Birth of Jesus

THE ROAD from Nazareth to Jerusalem was busy with others traveling under the mandate of Rome and/or to observe the Feast of Dedication. Because Mary was so far along, their journey took longer than it would have otherwise. When they reached Jerusalem, they found the streets crowded with people trying to find accommodations. Joseph feared they would find the same confusion in Bethlehem. They pressed on.

When they reached Bethlehem, Joseph's fears were confirmed. With so many people there to register for the Roman census, it was impossible to secure lodging. Joseph was desperate to find anything he could and at last, an inn keeper offered his stable. The people of Bethlehem were more than aware of the prophecy that the Messiah would be born in their city and had they known who Joseph and Mary were, they would have made room. But they were just two among many, and so a humble stable became the temporary shelter of Mary and Joseph and the birth place of the Savior of the world. Joseph did all he could to make Mary comfortable, not refusing and even soliciting the assistance of sympathetic acquaintances, new and old.

As dusk gave way to night, Joseph saw a star in the eastern sky shining with increasing intensity as the light of the sun faded. It was a new star; large and outshining all the others. Mary had already been experiencing labor pains and the star confirmed it; this was the night of the Savior's birth.

The Star

THE ANONYMOUS ARRIVAL of Mary and Joseph in Bethlehem was contrasted by a universal proclamation of Jesus' entry into mortality. A sign that only God, His Father, could provide was given as a star, placed in its appointed course in the eternities to appear at precisely the right time, to herald this great event in the eternal lives of all mankind. As I view this wonderful phenomenon, I ask myself *why a star? Why not a voice of thunder to shake the earth and proclaim the Son of God?* As I pondered this I began to realize that the sign was given in such a way that only those watching would see it. An undeniable proclamation would have been a compromise of agency, requiring that everyone acknowledge their king. Another reason for a star is that the sign had to be visible to ALL the creations made by the Son and "…put into his power…" (D&C 76:42-43) The birth of the Savior was of universal importance and the sign had to be one visible, not only to our earth, but to every earth that had an interest in the life and mission of Christ. (D&C 88:43-61) (see Hel. 14:4 and 3 Ne. 1:21) The star bears witness that our earth is center stage for the work and glory that engages the Father and the Son and includes worlds without number.

Shepherds

IN ADDITION to the witness of the Star, angelic visitations also bore witness of the Holy Birth. There were shepherds tending their flocks in the hill country surrounding Bethlehem. They were good and honorable men, worthy of revelation in answer to lifelong prayers. When the light and glory of an angel suddenly illuminated their camp, they were understandably startled. They were immediately put at ease when the angel addressed them. "Fear not: for, behold, I bring you good tidings of great joy…" (Luke 2:8-18)

The angel explained to these good shepherds that the Savior, Christ the Lord, was born and they would find him wrapped in swaddling clothes and lying in a manger. In the moment of this glorious scene, the covering that separates heaven and earth was parted and the shepherds saw and heard a multitude of the heavenly hosts. As I witness this great event in my heart and mind, I am struck by the possibility and even likelihood that I was among those in that heavenly host. The importance of that humble birth was understood better and by more in heaven than it was on earth.

When the angels withdrew and the covering over the earth was closed, the shepherds left immediately for Bethlehem in search of the Lord. They knew their search was for a stable and it did not take long for them to find one with lamps burning. As the shepherds made their way through a gathering crowd, they felt the same inner burning they felt earlier when the angel appeared and the heavens opened. As foretold, they entered the stable and found the baby Jesus, wrapped and resting in a manger. With humble hearts and tear streaked faces they worshiped their Savior and testified to Mary and Joseph of the heavenly manifestation that brought them to the stable. The shepherds bore witness of all they had seen and heard to the small crowd and then returned to their flocks, bearing witness to all they met. The people marveled and "Mary kept all these things, and pondered them in her heart." (Luke 2:16-20)

SHORTLY AFTER the birth of Jesus, Joseph was able to find lodging. Word of the birth spread quickly as a matter of wonderful testimony to some and to others, only rumor, to which they were indifferent. Zacharias and Elisabeth began preparations to go to Bethlehem as soon as they saw the star. Elisabeth was especially anxious to see Mary and to bring their sons together.

Mary and Joseph received many visitors in their Bethlehem home as the word of Jesus' identity spread. According to the custom of purification, Jesus' circumcision and formal naming took place when he was eight days old. Then thirty three days later, at the conclusion of the days of purification, Joseph took Mary and Jesus to Jerusalem to present her first born son in the temple as custom required. This was an important day for Mary and Joseph. Zacharias and Elisabeth were there, as were other family members and close friends.

There were others in the temple that had seen the star and heard the testimonies of the shepherds. The spirit was strong as was the feeling of anticipation. There was one man in particular who had come with a special purpose. Simeon was well advanced in years. The Holy Ghost had revealed to him that he would not die before seeing the Christ. On that special day, Simeon was prompted by the spirit to be there. When Joseph and Mary brought their baby in, Simeon immediately recognized the Lord and asked Mary if he might be permitted to hold him. "Then took he him up in his arms, and blessed God…" (Luke 2:28)

Simeon returned the child to Mary and testified of His divinity and prophesied of his mission. Then Anna, a prophetess, also in the temple, testified of the infant Savior. She and Simeon continued to give their witness and "…spake of him to all them that looked for redemption in Jerusalem." (Luke 2:38)

Joseph and Mary remained in Bethlehem, waiting for her and the baby to be strong enough to make the journey home.

WISE MEN

KNOWLEDGEABLE MEN AND WOMEN all over the world saw the sign of the star. In a country east of Judea, men of faith made preparations to follow the star. They were leaders among a branch of followers of Christ. They knew that the star was the sign that had been prophesied to herald the birth of the King of the Jews. This was of great importance to them and they began making preparations to travel west, across the desert, to pay homage and witness for themselves the Lord's coming. For practical reasons, they traveled with servants, family and other interested individuals.

By the time the travelers from the east arrived in Judea, they knew that they were no longer looking for an infant. Familiar with the prophecies, they knew that the birthplace was Bethlehem, but they made a courtesy visit to Jerusalem and the royal court. They thought it reasonable that one as important as the Messiah might actually be in Jerusalem; in the heart of Judaism.

The leaders of the company from the East, called on Herod. They explained that they had seen the star and asked where they might find the child that had been born King of Jews. In spite of Herod's proximity to the sacred event and the news of it spreading throughout the land, Herod was not aware and was actually troubled by what he heard. His advisors reminded him of the prophecies.

Learning nothing more than they already knew, the delegation from the east continued on, roughly eight miles to

Bethlehem. It was not difficult to find Joseph and Mary. Everyone in Bethlehem knew about the birth and the glorious events associated with it. "And when they were come into the house, they saw the young child...and fell down, and worshipped him..." (Mat. 2:11)

The faithful travelers from the east stayed in Bethlehem long enough to purchase food and supplies for their return trip. During that time, members of the party made frequent visits to Joseph and Mary's home to honor the Messiah, and to simply be near him; it would be difficult for them to leave. They left gifts to show their love and adoration.

When Herod directed the travelers to Bethlehem, he told them to return with the location of Jesus, "...that I may come and worship him also." (Mat. 2:8) But, it was a terrible plot; Herod had no intention of worshiping Mary's son. God warned the travelers in a dream not to return to Herod and so they went another way, avoiding Jerusalem.

Herod-Egypt

HEROD WAS a wicked man and did not believe the prophecies regarding the Messiah. Personally, he could not have been more indifferent, but it was clear to him that Israel did believe. To him the birth of a king was a threat. Herod waited anxiously for the information the travelers from the east were to bring. When it became clear that they were not coming, he took matters into his hands and devised a plan that would rid him of a threat to his authority. His plan was not new or unique, nevertheless it was cruel and heartless. Unsure of the actual age of Jesus, Herod ordered the death of all baby boys in Bethlehem to the age of two.

When the eastern travelers had gone, life in Bethlehem began to resume a sense of normalcy. It was a happy time for Mary and Joseph, surrounded by friends and family. However, their happiness was short lived. The angel returned to Joseph in a dream and warned him of the impending danger. The angel instructed Joseph to take Mary and Jesus into Egypt and remain there until it was safe to return. Quickly, but quietly, Joseph made preparation to join a caravan for the nearly eight hundred mile journey.

Their exile was relatively short. An angel appeared to Joseph again and told him that Herod and all those who sought Jesus' life were dead. On the return trip, Joseph learned that it was Herod's son, Archelaus, who sat on the throne. Fearing that the threat may still be real, Joseph avoided Jerusalem and took Mary and Jesus by another way to Galilee; back to Nazareth.

Jesus of Nazareth

NEWS OF THE SAVIOR'S birth had spread quickly among the believers in Palestine. Galileans were the most devout of all the Jews and so they saw the Star with great interest. They spoke widely of the Holy Birth. However, by the time Joseph and Mary returned to Nazareth, it was not the subject of conversation as it had been. They did not know the identity of Jesus so he came to Nazareth as the carpenter's son.

Jewish parents faithfully taught their small children the history and customs of their people, reciting verses from the Torah in preparation for their formal education. Joseph and Mary were particularly diligent in this regard and Jesus was an apt student.

One of the first things Joseph did upon returning to Nazareth was to enroll Jesus in elementary school where he studied and learned alongside other children. School was held in the synagogue and taught by the Rabbi. The Rabbi held no particular station or office, but was honored and revered as a teacher. For his text, he relied solely on the Torah from which the students learned to read and to write. The synagogue's Torah was the only copy in Nazareth and, since the students were expected to know the Torah, much of the time was devoted to reciting and memorizing in order to commit it entirely to memory. Not all students did this, but Jesus surpassed all expectations.

Jesus still had time to be a boy. The streets of Nazareth echoed the clamor and laughter of happy children playing games and challenging each other as children do and have always done. The unwelcome Roman presence in Palestine influenced the games the boys played. They had their own versions of 'cowboy and indians' or 'cops and robbers.' Pretended contests between David and Goliath occupied the boys for hours on end. Jesus participated in the games and activities common to his age and in so doing he developed physical and social skills and began early to gain favor in the eyes of his peers.

In addition to his schooling, Jesus learned the family trade, working alongside Joseph in his carpentry business. He worked hard, but he was unusually devoted to his studies and prone to meditation. Joseph and the business might have benefited from a little more labor, but Joseph was pleased to see Jesus' dedication to the purpose for which he was born.

Joseph and Mary went to Jerusalem every year to observe the Passover. Jesus looked forward to these and other trips. The close relationship he had developed with John was only made stronger by the miles that separated them. No two boys were ever happier in each other's company. He and John loved to explore Judea's hill country where John felt so much at home. But more than that, they cherished their days together that allowed them to be themselves. Their mutual love for the scriptures carried them into unique and wonderful relationships with Moses, Isaiah, Jeremiah and all the prophets that preceded them. Those days were all too few and cut short by Jesus' return to Nazareth.

At age ten, as was the custom, Jesus advanced from *Beth Sefer* (elementary school) to *Beth Midrash* (secondary school). At this point, he had memorized the entire Torah; not necessarily unusual, but the depth of his understanding was. To this point his education had been focused on the written word. The next five years would focus on rhetorical debate, developing the skill of exploring meaning by answering a question with another question rather than simply recalling answers from stored knowledge. This kind of debate was considered the highest form of learning and was essential preparation for one with hopes of becoming a *Talmid* (disciple) and then a Rabbi.

As I, or any of us, try to walk where Jesus walked, the experience is limited by a scarcity of information. Each of us is free to make assumptions based on what information we have. We are aided in our assumptions by a look at the typical and customary life of a Jewish male. Boys (and girls) were taught in their home and prepared for elementary school at age five. At age ten, the students were ready for secondary school. Age thirteen the boys became *Bar Mitzvah* (son of the commandment). Age eighteen; marriage (For the devout Jews this was a sacred responsibility; to marry and 'multiply and replenish the earth'. This was taken so seriously that one not married past the age of twenty was sometimes ordered by the council to marry or be considered unworthy.) At age twenty the young man was ready to pursue a vocation and at age thirty, if he chose to, he could teach; be a Rabbi.

Jesus was an exceptional student in his secondary studies. He looked forward to his visits with John and the wonderful debates they had. Together they sharpened their understanding of the scriptures. On one of the Passover visits, just prior to his becoming *Bar Mitzvah*, Jesus went to the temple. This was not his first visit to the temple since his "[presenting] to the Lord, (Luke 2:22-23) but it was his first as one of age and preparation to debate the scriptures. Simeon and Anna had passed on, but there were others there that remembered Mary's child. To them, Jesus was more than a curiosity and remarkable boy. Many of these learned men knew who He was and so, even though they had not yet seen the wonder of miracles or witnessed a resurrection, they would, indeed, listen to Jesus. Not surprisingly, they "were astonished at his understanding and answers." (Luke 2:47)

At some point in their secondary education, the very gifted students sought out a renowned Rabbi and made application to be one of his *Talmidim* (disciples). They were accepted or rejected on the basis of the Rabbi's assessment of their ability to learn and emulate him. The priests and elders in Nazareth couldn't understand why Jesus did not become a Talmid, choosing rather to be a carpenter. They didn't know his Father was his Rabbi. Jesus spent many hours in solitude in Nazareth's hills and mountains, being tutored by God. The people saw no traditional Rabbi and later would say, "Is this not the carpenter's son? Is not his mother called Mary?..." (Matt 13:55) Others would marvel "saying, How knoweth this man letters, having never learned?" (John 7:15)

By age twenty, Jesus had married and with Joseph's health failing, Jesus worked hard to support his family as well as his mother and Joseph. His regular meetings with John took on greater importance and urgency as time went on. Their wives cherished the time they had together. They were like sisters and shared a bond very much like that of Mary and Elizabeth.

John the Baptist

THE SPIRIT had been John's teacher as well and he felt very much at home on the slopes of Judea's mountains. Jesus met him there and together they made preparations for the ministries that were about to begin.

Three months after his twenty ninth birthday, Jesus was in Jerusalem again for the Passover. As always, John was there as well and together they went into the mountains to receive instruction and ready themselves for the beginning of John's ministry, just three months away. They felt confidence and great resolve in each other's company and the spirit gave them strength to go on in the face of what the spirit of prophecy told them about their missions and fate. Jesus returned to Nazareth with his family and his mother. With Joseph's passing, Jesus assumed responsibility for her wellbeing.

Just prior to his thirtieth birthday, John spent the majority of his available time in the solitude of the wilderness. Immersed in God's creations, he found all the strength and nourishment he needed, both physical and spiritual. When he began to openly teach, he was seen by many as one coming out of the wilderness.

John had been ordained to his ministry by an angel when he was eight days old, but he spoke with such power and conviction, no one thought to question his authority. Word of a new teacher [Rabbi] spread quickly, reaching as far as northern Galilee. The timing of John's public ministry was seen as more than a curiosity. It had been thirty years since the star had been seen. Devout men and women were looking for the advent of the Messiah's reign. John soon had a following and in anticipation many wondered if he was indeed the Christ. (Luke 3:15) John assured them that he was not. With power and conviction, born of humility and love for Jesus, John proclaimed the coming of one "...the latchet of whose shoes [he was] not worthy to unloose..." (Luke 3:16) He explained that his message was one of repentance and that he baptized with water, but when the Christ came, He would baptize with fire and the Holy Ghost.

Soon after John began his formal ministry, Jesus returned to Jerusalem to observe the Feast of Tabernacles, but more importantly, to talk with John. Jesus was soon to turn thirty and begin his ministry. He and John had spent their lives preparing for this and as they dined together in John's home, the mood was sober and yet there was also a sense of eagerness. Their wives sat silently, arm in arm, wondering what exactly lay ahead. Jesus' baptism would be the initiation of His ministry and they talked of how important it was that they set this example for all mankind. John had been teaching and baptizing in the vicinity of Bethabara. Jesus told him to watch for him there.

Jesus returned to Nazareth and John continued to teach repentance and baptism. By the power of the spirit many were convinced that he was a prophet. Multitudes sought him out to be baptized. John's discipleship grew quickly and was not limited to those of Judea; it included men from Galilee and other regions. Among these were John and Andrew, devout men from Bethsaida in northern Galilee.

Jesus' Baptism

As the time of the Feast of Dedication approached, Jesus' family prepared for the journey with an anticipation that had not accompanied other trips. They were looking forward to the commencement of Jesus' ministry. They knew very well what John was doing; they were looking forward to their baptisms.

The hospitality of family and friends was very welcome at the end of a week on dusty roads. John was able to spend more time with his family during the customary observance of the Feast of Dedication, an eight day custom observed primarily by families in their homes. He joyfully received Jesus and his family. Together they observed the Feast, after which John returned to Bethebara. A feeling of fulfillment was already swelling inside of him; he knew that the day he and Jesus had been preparing for was at hand. Jesus and his family readied themselves to meet John at Bethebara.

Disciples and curious others were gathered around, listening carefully to John's message. John had positioned himself so that he had a good westward view toward Jerusalem. As he spoke, he watched people approaching singly and in small groups. With each group of people he saw, his heart jumped. Then, at last, he saw Jesus coming down the slope at the head of his family. The time had come. Years of preparation came to bear on this long awaited moment when he would at last be able to speak the words he longed to say, to proclaim the Messiah, the Son, the Lamb of God, the Holy One of Israel.

John had assured the people that he was not the Christ, but that He would be coming. When he was sure that it was Jesus approaching, the spirit swelled in his chest as he stepped to higher ground. He turned to the people and said, "Behold the Lamb of God, which taketh away the sin of the world. This is he of whom I said, After me cometh a man which is preferred before me…" (John 1:29-30) A hush fell over the congregation as their eyes were trained on Jesus. A few of them had seen Jesus before and were surprised at John's pronouncement, but the spirit was so strong that surprise was replaced by wonder. As Jesus drew closer John walked toward him. Tears streamed down their cheeks as they embraced.

Few words were exchanged as they stepped down into the river. John raised his arm to the square and by divine authority repeated the words of the baptismal covenant. He then immersed Jesus in the water and brought him up again. Their eyes were still moist as they embraced again, filled with joy. As they embraced, the heavens were opened and the spirit of the Lord was shed upon all who witnessed. The sign of the dove was given and the voice of God was heard, "This is my beloved son in whom I am well pleased." (Mat. 3:17)

John and Jesus stood in the water for a moment while their families, thrilled and silent looked on. As Jesus and John stepped out of the river, John turned to face Jesus and humbly petitioned, "...I have need to be baptized of thee..." (Mat. 3:14) Lovingly, Jesus looked into John's eyes, "...Suffer it to be so now: for thus it becometh us to fulfill all righteousness..." (Mat. 3:15) John was filled with the gift and power of the Holy Ghost; the baptism of fire of which he had taught and prophesied.

Jesus stood on the bank of the river and witnessed the baptism of his mother and each member of his family. When the last ordinance was complete, John came up out of the river and embraced Jesus again. Jesus held his arm firmly and asked that he take care of his family as the spirit had directed him to go into the mountains. This was not at all unusual and John humbly agreed. John, in company with the first of Jesus' disciples walked slowly, with full hearts toward the setting sun. They turned to see the silhouette of Jesus fade and disappear over the brow of a hill.

Ministry

Jesus was led by the spirit into the wilderness to be with His Father. This was a time of purification and spiritual preparation to begin His formal ministry. Under overhanging rock formations, he built a small fire for warmth. As he slept the spirit sheltered him and in visions of the night he was instructed and encouraged by heavenly ministrations. The following day was spent in prayer and fasting and communication with His Father.

At the conclusion of the day's fast, Jesus prepared another fire for the night. The Devil came and began to tempt him. The devil made three attempts to persuade Jesus to abandon his mission, but Jesus resisted and "...gave no heed unto them." (D&C 20:22) The next day, when Jesus came out of the hills, John saw him, as he was again teaching and baptizing at Bethebara.

On the road to Jerusalem, it was about three o'clock in the afternoon when Jesus passed by the place where John was teaching. John was thrilled to see Him and eagerly he turned to two of his disciples, John and Andrew, and said, "Behold the Lamb of God." (John 1:36) Eagerly, the two disciples from Galilee gathered those that were with them and hurried to catch up with Jesus. As they came near, Jesus turned and asked them what it was they wanted. Their hearts raced at this sudden and unexpected audience with the man that was, according to John, the very Messiah they were looking for. They asked Jesus where he was living. Jesus kindly put them at ease and invited the entire party to "come and see." (John 1:39)

John and Andrew did not hesitate at the invitation. They felt the spirit that emanated from Jesus and gladly followed him. Jesus introduced his new disciples to his hosts and to his family and invited them to stay. As evening approached, John and Andrew were anxious to tell the rest of their family and friends from Galilee that they had found the Messiah. Andrew was especially eager to tell his brother, Peter. Jesus invited them to return and they hurried away while they still had some light to see their way.

Andrew rushed ahead and found Peter. While still trying to catch his breath, he told him that they had found the Messiah. Peter was thrilled, but the hour was late. He did not sleep well in anticipation of meeting the Christ. The next morning Andrew took Peter to meet Jesus. A large group of Galilean pilgrims followed.

When Jesus saw Peter, he spoke prophetically, "…Thou art Simon the son of Jona: thou shalt be called [seer]…" (John 1:42)

Jesus spent the better part of the day teaching and becoming acquainted with his new disciples and friends from Galilee. In late afternoon the families returned to their own lodgings to make preparations to return to their homes in Bethsaida, Capernaum and other cities.

The following day Jesus and his party joined an already large group on the road north. Most were on foot. The air was crisp and invigorating and the winter sun hung low in the sky. Its rays were welcome warmth on the hardened faces of fishermen and others far from their homes. Word of Jesus spread quickly through the caravan and when they stopped to rest people crowded around him. He recited the scriptures and taught them. They were reluctant to leave, but the caravan began to move again and everyone left to rejoin their families. A man from Bethsaida hung back, not wanting to leave. His name was Phillip. He was a friend of Peter and Andrew and was one of the devout men from Galilee who had come specifically looking for the Messiah. Peter and Andrew told him that Jesus was the man they had come to find. Jesus saw the longing in his eyes and invited Phillip to join his *Talmidim*.

Overjoyed, Phillip rushed to find his friend, Nathanael. When Phillip told him that they had found the Messiah and that it was Jesus of Nazareth, Nathanael questioned. He knew that it had been foretold that the Messiah would be born in Bethlehem and he asked Phillip if the Messiah could be from Nazareth. Phillip simply said, "come and see." (John 1:46) As they hurried along the way, the spirit filled Nathanael's heart and he picked up his pace. When Jesus saw him he said, "behold an Israelite indeed, in whom is no guile." (John 1:47) Surprised, Nathanael asked Jesus how he could possibly know him. When Jesus said that he had seen him in a vision, Nathanael replied, "Rabbi, thou art the Son of God; thou art the King of Israel." (John 1:49)

As they traveled, Jesus continued to teach the people in the caravan. Because he stopped to teach in synagogues along the way, the caravan went ahead of Jesus, and so his fame preceded him throughout Galilee.

Jesus knew that he would not be well received in Nazareth. He did not try to teach there and stayed only long enough to settle his affairs and make preparations to take his family and mother to the northern shore of the Sea of Galilee; to Capernaum where he had friends and a loyal following. When Jesus did return to Nazareth, his declaration that he was the Messiah was more than the people there could accept. They remembered him only as the carpenter's son. They were so incensed at what he said that they forcibly took him out of the city with the intent of throwing off a cliff. The spirit of God was with him and confused the people to the point he was able to simply walk away unharmed. He did not return to Nazareth.

After making sure his family was secure in Capernaum, Jesus did not stay long. He returned to Jerusalem for the Feast of the Passover. His *Talmidim* followed him on this and every other pilgrimage. Jesus invited everyone to accept his yoke (his doctrine) but he was particularly intent on teaching and grooming his *Talmidim*. They were eye witness to the power and glory of God as he healed the sick, restored sight to the blind, made the lame to walk and raised the dead.

In addition to his pilgrimages to Jerusalem, Jesus left his family periodically to travel throughout Palestine and surrounding regions, always taking with him his *Talmidim*. He was well received everywhere he went, but not without opposition as well. Ironically, those who opposed him were the very ones who should have been first to acknowledge him. The well educated Pharisees and Sadducees of the Sanhedrin were versed in the scriptures and prophecies, but they viewed Jesus not as the Messiah, but as a threat to their established order. They began early in his ministry to find a way to kill him. The people, especially in Jerusalem, would not speak openly of Jesus, for fear of the Sanhedrin.

After about a year and a half of teaching and training, Jesus selected twelve from among his *Talmidim*. He ordained them to be his apostles, gave them priesthood authority and commissioned them to go among the people and do the things they had seen him do. He later called the seventy and gave them the same commission.

When the twelve apostles returned, Jesus began to instruct them and prepare them more specifically for the time when he would be gone. He had already selected Peter, James and John for leadership and had included them in ministrations apart from the other nine. To further prepare them for the roles they would assume, Jesus took them to a mountain near Cesarea Phillipi where they became part of a glorious vision. Jesus was transfigured before them and they heard the voice of God, "This is my beloved Son..." (Luke 9:35). Moses and Elijah appeared and conferred upon them the keys of presidency and of the kingdom. Jesus told them again about the necessity of his death and told them to say nothing of the things they had seen and heard until after his resurrection.

In early spring of the third year of his ministry, preparations were made to travel again to Jerusalem to observe the Passover. Jesus was fully aware that this would be his last pilgrimage. He took strength and comfort in the company of his mother and family, as well as his beloved apostles. Many of his disciples set out with him and they were joined along the way by still others.

When the company came to Bethany, a town on the east edge of Jerusalem, Jesus sent two disciples into a neighboring village where they would find a colt. They were told that if anyone should question them about the colt, they should respond, "...the Lord hath need of him." (Luke 19:31) "...They cast their garments upon the colt, and they set Jesus thereon. And as he went, they spread their clothes in the way. And when he was come nigh, even now at the descent of the mount of Olives, the whole multitude of the disciples began to rejoice and praise God with a loud voice for all the mighty works that they had seen; Saying, blessed be the King that cometh in the name of the Lord; peace in heaven, and glory in the highest." (Luke 19:35-38)

Not all were pleased with Jesus' triumphal entry into Jerusalem. Some of the Pharisees told Jesus to silence his disciples. Jesus told them that if they were silent, "…the stones would immediately cry out." (Luke 19:40) His entry into Jerusalem was publically celebrated, but in the shadows infamy was in the making. Judas was conspiring with the chief priests and scribes. He promised them that he would deliver Jesus where the multitude could not intercede.

On the day of the feast, Jesus sent Peter and John ahead to make preparations for the Passover meal. Knowing that this would be the last time he would dine with his family and apostles and fully aware of Judas' treacherous betrayal, Jesus' heart was heavy.

Jerusalem had become volatile, with an element bent on the death of Jesus and the demise of his *Talmidim*. Even in the face of his own death, Jesus' greatest concern was for the safety of all of his disciples, and especially his family and apostles. He felt a sense of urgency, knowing he had little time to prepare them for what was about to befall him and the great responsibility they, particularly Peter, would shoulder. He had to insure their safety for the sake of his church and the spread of his gospel.

In the upper room of a friend's home, Jesus welcomed his disciples and told them of his great desire to observe the Passover with them before his suffering. (Luke 22:15) As was customary, Jesus washed the feet of his apostles, but this washing was more than just a custom. He asked them if they knew what he had done and then explained, "Ye call me Master and Lord and ye say well; for so I am. If I then, your Lord and Master, have washed your feet; ye also ought to wash one another's feet." (John 13:12-14) What had been a common practice was now a sacred ordinance.

Following the ritual of the passing of the cup, (Luke 22:17) Jesus blessed and served bread and wine. He explained that this was to be an ordinance observed often, that the bread and wine were symbolic representations of his body and blood, sacrificed for mankind. This would be a means of remembering him. Before the Feast had concluded, Jesus turned to Judas and dismissed him, "…that thou doest, do quickly." (John 13:27)

When Judas left, his evil spirit went with him and Jesus felt a measure of relief. He turned to the remaining eleven of his apostles and spoke lovingly; "…Little children, yet a little while I am with you…A new commandment I give unto you, that ye love one another…In my Father's [presence] are many mansions…I go to prepare a place for you…If ye love me, keep my commandments. And I will pray the Father, and he shall give you another Comforter…which is the Holy Ghost…he shall teach you all things, and bring all things to your remembrance…Peace I leave with you, my peace I give unto you: not as the world giveth…Let not your heart be troubled, neither let it be afraid…" Tears flowed freely as the apostles and disciples listened with the greatest intent. They felt a sense of farewell and finality in Jesus' tender words. Lovingly he added, "…be of good cheer; I have overcome the world." (John chapters 13-16) Jesus then offered a prayer on behalf of the apostles, speaking as though he had already departed, "…And now I am no more in the world, but these are in the world, and I come to thee, Holy Father, keep through thine own name those whom thou hast given me, that they may be one, as we are…" (John 17:1-26)

Jesus looked into the eyes of his eleven; "Ye are they which have continued with me in my temptations." (Luke 22:28) His heart swelled with compassion for them as it ached for Judas. He knew that Judas' betrayal had already set into motion the events that would ultimately take his life. "I appoint unto you a kingdom, as my Father hath appointed unto me; that ye may eat and drink at my table in my kingdom, and sit on thrones judging the twelve tribes of Israel." (Luke 22:29-30) Jesus looked at his disciples with love eternal in his eyes. He turned again to his apostles and as he spoke his tone and demeanor reflected the gravity and reality of the moment. For their safety, he gave them specific instructions that each of them were to distance themselves from him that very night and then rendezvous with him in Galilee after he had risen from the dead. (Mat. 26:31-32) As he often did, Peter spoke for the apostles, "...though all men shall [abandon] thee, yet will I never [abandon] thee." (Mat. 26:33) Knowing that his chief apostle was a man of great faith, courage and loyalty, Jesus turned to Peter and tenderly, but urgently told him that Satan wanted him so that he would be able to do whatever he chose with all the children of men. Jesus continued, "But I have prayed for thee, that thy faith fail not: and when thou [art my presiding authority], strengthen thy brethren." Peter assured Jesus again that he was ready to die with him. But that was the whole point; it was imperative that Peter, the apostles remain alive to carry on the work. Jesus looked into Peter's anxious and loving eyes and told him that before the cock would crow, it would be necessary for him to deny their association three times. (Luke 22:31-34) The disciples then sang a hymn and Jesus walked ahead of his apostles to the Mount of Olives. (Mat. 26:30)

Arriving at the Garden of Gethsemane, on the Mount of Olives, Jesus took Peter, James and John and asked the other eight to wait at the entrance. The three followed Jesus into the Garden. The weight of the world was on Jesus and he asked them pray for him. He went a short distances and fell to his knees under the burden of the pain, suffering and sin of mankind. Jesus knew that he had arrived at the point for which he was born; to intercede on behalf of all of us. Willingly, and with the resolve that was the hallmark of his ministry, he approached the terrible reality of the covenant he had made with His Father and with each of us. Knowing how eternally essential his atonement was to the salvation and eternal life of mankind, he prayed for the physical and spiritual strength it would require. He prayed metaphorically, referencing the Passover Cup; that it would not pass from him until he had drunk deeply, even to the bitter dregs and that in all things he would do the will of the Father.

Under the circumstances, given all that Jesus had predicted, Peter, James and John were tense and distracted when Jesus returned to them. He admonished them to pray and to be vigilant. Jesus returned and prayed as he had done previously. He again admonished his three apostles and returned to pray again. An angel from heaven appeared, giving him the strength he had pled for. Returning a third time, he told Peter, James and John, "…behold, the hour is at hand, and the Son of man is betrayed into the hands of sinners." (Mat. 26:45)

Judas was well acquainted with Jesus' movements and knew that the Garden of Gethsemane was a favorite retreat. The chief priests and Pharisees had given him charge of a band of men and officers and he led them, armed as they were with torches and weapons. Knowing very well who they were and what they wanted, Jesus asked them who they were looking for. "They answered, Jesus of Nazareth…" (John 18:5) Judas stepped forward and kissed Jesus on the cheek. In humble affirmation of his treachery, Jesus said, "Judas, betrayest thou the Son of man with a kiss?" (Luke 22:48) Jesus turned to the band of men and said, "I am he." He spoke with such calm and dignity that the men were taken aback and fell to the ground. Jesus asked them again who it was they were looking for. Regaining their composure, they replied, Jesus of Nazareth. In spite of the threat and personal danger to him, Jesus was concerned for his apostles and did not want to lose even one. He responded, "I have told you that I am he; if therefore ye seek me, let these go their way:…" (John 18:8-9)

The apostles slipped away into the safety and cover of the night; all but Peter. Showing that he was ready to make good his willingness to remain and even die with Jesus, he drew his sword and cut off the ear of one of the chief priest's servants. Jesus immediately healed the servant's ear and told Peter to put away his sword. Fear and anguish surged inside of Peter as he watched his Rabbi, his Lord, the Messiah forcibly taken. He stood helpless as the terrible realization that everything Jesus had predicted was unfolding before his eyes.

Jesus was made to endure an illegal mockery of a trial, where he was subjected to false accusations and gross and inhumane torture. Peter and John did as they had been instructed. They distanced themselves, but followed close enough to observe the proceedings. Unable to do more than watch, Peter's heart was braking. Then, to add to his pain, in order to be obedient to the Lord's command, it became necessary for him to deny his association with Jesus; not once or even twice, but three times. Peter heard the crowing of a rooster and felt a terrible emptiness come over him as he remembered Jesus' words. Peter knew that everything would happen just as Jesus had said. Jesus was about to be killed. He looked up and caught the gaze of his Master. Even then, there was no pain or pity in Jesus' eyes, only sweet assurance and love for his chief apostle. Powerless to render aid or comfort, Peter went away and wept bitterly.

The so-called trial revealed no guilt on Jesus part, but did reveal the merciless and hypocritical hearts of his accusers. Even though Pilate had found no cause worthy of death, the Jews insisted that Jesus be crucified. Jesus was taken to Golgotha and hung on a cross between two thieves. While the Jews, the scribes and Pharisees, gloated in victory, Jesus' disciples anguished in pain at the unspeakable suffering he endured. Even in physical and spiritual agony, Jesus was able and willing to forgive his killers. Mary knew that her son was born to die for the redemption and salvation of mankind, but that did nothing to ease the pain of a mother forced to watch the pain and death of her son.

Because murder was there intent, the evil Jews were guilty and yet they did not kill him. Jesus had made a covenant that he would give his life for all who would repent. When the demands of the covenant were satisfied on the cross, he voluntarily surrendered his life and committed his spirit into the hands of his Father, consummating the covenant that made us all subject to him before the world began.

Thanks to the generosity of one of his disciples, Jesus' body was hastily placed in a borrowed tomb. His mother and family postponed their return to Galilee and remained with their friends so that they could revisit the tomb and more properly anoint and prepare the body. On the third day after Jesus' death, Mary, his mother and Mary Magdalene, along with other women, came to the sepulcher, but found it empty. Distraught, the women returned to the city. Mary Magdalene rushed ahead of them to find Peter and John. For fear of what might have happened and partly in the hope that Jesus was in fact alive, they ran to see. Mary followed after them. Finding the tomb empty Peter and John returned to the city. Heartbroken, Mary remained at the tomb. Angels asked her why she was crying. She explained, "Because they have taken away my Lord, and I know not where they have laid him." (John 20:13) She heard another voice asking why she was crying. She turned toward the voice. With tear filled eyes she did not recognize Jesus, but assumed he was the gardener. Jesus spoke her name lovingly as he had done so many times. Inexpressible joy propelled her to her feet. She ran and threw her arms around him. The tenderness of the moment captured the attention of eternity. They walked arm in arm in the perfect peace and serenity of the garden that had become a sacred place. Mary did not want her moment to end, but at last Jesus told her she would have to let him go, as he had not yet ascended to his Father. He instructed her to go and tell the disciples.

On that resurrection day, Jesus showed himself to Peter, his beloved chief apostle and to two disciples on the road to Emmaus. He also appeared to women on the road, not far from the tomb, and told them to tell the disciples and remind them that he would meet them in Galilee. Toward evening, he appeared again in the upper room where the apostles and other disciples had secluded themselves.

The Jews were afraid that Jesus' disciples would make some claim that Jesus had resurrected and so the threat to them was very real. The apostles and other disciples remained in hiding for several more days, during which time, Jesus appeared to them again. Jesus appeared to many others and it was soon being talked about to the point it was safe for the apostles and their families to make their way to Galilee.

Jesus had promised that he would meet his disciples in Galilee when he was risen from the dead. While they waited for his coming, they returned to their employment to see to the needs of their families and their homes. Peter, James and John, along with Thomas and three other disciples, returned to their nets. They fished through the night and caught nothing. When the morning came, Jesus stood on the shore and called to them, asking if they had caught anything. When they replied that they had not, he told them to cast their nets on the right side of the boat. Reminiscent of an earlier experience, they did as they were instructed. They caught so many fish they were unable to bring them in. Realizing who it was, John said to Peter, "it is the Lord." Immediately, Peter jumped into the water. His joy and enthusiasm propelled him to shore.

Peter, as well as the others had already seen Jesus, but now he was inviting them to dine with him, to actually be with him again. Peter especially was grateful. He still carried the pain of having to disassociate himself at Jesus' trial and saw this as a chance to renew his love. Jesus knew the heart his apostle, now president of the quorum of the twelve apostles and presiding authority on the earth. In perfect love and charity, he asked Peter if he loved him. Peter looked into Jesus' eyes as he had done on that fateful night and without hesitation, answered in the affirmative. Jesus asked him again if he loved him, to which Peter gave affirmation. A third time Peter received the same question to which he responded, "...Lord, thou knowest all things; thou knowest that I love thee." (John 21:17) To each of Peter's affirmations, Jesus reiterated his charge to strengthen his brethren. Each time he told him to feed his sheep.

Jesus had done all that he was sent to do. He established the doctrine of the Father, the gospel of Jesus Christ, he established his Church with a foundation of apostles and prophets. He empowered them with the gift of the Holy Ghost and commissioned them to "Go…into all the world, and preach the gospel to every creature." (Mark 16:15) He suffered and died for all mankind that sins might be forgiven and made exaltation available to all who would accept the Father's will as their own and be willing to walk as he walked.

Jesus of Nazareth is indeed the Son of God. As I have walked with him, I have come to know and to love him. He is my Savior and my advocate with the Father. I know that he is yet pleading my cause. (see D&C 45:3-5) It is my prayer that people everywhere will accept his invitation to walk with him as a true disciple.

49277924R00172

Made in the USA
San Bernardino, CA
19 May 2017